THE FAMILY FAVORITES COOKBOK

READER'S DIGEST
BOOKS FOR COOKS

THE FAMILY FAVORITES COOKBOOK

READER'S DIGEST
BOOKS FOR COOKS

The Reader's Digest Association, Inc.
Pleasantville, New York/Montreal

Edited and designed by Media Projects Incorporated

Portions of this book were previously published in
Reader's Digest Creative Cooking Club.

The credits that appear on page 144 are hereby made a part of this copyright page.

Library of Congress Cataloging in Publication Data

The Family favorites cookbook.
    p.   cm.—(Books for cooks)
    Includes index.
    ISBN 0-89577-490-9
    1. Cookery.   I. Series.
        TX714.F343   1993
        641.5—dc20   93-16408

Printed in the United States of America

TABLE OF CONTENTS

One of life's great pleasures is sharing a meal with family. Mealtimes are quality times, occasions to catch up on the day and make plans for the future. And, as hectic as today's schedules are, a foolproof way to encourage family togetherness is by providing meals that are satisfying, healthful, and delicious.

The Family Favorites Cookbook celebrates the tradition of the family meal. Its goal is to offer exciting home-cooked recipes that are full of family appeal—hearty soups and stews, robust chilis, melt-in-the-mouth pot roasts, roast poultry and meats with all the trimmings, crisp salads, vegetable bakes, flavorful pasta dishes, chocolate cake, muffins, and so much more.

But what's special about these recipes is how they've been revised and updated for today's tastes and time constraints. The emphasis is on fresh and imaginative ingredients and cooking techniques that transform popular dishes into something unique. For instance, chicken stew is made better than ever with the use of homemade stock and light as air dumplings. And, the entire family will rave about Lattice-Topped Meat Pie (pages 40-41), an irresistible version of the classic meat and potatoes, featuring a spicy beef filling topped by a crusty lattice of mashed potatoes.

Many of the dishes have an international inspiration but have been revised to cater to the family's palate. For fans of Italian food, there's Veal Parmigiana (page 55) made with bell peppers, mushrooms, and a touch of fresh basil. And, for lovers of German food, a recipe for Sweet and Sour Red Cabbage (page 84) is given; it will make a great accompaniment to pot roast.

Whether it's a great beginning to a family meal or celebration or a memorable finale—or something in between—*Family Favorites* has a recipe that's sure to get wows. Chicken wings with a flavorful Asian sauce, a warming soup made with chicken, vegetables, and rice, meatloaf that features Southwestern accents, an unusually tasty fish-filled lasagne, spaghetti tossed in an especially hearty chicken-liver-based Bolognese sauce, and baked apples with an almond filling are just a few of the recipes that have received the *Family Favorites* treatment and tasters' approval. And, all the dishes have been kitchen-tested for convenience, ease of preparation, and accuracy so that the recipes will come out perfectly every time.

Hearty Chicken and Rice Soup (page 25) will provide a warming start to a family meal or a one-pot meal that only requires chunks of bread to complete it. It's a soup that "says" homemade, and yet it's surprisingly simple to prepare. The blend of ingredients will please everyone's palate and will whet the appetite for the entrée to come. The soup is also versatile and lends itself to vegetable variations.

Family cooks will find the recipes a pleasure to cook from because everything they need to know is provided. The number of servings and preparation and cooking times accompany each recipe to help with planning. The steps are clearly numbered and the instructions are very easy to follow. Where appropriate, the ingredients list contains frozen or canned alternatives for seasonal items. And, as a bonus, each recipe includes an equipment list that specifies exactly what tools and utensils will be needed, thereby streamlining food preparation.

Many of the recipes contain tips and helpful hints that guide cooks every step of the way—from purchasing food to getting it on the table in record time. Discover what to look for when buying fresh tuna, an easy method to cook dried beans, and how to freeze noodle pudding. Recipe variations explain how to add different ingredients to the basic dish for a change of pace. And, the serving suggestions provide complete menus at-a-glance, so there's no need to fret about what to serve with a dish.

Family Favorites also takes the stress out of special occasion meal planning. It presents three complete and easy-to-prepare menus—with hints on advance preparation. Plus, the family's health needs are catered to by the inclusion of nutritional information for each recipe. Simply turn to the special section at the back of the book.

Finally, more than half of the recipes in the book are illustrated with beautiful color photographs so that cooks can see what the finished dish will look like.

Who can resist meat and potatoes, especially if they're prepared in a novel way? This recipe for Lattice-Topped Meat Pie (pages 40-41) is wonderfully tasty and offers an eye-catching presentation, which makes it perfect to serve to family and guests alike. A single serving is very satisfying but don't be surprised if seconds are asked for.

On the lookout for a chocolate cake that tastes so scrumptious that the recipe will be requested again and again? Then try Chocolate-Walnut Cake with Chocolate Frosting (page 127) —a chocoholic's dream. The cake is rich but not overly sweet and the walnuts lend it something extra. As a centerpiece for a family gathering it is unsurpassed.

Shopping Shortcuts

The most important time-saver is to prepare a shopping list, as this reduces the temptation to buy on impulse and will also cut down on emergency shopping runs.

For efficiency, plan the list for a week's worth of meals so there's no need to worry about what goes on the table every night. Keep in mind how many meals will be needed and the number of family members who will be home each evening. Think about what food could be used from one meal to form the basis for another later in the week. Follow the list as much as possible with the exception of fresh produce, which should be selected on the basis of what looks best. Check supermarket specials to prepare freezable favorites. And, if possible, try to limit shopping to one or two supermarkets; knowing the layouts will make it simpler to find everything fast.

Tools of the Trade for the Family Favorites Kitchen

Listed below is all the equipment used in this cookbook. It is not essential to own every item. A blender can often double as a food processor; a large, heavy skillet can replace a wok. To improvise a double boiler, use a heatproof bowl set over a saucepan of simmering water. To make a baking pan substitution, choose one with the same volume and a similar depth. To determine volume, measure the amount of water the pan holds when filled to the rim. Allow more baking time when using a deeper pan than the one called for in the recipe.

EQUIPMENT
Small bowl, 2 cups to 1½ quarts
Medium-size bowl, 2 to 3 quarts
Large bowl, 4 to 5 quarts
Blender
Electric hand mixer
Food processor with metal blades
6-cup ring mold
Shallow glass dish, 11″ x 7″ to 9″ x 13″
Toaster oven or toaster
Vegetable steamer
Waffle iron

BAKING
Baking pan, 9″ x 13″
Baking pan, 8″ square
Baking sheets, 12″ x 18″ or 11″ x 15″
Bundt pan, 10″
Jelly roll pan, 15½″ x 10½″
2 layer cake pans, 9″
2 loaf pans, 9″ x 5″
Pie pan, 9″
Tube pan, 9″
Cookie cutters, 2″ and 3″, round and other assorted shapes
Muffin pan, standard size (12-cup)
Pastry bag with plain, star, and other assorted tips
Pastry blender
Pie weights
Rolling pin, 10″ to 12″
Sifter
Wire racks

MEASURING
Glass measuring cups for liquids, 1 to 4 cups
Measuring cups for dry ingredients: ¼ cup, ⅓ cup, ½ cup, and 1 cup
Measuring spoons: ¼ teaspoon, ½ teaspoon, 1 teaspoon, and 1 tablespoon
Kitchen scale

POTS, PANS, AND CASSEROLES
Small saucepan with lid, 2 cups to 1½ quarts
Medium-size saucepan with lid, 2 to 4 quarts
Large saucepan with lid, 5 to 6 quarts
Double boiler
Stockpot with lid, 8 quarts
Small skillet, 6″ to 8″
Medium-size skillet with lid, 8″ to 10″
Large skillet with lid, 10″ to 12″
Nonstick skillet, 8″ to 10″
Crêpe pan, 8″
Broiler pan
Griddle
Deep-fat fryer with removable basket
Paella pan
Wok
Baking dishes, 1½, 2, and 3 quarts
Casserole with lid, 2 quarts
Dutch oven, 4 to 6 quarts
Individual gratin dishes, 1 to 2 cups
Roasting pan with rack, 16″ x 11″ x 5″
Soufflé dish, 1½ quarts

UTENSILS
Apple corer
Bulb baster
Cake testers
Can opener
Candy thermometer
Carving board
Citrus juicer
Colander, 8″ to 10″
Corkscrew
Cutting board
Fine wire mesh sieve, 2″ to 3″
Grater
Kitchen scissors
Kitchen timer
Kitchen tongs
Long-handled fork
Meat mallet
Meat thermometer
Melon-ball cutter
Mortar and pestle
Oven thermometer
Pastry brushes
Pepper mill
Potato masher
Poultry shears
Salad servers
Salt shaker
Skewers, metal or wooden, 10″ to 12″
Spaghetti fork
Vegetable brush
Vegetable peeler
Wire mesh strainer, 6″ to 8″
Wire whisk, stainless steel, 8″ to 12″
Yeast thermometer

KNIVES
Paring knife, 3″ to 4″ blade
Boning knife, 5″ to 6″ blade
Utility knife, 6″ to 8″ blade
Serrated knife, 8″ to 9″ blade
Chef's knife, 8″ to 10″ blade
Carving knife and fork, 10″ blade
Knife sharpening steel

SPATULAS
Large, metal spatula
Rubber spatula
Thin, metal spatula

SPOONS
Long-handled metal kitchen spoons
Slotted stainless steel spoon
Soup ladle
Wooden spoons

SUPPLIES
Airtight plastic containers in assorted sizes
Aluminum foil
Cheesecloth
Kitchen twine
Muffin pan liners, paper or foil
Paper towels
Plastic food storage bags
Plastic wrap
Pot holders
Toothpicks
Wax paper

Equipping the Kitchen

Kitchen equipment can be as basic or elaborate as desired, depending on budget and available space. However, it makes sense to invest in a few good pieces, as properly cared for kitchen tools can last forever. High-quality knives are essential, as are heavy-bottomed pots and pans that conduct heat more efficiently. Food processors and blenders are excellent timesaving investments as well and will last for years, even with frequent use.

Organize the kitchen with an uncluttered work space. Have frequently used equipment such as the food processor or electric blender nearby so it's handy for chopping and mincing tasks. Keep cookbooks and recipe files within easy reach and pot holders by the stove. And, if the kitchen is small, try a wall arrangement of pegboards and hooks or ceiling hangers to hold pots and pans to free up other storage space.

The Cook's Pantry

Creating quick meals for family or guests is never a problem when the pantry is full. Keep a supply of interesting pastas, beans, and grains, which are good bases for a wide range of dishes. Canned foods, such as assorted fish, fruits and vegetables, tomato paste, broths, juices, and specialty sauces, are also handy basic items. Stock up on dried herbs and spices, too.

Condiments, like salsas, mustards, chutney, pickles, roasted red peppers, and capers, add zest to many foods with no additional preparation. Special oils and vinegars, including balsamic vinegar and extra virgin olive oil, can be used to make fast, tasty salad dressings. And, if unexpected guests are the rule rather than the exception, then reserve a special kitchen shelf for "company" goods, such as jarred pesto sauce, sun dried tomatoes, olives, nuts, and canned fish, such as smoked oysters and clams. Regular inventories will ensure that adequate supplies are always on hand for rushed weekday dinners or impromptu gatherings.

Lay out the pantry in a sensible way, storing all like and complementary items together in one area: oils with vinegars and legumes with grains. Consider lazy Susan turntables as a way to organize cabinet space.

Vegetarian Baked Beans (page 86) has been devised as a dish that will appeal to both meat eaters and non-meat eaters in the family. Based on traditional baked beans, it omits the pork and bacon and yet remains extremely flavorful and full of texture. What's more, it can be prepared primarily from pantry items. Vegetarian Baked Beans can also be served for barbecues and buffets.

Family Meals
from the Refrigerator and Freezer

The secret to creating delicious and easy family meals is planning ahead. This means, in part, making the best use of the refrigerator and freezer to cut preparation and cooking times to a minimum.

Do-ahead dishes that can be refrigerated for a few days, such as stews and casseroles, are very convenient. Reheat them, covered, in a moderate oven or over low heat on the stovetop. Savory pies and quiches, pasta salads, and many appetizers and desserts can also be made in advance, then refrigerated until needed. Even when a whole recipe can't be prepared ahead of time, it's usually possible to ready part of it beforehand. Potatoes can be peeled and sliced a day ahead, and kept refrigerated in a bowl of water. Croutons, salad dressings, and pasta sauces can also be prepared in advance and stored in the refrigerator until required.

To ease the weekday breakfast rush, consider making hard-cooked eggs, cutting fresh fruit, and slicing cheese and storing them. Also, figure on some dinners with built-in leftovers such as meatloaf or roast chicken, which taste even better the next day. Be sure to cover refrigerated foods tightly, preferably with plastic wrap plus aluminum foil, to prevent drying and to seal out odors.

Purchase poultry, meat, and fish in quantity when they are on sale, wrap airtight, and freeze until needed. Use a food processor or blender to grate cheese, make fresh bread crumbs, chop carrots, celery, onions, and nuts in quantity and store them, tightly wrapped, in the freezer. They can be frozen for months and used directly from the freezer without thawing. Dishes can be cooked in bulk and leftovers frozen in serving-size containers for times when different numbers of family need to be catered for.

For safety, always defrost entrées overnight in the refrigerator—never on the kitchen counter—or in the microwave oven as the manufacturer directs. When freezing food, wrap it properly to keep it in peak condition. Use moisture- and vapor-proof wraps, such as heavy-duty foil, freezer paper, freezer bags, or plastic containers with tight fitting lids. Press or squeeze out as much air as possible as excess air causes freezer burn. However, leave a little space when packing semisolid food in rigid containers, since liquids expand slightly when frozen. Always label and date each item and be sure to use the foods frozen the longest first.

Using the freezer to help plan for special family gatherings helps eliminate last-minute shopping and fuss. So always keep a few hors d'oeuvres frozen and ready to bake or reheat. For quick desserts, stock frozen pound cake, fancy cookies, and canned or frozen fruits that can be puréed for a sauce for ice cream.

RECIPES FOR GOOD HEALTH

- **EAT SMART:**
  Eat more complex carbohydrates, fruits, and vegetables, and cut back on saturated fats (from animal products), cholesterol, sodium, sugar, and alcohol.

- **MAKE SMART CHOICES:**
  Select a variety of foods and balance food choices. Substitute healthier foods, where possible, for instance serve pasta with a tomato rather than a cream sauce.

- **COOK SMART:**
  Rely on low-fat cooking techniques, such as steaming vegetables or broiling meat on a rack so the fat can drip away. Sautéing and stir-frying with very little added oil are other healthy methods.

Pasta is always a dish of choice and the Bolognese Sauce (page 104) makes it a real winner. Hearty and colorful, the sauce contains a surprise ingredient—chicken livers—which give it an especially delicious flavor and robust texture. When preparing the sauce, make extra and freeze it in a covered plastic container. Use it as a lasagne filling or try it with other pasta shapes.

Getting Started

Begin each recipe by reading it through very carefully to get a sense of the preparation sequence, ingredients, and equipment. Refer to the general equipment list as necessary for such specifics as pan sizes and recommended measuring cups. Gather all the ingredients and tools together, then chop and measure before combining the ingredients. Prepare the pans and preheat the oven if necessary.

Don't feel restricted by the ingredients listed. Some substitutes contribute to a healthier diet, while others are a matter of choice. Canned chicken broth may be handier than homemade chicken stock; frozen vegetables can be used any time of year. However, remember that for some recipes such as Peach and Pistachio Dessert Soup (page 27), it really is best to use the fresh fruit called for.

Cooking for Family Celebrations

When entertaining, remember that good food need not be fussy. To prevent overloading the stovetop and oven with last-minute cooking, offer a combination of hot and cold dishes. Casseroles that can be made ahead and frozen are also good for a party. Or, serve a meal of cold salads that can be made in advance.

Cook and prepare ahead as much as possible. The day before the party prepare the ingredients needed for each recipe, wrap them individually, label, and refrigerate. Keep tabs on where everything is, listing what is in the freezer or fridge.

When setting the table, enhance the festive mood with attractive fabrics, bright crockery, flowers, and unscented candles. Or, consider an arrangement of seasonal fruits and vegetables for the center of the table.

Family Favorites is just the ticket to make meal planning easy, nutritious, and delicious. With this array of recipes to choose from, every member of the family is sure to find a favorite. Happy, healthy eating!

This menu for an Autumn Celebration Dinner (pages 130-131) takes the anxiety out of menu planning because it's so easy and yet it gives the impression that the home cook has slaved for hours in the kitchen. The stuffing for the chicken is prepared with dried fruit and is very tasty; the marinated vegetables are a snap; and the squash soufflé makes a stunning finale. The autumn theme can be carried through with table decorations.

*K*ick off everyday or special occasion meals with one of the appetizers in this chapter. A wonderful selection is offered, including pâté, individual carrot soufflés, spicy chicken wings, open-faced shrimp and avocado sandwiches, and a filled Edam cheese.

Bruschetta.

Bruschetta

4 large cloves garlic
4 medium-size ripe tomatoes, peeled, seeded, and coarsely chopped (4 cups)
2 tablespoons chopped fresh basil, or 2 teaspoons dried basil leaves, crumbled
½ cup extra-virgin olive oil
¼ teaspoon salt, or to taste
Freshly ground black pepper
4 slices Italian bread, cut ¾" thick
Sprigs of fresh basil (optional)

Classic Roman Bruschetta is a simple affair of grilled Italian bread rubbed with garlic and drizzled with fruity olive oil. This recipe goes a step further and features ripe tomatoes and fragrant chopped fresh basil.

For a party, try serving it as an hors d'oeuvre by cutting the bread into smaller pieces. If using it as a first course, leave the bread slices whole. Or, for a delicious summer lunch, place a thin slice of fresh mozzarella cheese on top of the warm, garlic-rubbed bread slices, and then top with the tomato-basil mixture. Allow 2 slices per serving.

1 Reserve 1 clove of garlic and slice the remaining 3 in half. In a medium-size bowl, combine the halved garlic, tomatoes, chopped basil, and oil. Season to taste with the salt and pepper. Cover with plastic wrap and let the mixture stand at room temperature for at least 45 minutes to allow the flavors to blend. Remove and discard the garlic from the tomato-basil mixture.

2 Prepare a charcoal grill until the coals form white ash, preheat a gas grill to high, or preheat the broiler.

3 Place the bread slices on the grill or under the broiler 4" from the heat source. Grill or broil the slices for 2 minutes on each side, or until golden brown.

4 Slice the reserved clove of garlic in half. While the bread is still warm, rub the bread slices with the garlic. Discard the garlic.

5 Transfer the bread slices to individual serving plates and generously spoon the tomato-basil mixture over them. Garnish with sprigs of fresh basil, if desired. Serve immediately.

4 SERVINGS
PREP TIME: 25 MINUTES PLUS
45 MINUTES TO MARINATE
COOKING TIME: 4 MINUTES

EQUIPMENT LIST
Paring knife
Serrated knife
Pepper mill
Medium-size bowl
Kitchen spoon
Plastic wrap
Charcoal or gas grill or broiler pan
Large, metal spatula

Cheese and Nut Filled Edam

6 strips lean bacon, chopped
1 2-pound Edam cheese, at room temperature
1 3-ounce package cream cheese, softened
4 green onions (including tops), finely chopped (½ cup)
1 ounce chopped walnuts (¼ cup)
2 tablespoons chopped fresh parsley
2 teaspoons Worcestershire sauce
Sprigs of fresh parsley (optional)
Assorted crackers (optional)
Toasted pita bread (optional)

This dramatic and easy-to-make appetizer can be prepared ahead, covered with plastic wrap, and refrigerated for up to a day. Remove from the refrigerator and let it stand for an hour before serving. If Edam cheese is unavailable, substitute two 1-pound Gouda cheeses. Proceed as directed, dividing the mixture between the cheese shells.

1 Cook the bacon in a medium-size skillet over moderate heat for 8 to 10 minutes, or until crisp. Using a slotted spoon, transfer the bacon to a plate lined with paper towels to drain.

2 Meanwhile, cut a ½" slice from the top of the Edam cheese. Using a curved knife such as a grapefruit knife, and a spoon, scoop out the cheese, leaving a ¼" thick shell. Shred the cheese with a hand grater or food processor.

3 In a large bowl, mix together the shredded cheese, bacon, cream cheese, green onions, walnuts, chopped parsley, and Worcestershire sauce until well blended. Spoon the cheese mixture into the Edam shell. Garnish with sprigs of fresh parsley and serve with assorted crackers or toasted pita bread, if desired.

20 SERVINGS
PREP TIME: 20 MINUTES
COOKING TIME: 10 MINUTES

EQUIPMENT LIST
Utility knife
Grapefruit or curved knife
Medium-size skillet
Slotted spoon
Kitchen spoons
Plate
Paper towels
Grater
Large bowl

Avocado-Shrimp Sandwiches

Serve these elegant open-faced sandwiches as a first course or cut them diagonally in half and serve as hors d'oeuvres. The recipe can easily be increased to accommodate a large gathering.

⅓ cup olive oil
¼ cup fresh lime juice
6 cooked jumbo shrimp, shelled, deveined, and halved lengthwise
⅛ teaspoon salt, or to taste
Ground white pepper
6 slices white bread, crusts removed
Sprigs of fresh cilantro (coriander leaves) or fresh parsley (optional)

GUACAMOLE (¾ CUP)

1 large ripe avocado
2 teaspoons fresh lemon juice
1 small jalapeño pepper, cored, seeded, and finely chopped (1 tablespoon) (optional)
1 teaspoon red wine vinegar
1 tablespoon finely chopped cilantro (coriander leaves) or fresh parsley
¼ teaspoon salt, or to taste

1 In a small glass or enamel bowl, combine the oil and lime juice. Add the shrimp, tossing to coat. Season to taste with the ⅛ teaspoon of salt and pepper. Marinate the shrimp at room temperature for 30 minutes to allow flavors to blend. Stir the shrimp occasionally.

2 Meanwhile, make the Guacamole. Split the avocado, remove and discard the pit, and peel. Cut 6 thin slices from the avocado and place on a small plate. Sprinkle the slices with 1 teaspoon of the lemon juice and set aside.

3 Chop the remaining avocado and place in a medium-size bowl. Using a fork, mash the avocado until smooth. Stir in the jalapeño pepper, if desired, the remaining 1 teaspoon of lemon juice, vinegar, and chopped cilantro. Season to taste with the ¼ teaspoon of salt. Cover the bowl with plastic wrap and set aside.

4 Preheat the broiler. Place the bread slices under the broiler 4″ from the heat source. Broil the slices for 1 minute on each side, or until golden brown.

5 Drain the shrimp and discard the marinade. Spread each slice of bread with some of the guacamole. Arrange 2 drained shrimp halves and a slice of avocado on each bread slice. Garnish each sandwich with a sprig of fresh cilantro, if desired, and serve immediately.

6 SERVINGS
PREP TIME: 20 MINUTES PLUS
30 MINUTES TO MARINATE
COOKING TIME: 10 MINUTES

EQUIPMENT LIST

Citrus juicer
Paring knife
Serrated knife
Small glass or enamel bowl
Medium-size bowl
Kitchen spoons
Small plate
Fork
Plastic wrap
Broiler pan
Large, metal spatula
Colander

Shrimp and avocado are here combined in a delicious open-faced sandwich.

Chicken Liver Pâté

This pâté has a rich taste and smooth texture and, because gelatin is added, it has a good molding consistency. Serve it with sliced French bread.

3 tablespoons unsalted butter
1 pound chicken livers, trimmed, rinsed, and patted dry
1 cup chicken stock or canned broth
1 envelope (¼ ounce) unflavored gelatin
½ cup sour cream
3 tablespoons finely chopped red onion
2 tablespoons Dijon-style mustard
2 tablespoons dry sherry (optional)
¼ teaspoon coarsely ground black pepper
1 large hard-cooked egg, finely chopped (optional)
Sliced French bread (optional)

1 Lightly grease a 4-cup pâté mold or bowl and set aside. In a large skillet over moderate heat, melt the butter. Add the chicken livers and sauté for 8 minutes, or until cooked through. Using a slotted spoon, transfer chicken livers to a plate lined with paper towels to drain.

2 Place ¼ cup of the stock in a small bowl and sprinkle with the gelatin. Let stand for 3 minutes, or until softened.

3 In a small saucepan, bring the remaining ¾ cup of stock to a boil over high heat. Remove the pan from the heat and set aside.

4 Meanwhile, in a blender or food processor fitted with the metal blade, combine the chicken livers, sour cream, onion, mustard, sherry, if desired, and pepper. Blend or process for 2 minutes, or until smooth, scraping down the side of bowl whenever necessary.

5 Pour hot stock over the gelatin mixture and stir until gelatin is dissolved. Add to the chicken liver mixture and blend or process for 2 minutes more. Pour chicken liver mixture into the mold, cover with plastic wrap, and chill in the refrigerator for 2 hours, or until firm.

6 Invert the pâté onto a serving platter. Garnish with the chopped egg and serve immediately with sliced French bread, if desired.

8 SERVINGS
PREP TIME: 15 MINUTES PLUS
2 HOURS TO CHILL
COOKING TIME: 11 MINUTES

EQUIPMENT LIST

Utility knife
Paper towels
Plastic wrap
4-cup pâté mold or bowl
Small bowl
Large skillet
Kitchen spoon
Slotted spoon
Plate
Small saucepan
Blender or food processor with metal blade
Rubber spatula

Individual Carrot-Dill Soufflés

These light and airy soufflés make an unusual prelude to a smoked chicken or turkey salad entrée.

2 tablespoons grated Parmesan cheese
5 small carrots, peeled and coarsely chopped (2½ cups)
¼ cup part-skim ricotta cheese
¼ teaspoon ground cumin
¼ teaspoon salt, or to taste
Freshly ground black pepper
4 large eggs, separated
2 tablespoons chopped fresh dill, or 2 teaspoons dried dill weed

1 Preheat the oven to 425° F. Grease six 1½-cup soufflé dishes or ramekins. Coat the insides with the Parmesan cheese.

2 Bring a large saucepan of water to a boil over high heat. Cook the carrots in the boiling water for 15 minutes, or until very tender. Drain and pat dry with paper towels.

3 Place the carrots in a blender or food processor fitted with the metal blade. Add the ricotta cheese, cumin, salt, and pepper. Blend or process for 1 minute, or until smooth, scraping down the side of the bowl whenever necessary. Transfer the purée to a large bowl. Add egg yolks and the dill to the purée, whisking until well blended.

4 In a medium-size bowl, using an electric mixer set on high speed, beat the egg whites to stiff peaks. Gently and thoroughly fold the egg whites into the carrot mixture.

5 Place prepared soufflé dishes on a baking sheet. Spoon the soufflé mixture into the dishes. Clean the rims to remove any overflow, which could prevent the soufflés from fully rising. Bake for 10 to 12 minutes, or until the soufflés have risen and are set. Remove the baking sheet from the oven. Serve the soufflés immediately.

6 SERVINGS
PREP TIME: 15 MINUTES
COOKING TIME: 27 MINUTES

EQUIPMENT LIST

Vegetable peeler
Utility knife
Pepper mill
2 small bowls
Large bowl
Medium-size bowl
6 1½-cup soufflé dishes or ramekins
Large saucepan
Colander
Paper towels
Blender or food processor with metal blade
Rubber spatula
Wire whisk
Electric mixer
Baking sheet
Kitchen spoon

Chinese Chicken Wings with 5-Spice Mayonnaise

6   large chicken wings, tips removed, divided at the joints (12 pieces) (1¾ pounds)
½   cup cornstarch
2   teaspoons Chinese 5-spice powder
¼   teaspoon salt, or to taste
Freshly ground black pepper
Vegetable oil
Chopped hazelnuts (optional)

5-SPICE MAYONNAISE (1 CUP)

1   cup reduced-calorie mayonnaise
2   tablespoons Dijon-style mustard
1   teaspoon low-sodium soy sauce
½   teaspoon Chinese 5-spice powder
Sprig of flat-leaf parsley (optional)

In this recipe, chicken wings are given an Asian touch with the use of Chinese 5-spice powder, which is available in Asian food stores and many supermarkets. Try substituting 12 small drumsticks for the chicken wings.

1 Rinse the chicken wings under cold running water and pat dry with paper towels. In a shallow dish or pan, sift the cornstarch with the 2 teaspoons of 5-spice powder. Season with the salt and pepper. Dredge the chicken wings in the cornstarch mixture, coating them completely and shaking off the excess.

2 In a large, deep skillet, heat 2″ of oil over moderately high heat for 5 minutes, or until it reaches 375° F. Add the chicken wings and cook, turning frequently, for 15 minutes, or until golden brown and cooked through. Using a slotted spoon, transfer the chicken wings to a plate lined with paper towels to drain. Keep warm.

3 Meanwhile, make the 5-Spice Mayonnaise: In a small bowl, mix together the mayonnaise, mustard, soy sauce, and the ½ teaspoon of 5-spice powder. Transfer to a serving dish and garnish with a sprig of flat-leaf parsley, if desired.

4 To serve: Dip the chicken wings in the 5-Spice Mayonnaise and then into the chopped hazelnuts, if desired.

6 SERVINGS
PREP TIME: 15 MINUTES
COOKING TIME: 20 MINUTES

EQUIPMENT LIST

Poultry shears
Pepper mill
Paper towels
Shallow dish
Sifter
Large, deep skillet
Kitchen tongs
Slotted spoon
Kitchen spoon
Plate
Small bowl

For finger food with an Asian flavor, try these chicken wings.

Apple-Walnut Salad

The whole family will love this crunchy tossed salad. Serve it as a refreshing start or accompaniment to an entrée of grilled pork or poultry.

1 ounce chopped walnuts
(¼ cup)
2 medium-size Red Delicious apples, peeled, cored, and chopped (2 cups)
2 teaspoons fresh lemon juice
4 cups Romaine lettuce, rinsed and torn in pieces
1 small yellow onion, finely chopped (½ cup)

HONEY-WALNUT DRESSING
(½ CUP)

2 tablespoons white wine vinegar
2 teaspoons honey
1 teaspoon lemon juice
3 tablespoons walnut oil
2 tablespoons vegetable oil
Freshly ground black pepper

1 Preheat the oven to 350° F. Spread the walnuts in a thin layer on a baking sheet. Toast in the oven for 7 to 10 minutes, or until golden. Stir the walnuts occasionally while toasting to prevent burning. Remove the baking sheet from the oven, transfer walnuts to a small bowl, and set aside.

2 Meanwhile, make the Honey-Walnut Dressing: In a small bowl, combine the vinegar, honey, and the 1 teaspoon of lemon juice. Slowly add the walnut and vegetable oils, whisking vigorously until well blended, or place the ingredients in a small jar with a tight-fitting lid and shake to blend. Season to taste with the pepper.

3 To make the salad: In a medium-size bowl, toss the apple pieces with the 2 teaspoons of lemon juice. Pour the dressing over the salad, tossing to coat. Transfer the salad to individual serving plates. Add the lettuce and onion to the bowl with the apple, stirring gently to combine. Sprinkle with the walnuts. Serve immediately.

4 SERVINGS
PREP TIME: 10 MINUTES
COOKING TIME: 10 MINUTES

EQUIPMENT LIST

Vegetable peeler
Utility knife
Citrus juicer
Colander
Pepper mill
Baking sheet
2 small bowls
Medium-size bowl
Kitchen spoon
Wire whisk
Salad servers

Tuna-Anchovy Stuffed Eggs

This variation of the classic deviled eggs is wonderful for a spring luncheon or brunch. For a decorative effect, pipe the filling onto the cooked egg whites using a pastry bag fitted with a large plain tip.

6 large eggs
¼ cup chopped, pitted black olives
1 ounce anchovies, drained, rinsed, and chopped
1 teaspoon capers, drained and rinsed
3 teaspoons fresh lemon juice
1 3½-ounce can solid white tuna in water, drained and flaked
3 tablespoons tomato juice
1 teaspoon Worcestershire sauce
1 teaspoon Dijon-style mustard
¼ cup olive oil
⅛ teaspoon salt, or to taste
Freshly ground black pepper
1 medium-size head red leaf lettuce, rinsed and torn in pieces (6 cups)
1 medium-size head Belgian endive, rinsed and torn in pieces (2 cups)
Sprigs of fresh parsley (optional)

1 Place the eggs in a medium-size saucepan with enough cold water to cover. Bring to a boil over high heat. Reduce the heat to low and simmer the eggs, uncovered, for 15 minutes. Drain well. Place the eggs in a large bowl, cover with cold water, and let stand for 15 minutes.

2 Peel the eggs and discard the shells. Cut the eggs in half lengthwise. Using a small spoon, scoop out the yolks and divide them between 2 medium-size bowls. Place the egg whites on a large plate and set aside.

3 Add the olives, anchovies, capers, and 2 teaspoons of the lemon juice to 1 bowl of the egg yolks. Add the tuna and mix until well blended. Fill each egg white half with 2 teaspoons of the filling.

4 Add the remaining teaspoon of lemon juice, the tomato juice, Worcestershire sauce, and mustard to the second bowl of egg yolks. Mix until smooth. Slowly whisk in the oil until well blended. Season to taste with the salt and pepper.

5 Place the lettuce and endive in a large bowl. Pour the tomato-egg yolk mixture over the salad greens, tossing to coat.

6 Arrange the salad greens on individual serving plates and place 2 stuffed egg halves on top. Garnish with sprigs of fresh parsley.

6 SERVINGS
PREP TIME: 25 MINUTES PLUS
15 MINUTES TO STAND
COOKING TIME: 15 MINUTES

EQUIPMENT LIST

Utility knife
Strainer
Colander
Citrus juicer
Pepper mill
Medium-size saucepan
2 large bowls
2 medium-size bowls
Large plate
Teaspoon
Kitchen spoon
Plate
Wire whisk
Salad servers

*H*omemade soups are perfect for family dining. They're easy to prepare and economical, and they can be used as starters or complete meals. Choose from this chapter's wide selection—hearty vegetable soups, gumbo, flavorful chowders, even a fruit-based dessert soup.

Chunky Winter Vegetable Soup.

Chunky Winter Vegetable Soup

6	cups chicken stock or canned broth
1	medium-size white turnip, peeled and chopped (1 cup)
1	small acorn squash, peeled and cut in ½" cubes (1 cup)
1	large carrot, peeled and cut in ½" slices (1 cup)
1	large California white or other boiling potato, peeled and cut in ½" cubes (1½ cups)
1	medium-size leek (including some green tops), trimmed, rinsed, and sliced (½ cup)
2	stalks celery, chopped (1 cup)
2	cups shredded green cabbage
1	28-ounce can whole tomatoes
1	bay leaf
¾	teaspoon ground cumin
⅛	teaspoon salt, or to taste
	Freshly ground black pepper
1	small zucchini, trimmed and cut in ½" slices (1 cup)
1	cup frozen peas
4	ounces mushrooms, trimmed, cleaned, and sliced (1¼ cups)

Soup gains significance in the autumn and winter months when it often ceases being a first course and becomes a main course. Hearty, full flavored, and with a colorful array of vegetables, this soup has an added bonus. The ingredients can be varied according to availablity. What's more, pantry staples like canned chick peas or white kidney beans (one 15-ounce can, drained and rinsed) can be added to make the soup even more robust.

When preparing the soup, be sure to cut the vegetables into an even size so that they will all be done at the end of cooking time. Serve the soup in a tureen and accompany it with whole-grain bread and assorted cheeses.

1 In a large stockpot, combine the stock, turnip, acorn squash, carrot, and potato. Bring the vegetable mixture to a boil over high heat.

2 Reduce the heat to low. Add the leek, celery, cabbage, and tomatoes with their juice. Stir in the bay leaf and cumin. Season to taste with the salt and pepper. Cook, partially covered, for 1 hour.

3 Stir in the zucchini, peas, and mushrooms. Cook, partially covered, for 12 minutes, or until the vegetables are tender. Remove and discard the bay leaf.

4 Ladle the vegetable soup into individual soup bowls and serve immediately.

6 SERVINGS
PREP TIME: 30 MINUTES
COOKING TIME: 1 HOUR 15 MINUTES

EQUIPMENT LIST
Vegetable peeler
Utility knife
Pepper mill
Large stockpot with lid
Kitchen spoon

Tomato-Orange Soup

4	medium-size ripe tomatoes, peeled and quartered (4 cups)
4	cups chicken stock or canned broth
1	cup orange juice
1	medium-size carrot, peeled and thinly sliced (¾ cup)
1	small yellow onion, finely chopped (½ cup)
1	lemon, thinly sliced
5	black peppercorns
1	bay leaf
⅛	teaspoon salt, or to taste
3	tablespoons unsalted butter
3	tablespoons all-purpose flour
¾	cup half-and-half
6	thin orange slices (optional)

Hot or chilled, this soup makes a delectable first course or luncheon entrée accompanied by homemade melba toast. To chill: Transfer the soup to a large bowl, cover with plastic wrap, and chill in the refrigerator for 1 hour.

1 In a large, enamel or stainless steel saucepan, combine the tomatoes, stock, orange juice, carrot, onion, lemon slices, peppercorns, bay leaf, and salt to taste. Bring to a boil over moderately high heat. Reduce the heat to low and cook, uncovered, stirring occasionally, for 1 hour. Strain the soup through a fine sieve into a large bowl and discard the solids.

2 In a large saucepan over moderate heat, melt the butter. Stir in the flour and cook, stirring continuously, for 2 minutes, or until a pale straw color. Return the soup to the pan and bring the mixture to a boil over moderately high heat. Reduce the heat to low and cook, stirring frequently, for 5 minutes, or until the soup has thickened slightly. Remove the pan from the heat. Stir in the half-and-half.

3 Ladle the soup into individual soup bowls. Garnish with the orange slices, if desired, and serve immediately.

6 SERVINGS
PREP TIME: 10 MINUTES
COOKING TIME: 1 HOUR 10 MINUTES

EQUIPMENT LIST
Paring knife
Utility knife
Vegetable peeler
2 large, enamel or stainless steel saucepans
Kitchen spoon
Fine sieve
Large bowl

Louisiana Gumbo

½ cup plus 2 tablespoons vegetable oil

¾ cup all-purpose flour

1 small red bell pepper, cored, seeded, and finely chopped (½ cup)

1 small green bell pepper, cored, seeded, and finely chopped (½ cup)

1 medium-size white onion, finely chopped (1 cup)

1 large clove garlic, finely chopped

1 stalk celery, finely chopped (½ cup)

½ cup chopped fresh parsley

1 pound okra, trimmed, rinsed, and cut in 2″ pieces (3 cups), or 1 16-ounce package frozen okra, thawed and drained

8 cups chicken stock or canned broth

2 bay leaves

1 teaspoon dried thyme leaves, crumbled

¼ teaspoon crushed red pepper flakes

¼ teaspoon ground red pepper (cayenne)

2 tablespoons Worcestershire sauce

2 cups chopped cooked chicken

8 ounces Andouille or other smoked sausage, cut in ½″ slices

4-5 drops hot pepper sauce

Chopped green onion tops (optional)

This gumbo is a Southern specialty with taste power.

This popular Southern soup gets its earthy flavor and color from the roux, a mixture of flour and oil that is cooked until it is a mahogany color. Serve this soup as a main course, accompanied by corn sticks.

1 In a medium-size, heavy saucepan, heat ½ cup of the oil over moderate heat for 1 minute. Slowly add the flour, stirring until well blended. Cook over low heat, stirring frequently, for 30 minutes, or until the roux is mahogany. Remove the pan from the heat.

2 In a 5-quart Dutch oven, heat the remaining 2 tablespoons of oil over moderate heat for 1 minute. Add the red and green bell peppers, onion, garlic, celery, and ¼ cup of the parsley and sauté for 10 minutes, or until the vegetables are softened. Add the okra and sauté for 5 minutes, or until the "roping" has stopped. (The juices form spiderweb-like strings called "roping," which will begin to disappear as the okra cooks.) Add the roux and stir until well blended.

3 Stir in the stock, bay leaves, thyme, red pepper flakes, ground red pepper, and Worcestershire sauce. Cook, uncovered, stirring occasionally, for 30 minutes. Add the chicken, sausage, and hot pepper sauce and cook, stirring occasionally, for 40 minutes. Remove and discard the bay leaves. Stir in the remaining ¼ cup of parsley.

4 Ladle the soup into individual soup bowls. Garnish with the green onion tops, if desired. Serve immediately.

EQUIPMENT LIST

Utility knife
Colander
Medium-size, heavy saucepan
Kitchen spoons
5-quart Dutch oven

Beets, Beef, and Cabbage Soup

This robust soup is reminiscent of Russian Borscht. Accompany it with a mixed green salad and pumpernickel bread for a warming winter meal.

3	tablespoons vegetable oil
1	pound boneless beef chuck, cut in 1″ pieces
2	large carrots, peeled and sliced (2 cups)
4	stalks celery, sliced (2 cups)
1	medium-size red onion, sliced (1¾ cups)
1	medium-size California white or other boiling potato, peeled and cut in ½″ pieces (1 cup)
3	medium-size beets, peeled and sliced (3 cups)
3	cups beef stock or canned broth
3	cups water
¼	teaspoon salt, or to taste
4	cups shredded green cabbage
4	tablespoons sour cream (optional)

1 In a large saucepan, heat 2 tablespoons of the oil over moderately high heat for 1 minute. Add the beef and cook, stirring frequently, for 5 minutes, or until browned on all sides. Using a slotted spoon, transfer the beef to a plate.

2 Add the remaining 1 tablespoon of oil to the pan and heat over moderately high heat for 1 minute. Add the carrots, celery, onion, potato, and beets. Cook, stirring continuously, for 5 minutes, or until the vegetables are softened.

3 Return the beef, with any accumulated juices, to the pan. Add the stock, water, and paprika. Season to taste with the salt. Bring the mixture to a boil. Reduce the heat to low and cook, covered, for 1½ hours, or until the beef is tender. Add the cabbage and cook, uncovered, for 15 minutes more, or until the cabbage is tender.

4 Ladle the soup into individual soup bowls and garnish with sour cream, if desired. Serve immediately.

6 SERVINGS
PREP TIME: 25 MINUTES
COOKING TIME: 2 HOURS

EQUIPMENT LIST

Chef's knife
Vegetable peeler
Utility knife
Large saucepan with lid
Kitchen spoon
Slotted spoon
Plate

Chilled Fennel and Leek Soup

Fennel and leek make a tasty combination in this chilled vegetable soup. It can also be served hot: Return the puréed vegetables to the pan and heat over moderate heat, stirring frequently, for 5 minutes, or until heated through. Hot or chilled, serve it with lightly toasted whole-grain bread as an elegant start to a roast beef or poultry entrée.

2	tablespoons unsalted butter
1	medium-size fennel bulb, trimmed and roughly chopped, fronds reserved (3 cups)
1	medium-size leek (including green top), trimmed, rinsed, and sliced (1 cup)
1	small clove garlic, finely chopped
1	tablespoon all-purpose flour
2	cups milk
2	cups chicken stock or canned broth
¼	teaspoon ground nutmeg
⅛	teaspoon ground cinnamon
	Ground white pepper

1 In a large stockpot over moderate heat, melt the butter. Add fennel, leek, and garlic and sauté for 5 minutes, or until the vegetables are slightly softened.

2 Add the flour to the pan and cook, stirring continuously, for 2 minutes, or until a pale straw color. Add the milk and stock and bring to a boil. Cook, stirring continuously, for 3 minutes, or until smooth and thickened. Reduce the heat to low and simmer, uncovered, for 20 minutes, or until the vegetables are soft.

3 Place half the soup in a blender or food processor fitted with the metal blade. Blend or process for 1 minute, or until the mixture is smooth. Transfer the mixture to a large bowl. Repeat as directed with the remaining soup. Season to taste with the nutmeg, cinnamon, and pepper. Stir well, cover the bowl with plastic wrap, and chill in the refrigerator for 2 hours.

4 Ladle the soup into chilled individual soup bowls. Garnish with the reserved fennel fronds. Serve immediately.

6 SERVINGS
PREP TIME: 10 MINUTES PLUS
2 HOURS TO CHILL
COOKING TIME: 30 MINUTES

EQUIPMENT LIST

Utility knife
Large stockpot
Kitchen spoon
Blender or food processor with metal blade
Large bowl
Plastic wrap

Steamer Soup

24 little neck clams
1 tablespoon white vinegar
2 teaspoons vegetable oil
¼ cup finely chopped yellow onion
3 ounces cooked ham, cut in ¼" strips
1 small red bell pepper, cored, seeded, and finely chopped (½ cup)
1 small green bell pepper, cored, seeded, and finely chopped (½ cup)
1 small tomato, peeled, seeded, and chopped (½ cup)
2½ cups fish stock or bottled clam juice
¼ cup dry white wine (optional)
Freshly ground black pepper
2 tablespoons chopped fresh parsley (optional)

This soup, reminiscent of Manhattan clam chowder, is a treat for clam lovers. It's great as a first course or as a light supper served with crusty French bread. Small, hard-shell clams, such as little necks, are best to use. When purchasing clams, avoid any with cracked, broken, or opened shells that do not close when tapped.

1 Scrub the clams under cold running water and place them in a large bowl with lightly salted cold water to cover. Add the vinegar and let stand for 20 minutes. (The vinegar in the soaking water acts as an irritant and causes the clams to flush out their sand.) Drain the clams well.

2 In a 6-quart Dutch oven, heat the oil over moderate heat for 1 minute. Add the onion and sauté for 5 minutes, or until translucent. Add the ham, red and green bell peppers, and tomato and sauté for 2 minutes, or until the peppers are slightly softened. Stir in the stock and wine, if desired, and bring the mixture to a boil over high heat. Reduce the heat to moderately low and simmer, partially covered, for 15 minutes. Add the clams and cook, covered, for 3 to 4 minutes, or just until the shells open. Gently stir the clams once or twice to ensure even cooking.

3 Using a slotted spoon, divide the clams among individual soup bowls, discarding any that haven't opened. Ladle some broth over the clams. Season to taste with the pepper. Garnish with the chopped fresh parsley, if desired, and serve immediately.

4 SERVINGS
PREP TIME: 15 MINUTES PLUS
20 MINUTES TO STAND
COOKING TIME: 25 MINUTES

Equipment List

Paring knife
Pepper mill
Vegetable brush
Large bowl
6-quart Dutch oven
Kitchen spoon
Slotted spoon

Halibut and Vegetable Chowder

1 pound halibut or grouper fillet, skinned
2 tablespoons vegetable oil
4 stalks celery, sliced diagonally (2 cups)
2 medium-size carrots, peeled and chopped (1½ cups)
1 medium-size yellow onion, finely chopped (1 cup)
1 large clove garlic, chopped
1 large California white or other boiling potato, peeled and cut in ½" pieces (1½ cups)
1 teaspoon dried oregano leaves, crumbled
2½ cups milk
1 cup light cream
Freshly ground black pepper
3 tablespoons chopped fresh parsley (optional)

This chowder is the perfect choice for an easy Sunday supper. Round out the meal with a fresh fruit salad and an assortment of cheeses and crackers.

1 Rinse the halibut fillet under cold running water and pat dry with paper towels. Cut the halibut into 1" pieces and set aside.

2 In a large saucepan, heat the oil over moderately high heat for 1 minute. Add the celery, carrots, onion, and garlic. Cook, stirring frequently, for 5 minutes, or until the onion is translucent. Add the potato and oregano and sauté for 5 minutes, or until the potato is slightly softened. Add the milk and cream.

3 Cook, stirring occasionally, over moderate heat for 10 minutes, or until the potato is tender when tested with a fork. Add the halibut and cook, uncovered, for 5 to 7 minutes, or until the fish flakes easily when tested with a fork. Season to taste with the pepper.

4 Ladle the soup into individual soup bowls. Garnish with the chopped fresh parsley, if desired, and serve immediately.

4 SERVINGS
PREP TIME: 20 MINUTES
COOKING TIME: 28 MINUTES

Equipment List

Utility knife
Vegetable peeler
Pepper mill
Paper towels
Large saucepan
Kitchen spoon
Fork

French Onion Soup

6	tablespoons unsalted butter
1	teaspoon granulated sugar
2½	pounds yellow onions, thinly sliced (10 cups)
6	cups beef stock or canned broth
⅛	teaspoon salt, or to taste
	Freshly ground black pepper
6	slices French bread, cut 1″ thick
4	ounces shredded Gruyère cheese (1 cup)
3	tablespoons cognac (optional)
2	green onions (including tops), chopped (¼ cup)

Small cafés in the famous Paris market, Les Halles, used to serve onion soup to market workers and late-night party revellers alike. Sadly, the market has disappeared, but the soup lives on. Serve it as a first course, or as a meal in itself, accompanied by extra French bread and a salad of mixed greens with a vinaigrette dressing.

1 In a large saucepan over moderate heat, melt 4 tablespoons of the butter with the sugar. Add the onions, stirring well to coat. Reduce the heat to low and cook, uncovered, stirring frequently, for 30 minutes, or until the onions are evenly browned and caramelized. Take care not to let them burn.

2 Add the stock and season to taste with the salt and pepper. Increase the heat to high and bring the soup to a boil. Reduce the heat to moderately low and simmer, partially covered, for 1 hour.

3 Preheat the broiler. Place the bread slices under the broiler 4″ from the heat source. Broil the slices for 1 minute on each side, or until golden. Spread the slices with the remaining 2 tablespoons of butter.

4 Stir the cognac into the soup, if desired, and ladle into individual flameproof soup bowls. Top each bowl with a slice of bread and some of the cheese. Place the bowls under the broiler 3″ from the heat source. Broil for 30 seconds, or until the cheese melts. Sprinkle each bowl with the chopped green onions and serve immediately.

6 SERVINGS
PREP TIME: 15 MINUTES
COOKING TIME: 1 HOUR 30 MINUTES

EQUIPMENT LIST

Utility knife
Serrated knife
Pepper mill
Grater
Large saucepan with lid
Kitchen spoon
Broiler pan
Large, metal spatula
Flameproof soup bowls

Bring a taste of France to the table with this classic onion soup.

Hearty Chicken and Rice Soup

This recipe for chicken and rice soup is a one-pot meal that will soothe and satisfy the heartiest of appetites. Easy and inexpensive, it can be prepared in less than 2 hours yet tastes as if it had been simmering on the stove all day. For a different flavor, try adding other vegetables such as a cup of frozen corn kernels or peas, thawed and drained, after straining the stock.

2   whole chicken breasts, rinsed and patted dry (3 pounds)
1   medium-size parsnip, scrubbed and cut in 2″ pieces (1 cup)
1   medium-size yellow onion, quartered
5   cups chicken stock or canned broth
4   cups water
2   medium-size carrots, peeled and cut in ¼″ slices (1½ cups)
2   stalks celery, chopped (1 cup)
1   teaspoon dried oregano leaves, crumbled
½   teaspoon dried thyme leaves, crumbled
1   bay leaf
1   cup long-grain white rice
¼   cup chopped fresh parsley
¼   teaspoon salt, or to taste
Freshly ground black pepper
2   tablespoons fresh lime juice (optional)
Lime slices (optional)

1 In a large stockpot, combine the chicken breasts, parsnip, onion, stock, and water. Bring to a boil over high heat. Reduce the heat to low and cook, covered, for 30 minutes.

2 Using a slotted spoon, transfer the chicken breasts to a plate and set aside. Strain the stock through a fine sieve into a medium-size bowl, discard the vegetables, and then return the liquid to the pan.

3 Add the carrots, celery, oregano, thyme, bay leaf, and rice to the stock. Bring the mixture to a boil over high heat. Reduce the heat to low, and cook, covered, for 20 minutes, or until the vegetables and rice are tender.

4 Remove and discard the skin and bones from the chicken. Cut the meat into 1″ pieces.

5 Add the chicken pieces to the stock. Cook, covered, for 15 minutes. Stir in the parsley and season to taste with the salt and pepper. Stir in the lime juice, if desired. Remove and discard the bay leaf.

6 Ladle the soup into individual soup bowls. Garnish with lime slices, if desired. Serve immediately.

8 SERVINGS
PREP TIME: 20 MINUTES
COOKING TIME: 1 HOUR 5 MINUTES

EQUIPMENT LIST

Paper towels
Vegetable brush
Utility knife
Vegetable peeler
Pepper mill
Stockpot with lid
Kitchen spoon
Slotted spoon
Plate
Fine sieve
Medium-size bowl

This substantial soup is perfect for a chilly winter day.

Corn and Kidney Bean Soup

This soup will really keep the cold at bay. It can be quick to make, too, if canned beans and frozen corn are used. Either way, the results will be delicious. Serve the soup as an entrée with tortilla chips or warm flour tortillas, or as an appetizer to a grilled fish or chicken entrée.

1½ cups dried red kidney beans, or 2 15-ounce cans red kidney beans, drained and rinsed

4 medium-size ears of fresh corn, shucked, or 1 10-ounce package frozen corn kernels, thawed and drained

1 tablespoon vegetable oil

1 small green or red bell pepper, cored, seeded, and chopped (½ cup)

¼ cup finely chopped yellow onion

1 large clove garlic, finely chopped

1 28-ounce can whole tomatoes, drained and chopped

1¾ cups beef stock or canned broth

1½ cups tomato juice

1 tablespoon chili powder

1 teaspoon ground cumin

4 ounces shredded Cheddar cheese (1 cup)

Tortilla chips or warm flour tortillas (optional)

1 If using dried beans: In a large saucepan, place the beans and add cold water to cover. Bring to a boil over high heat and boil for 2 minutes. Remove the pan from the heat, cover, and let stand for 1 hour. Drain the soaking liquid and cover with fresh cold water. Bring to a boil over high heat. Reduce the heat to moderately low and cook for 1½ hours, or until the beans are tender. Drain well.

2 If using fresh corn, hold an ear of corn vertically over a shallow dish and, using a small, sharp knife, cut the kernels from the cob. Repeat cutting kernels from the remaining ears of corn as directed.

3 In a 6-quart Dutch oven, heat the oil over moderate heat for 1 minute. Add the bell pepper, onion, and garlic and sauté for 5 minutes, or until the onion is translucent. Add the beans, tomatoes, stock, tomato juice, and corn. Stir in the chili powder and cumin.

4 Bring the soup to a boil over high heat. Reduce the heat to low and cook, uncovered, stirring occasionally, for 15 minutes.

5 Ladle soup into individual soup bowls and sprinkle each with some of the cheese. Serve immediately with tortilla chips, if desired.

6 SERVINGS
PREP TIME: 15 MINUTES PLUS
1 HOUR TO STAND
COOKING TIME: 1 HOUR 50 MINUTES

EQUIPMENT LIST

Utility knife
Colander
Grater
Large saucepan with lid
Shallow dish
6-quart Dutch oven
Kitchen spoon

Highly spiced but not at the expense of flavor, this Tex-Mex style soup will prove to be very popular.

Chilled Peach and Pistachio Dessert Soup

4 medium-size ripe peaches
(1½ pounds)
1 tablespoon granulated sugar
¼ cup dry white vermouth, dry
white wine, or water
2 teaspoons fresh lemon juice
½ cup plain lowfat yogurt
¼ cup sour cream (optional)
2 tablespoons chopped
pistachio nuts

This healthful and refreshing dessert soup is an ideal showcase for the fresh, ripe peaches that are available in July and August. Serve it on its own or with a selection of delicate cookies. It will make a fabulous finale to a summer lunch and guests will never know how easy it was to prepare.

1 Peel, pit, and cut the peaches into ¼″ thick slices. Place the peaches, sugar, vermouth, lemon juice, and yogurt in a blender or food processor fitted with the metal blade. Blend or process for 1 minute, or until smooth. Transfer the mixture to a medium-size bowl, cover with plastic wrap, and chill in the refrigerator for at least 3 hours.

2 Ladle the soup into chilled individual glass soup bowls. Garnish with a spoonful of sour cream, if desired, and sprinkle with pistachio nuts. Serve immediately.

4 SERVINGS
PREP TIME: 10 MINUTES PLUS
3 HOURS TO CHILL

EQUIPMENT LIST

Citrus juicer
Vegetable peeler
Blender or food processor with
metal blade
Medium-size bowl
Plastic wrap

Pretty as a peach, this frosty dessert soup provides a perfect finishing touch to a summer meal.

Packed lunches, picnics, and Sunday brunch are all catered for here. Try an inside-out pizza bread, turkey tortillas, spicy meatballs in pita pockets, cheese and onion pie, salmon strudel, griddle cakes, and French toast served with honey and butter balls.

Herb Crêpes with Tomato-Garlic Topping.

Herb Crêpes
with Tomato-Garlic Topping

These crêpes are ideal for a light lunch or supper. For variety, substitute 1 tablespoon of chopped fresh basil or 1 teaspoon crumbled dried basil leaves for the tarragon; garnish with sprigs of fresh basil.

1   Preheat the oven to 350° F. Line 2 large baking sheets with aluminum foil.

2   To make the crêpes: In a small saucepan over moderate heat, melt the butter. Remove the pan from the heat. In a medium-size bowl, stir together the flour, salt, and pepper. Slowly add the buttermilk, egg, and melted butter, whisking until blended and smooth. Stir in the chopped parsley and tarragon.

3   Heat an 8″ crêpe pan or 8″ nonstick skillet over moderate heat for 1 minute, then lightly brush with some oil. Add ¼ cup of batter and swirl pan to coat the bottom evenly. Cook for 1 minute, or until bubbles form and edges are lightly golden. Using a large, metal spatula, turn the crêpe over and cook for 1 minute more, or until underside is lightly golden. Transfer crêpe to a prepared baking sheet. Cook the remaining batter as directed, adding more oil to the pan whenever necessary. Transfer crêpes, in a single layer, to the baking sheets.

4   Arrange the tomato slices, slightly overlapping in a circle, over each crêpe. Sprinkle the crêpes with the garlic. Season to taste.

5   Bake for 7 minutes, or until the tomatoes are softened and the crêpes begin to brown around the edges. Remove the baking sheets from the oven. Using a large, metal spatula, transfer the crêpes to individual serving plates. Sprinkle with the green onions. Garnish with sprigs of fresh parsley and tarragon, if desired, and serve immediately.

Ingredients

1   tablespoon unsalted butter
¾   cup sifted all-purpose flour
¼   teaspoon salt
⅛   teaspoon coarsely ground black pepper
1   cup buttermilk
1   large egg, lightly beaten
1   tablespoon chopped fresh parsley
1   tablespoon chopped fresh tarragon, or 1 teaspoon dried tarragon leaves, crumbled
Vegetable oil
Sprigs of fresh parsley (optional)
Sprigs of fresh tarragon (optional)

TOMATO-GARLIC TOPPING (6 CUPS)

12   ripe plum tomatoes, sliced ⅛″ thick (6 cups)
1   large clove garlic, chopped
¼   teaspoon salt, or to taste
2   green onions (including tops), thinly sliced (¼ cup)

6 SERVINGS OR 6 CRÊPES
PREP TIME: 15 MINUTES
COOKING TIME: 20 MINUTES

EQUIPMENT LIST

Sifter
Small bowl
Medium-size bowl
Wire whisk
Utility knife
2 large baking sheets
Aluminum foil
Small saucepan
Kitchen spoon
8″ crêpe pan or 8″ nonstick skillet
Pastry brush
Large, metal spatula

Spinach-Stuffed Baked Potatoes

Baked potatoes are delicious and healthful as a side dish or a complete meal. Potatoes themselves aren't fattening, and with the addition of a low-calorie filling and topping, this dish will be healthful and yet satisfying.

1   Preheat the oven to 425° F. Prick the potatoes with a fork and bake them in the oven for 40 to 45 minutes, or until the potatoes are tender when tested with a fork.

2   Remove the potatoes from the oven. Cut them in half lengthwise. Leaving a ¼″ shell, scoop out the flesh from each potato half into a medium-size bowl. Reserve the potato shells.

3   Squeeze out all of the excess liquid from the spinach. Add the spinach, butter, and milk to the potato flesh and mix well. Season to taste with the salt. Place the potato skins on a baking sheet. Spoon the mixture into the potato skins and bake in the oven for 15 to 20 minutes, or until heated through. Serve with the yogurt, if desired.

Ingredients

4   medium-size Idaho or other baking potatoes, scrubbed
1   10-ounce package frozen chopped spinach, thawed
2   tablespoons salted butter, softened
1   tablespoon milk
½   teaspoon salt, or to taste
½   cup plain lowfat yogurt (optional)

4 SERVINGS
PREP TIME: 10 MINUTES
COOKING TIME: 1 HOUR 5 MINUTES

EQUIPMENT LIST

Vegetable brush
Fork
Utility knife
Kitchen spoon
Medium-size bowl
Baking sheet

Pizza Bread

2   pounds frozen bread dough, thawed

1   large egg, lightly beaten

PIZZA FILLING

1   large yellow onion, finely chopped (1½ cups)

1   medium-size red bell pepper, cored, seeded, and finely chopped (¾ cup)

1   medium-size green bell pepper, cored, seeded, and finely chopped (¾ cup)

8   ounces pepperoni sausage, cut in small pieces

12   sliced, pitted black olives

1   teaspoon dried oregano leaves, crumbled

1   teaspoon coarsely ground black pepper

2   teaspoons fennel seeds

This bread recipe turns pizza outside-in as the traditional topping ingredients are incorporated into the dough before baking.

1 To make the Pizza Filling: In a large bowl, combine the onion, red and green bell peppers, sausage, olives, oregano, pepper, and fennel seeds. Set aside.

2 Divide the dough in half. On a lightly floured work surface, roll 1 dough half into a 15½″ x 10½″ rectangle ¾″ thick. Sprinkle half the filling over dough. Fold dough in half lengthwise to enclose filling. Roll out the dough again to a 15½″ x 10½″ rectangle and sprinkle with the remaining filling. Shape the filled dough into a ball and set aside.

3 Roll out the second dough half into a 15″ circle or a circle that is large enough to enclose the ball of dough completely. Place the dough ball in the center of the circle of dough, wrap the circle of dough around the ball, and pinch it into a knot to seal.

4 Place dough, knot-side down, on a lightly greased baking sheet and flatten to a 10″ circle. Cover loosely with plastic wrap and let rise in a warm, draft-free place for 30 minutes, or until doubled in volume.

5 Preheat the oven to 375° F. Remove the plastic wrap from the dough and make three or four slashes across the top. Brush the dough with beaten egg.

6 Bake the bread for 45 minutes to 1 hour, or until the top is golden brown and the bread sounds hollow when the bottom is tapped. Transfer the bread to a wire rack to cool for 15 minutes. Serve sliced.

1 LOAF OR 24 SLICES
PREP TIME: 30 MINUTES PLUS
45 MINUTES TO RISE AND COOL
COOKING TIME: 1 HOUR

EQUIPMENT LIST

Small bowl
Wire whisk
Utility knife
Paring knife
Large bowl
Kitchen spoon
Rolling pin
Baking sheet
Plastic wrap
Pastry brush
Wire rack

This pizza hides its true colors because the filling is on the inside, not on the outside.

Turkey Tortillas

2	tablespoons olive oil
1	pound uncooked turkey cutlets or boned breast meat, cut in small cubes
1	small yellow onion, finely chopped (½ cup)
1	small carrot, peeled and finely chopped (½ cup)
1	stalk celery, finely chopped (½ cup)
8	ounces mushrooms, trimmed, cleaned, and sliced (2¼ cups)
½	teaspoon ground cumin
8	10″ flour tortillas
1	cup mild or hot bottled salsa
8	ounces shredded Monterey Jack cheese (2 cups)
¼	cup pitted, sliced black olives
2	small tomatoes, quartered (optional)

1 Preheat the oven to 350° F. Lightly grease a large, shallow baking dish.

2 In a large, heavy skillet, heat the oil over moderate heat for 1 minute. Add the turkey pieces and sauté for 2 to 3 minutes, or until no pink color remains. Using a slotted spoon, transfer the turkey pieces to a plate and set aside.

3 Add the onion, carrot, and celery to the skillet and sauté for 5 minutes, or until the onion is translucent. Add the mushrooms and sauté for 5 minutes, or until softened. Stir in the cumin and the turkey pieces. Remove the skillet from the heat.

4 Lay 1 tortilla on a work surface. Spoon about ½ cup of the turkey mixture into the center of the tortilla. Top with 2 tablespoons of salsa, then sprinkle with 2 tablespoons of the cheese. Fold over 1 side to enclose the turkey mixture, then fold over the second side to cover the first. Place the filled tortilla, seam-side down, in the prepared dish. Repeat with the remaining tortillas, placing them side by side in the baking dish. Sprinkle the remaining cheese and the olives over the filled tortillas.

5 Cover the dish with aluminum foil and bake for 15 minutes. Remove the foil and bake for 5 to 10 minutes more, or until the tops of the tortillas are golden brown. Remove from the oven. Using a large, metal spatula, transfer the tortillas to individual serving plates. Garnish with the tomato quarters, if desired, and serve immediately.

4 SERVINGS
PREP TIME: 20 MINUTES
COOKING TIME: 30 MINUTES

EQUIPMENT LIST

Utility knife
Vegetable peeler
Grater
Large, shallow baking dish
Large, heavy skillet
Kitchen spoon
Slotted spoon
Plate
Aluminum foil

Salmon-Potato Strudel

6	medium-size California white or other boiling potatoes, peeled and quartered (6 cups)
¼	cup milk
1	15½-ounce can pink salmon, drained, boned, and flaked
2	large eggs, lightly beaten
2	tablespoons chopped fresh parsley
2	tablespoons chopped fresh dill, or 2 teaspoons dried dill weed
2	tablespoons finely chopped yellow onion
⅛	teaspoon ground red pepper (cayenne)
⅛	teaspoon salt, or to taste
1	10″ x 18″ sheet frozen puff pastry, thawed

1 Preheat the oven to 400° F. Place the potatoes in a large saucepan with enough cold water to cover. Bring to a boil over high heat. Reduce heat to moderately low and cook, uncovered, for 20 minutes, or until the potatoes are tender when tested with a fork. Drain well.

2 Place the potatoes in a large bowl. Using a potato masher or fork, coarsely mash the potatoes. Add the milk and mash until smooth. Stir in the salmon, half of the beaten egg, the parsley, dill, onion, and ground red pepper until well blended. Season to taste.

3 Lightly flour a work surface and a rolling pin. Roll pastry evenly, from the center outward, to a 14″ x 18″ rectangle. Carefully transfer pastry to a baking sheet. Spoon salmon mixture lengthwise down the center of the pastry to within 2″ of the top and bottom.

4 Fold the over top and bottom edges. Fold over 1 side to enclose the salmon mixture, then fold over the second side to enclose the first. Carefully turn strudel so the seam is underneath. Press top and bottom edges to seal. Brush the strudel with remaining beaten egg.

5 Bake for 30 minutes, or until the pastry is golden brown. Remove the baking sheet from the oven and place on a wire rack to cool for 15 minutes. Using a large, metal spatula, loosen the strudel from the baking sheet and transfer it to a serving platter. Serve warm.

8 SERVINGS
PREP TIME: 40 MINUTES PLUS
15 MINUTES TO COOL
COOKING TIME: 30 MINUTES

EQUIPMENT LIST

Vegetable peeler
Utility knife
Strainer
Small bowl
Large bowl
Wire whisk
Large saucepan
Fork
Potato masher
Kitchen spoon
Rolling pin
Baking sheet
Pastry brush
Wire rack

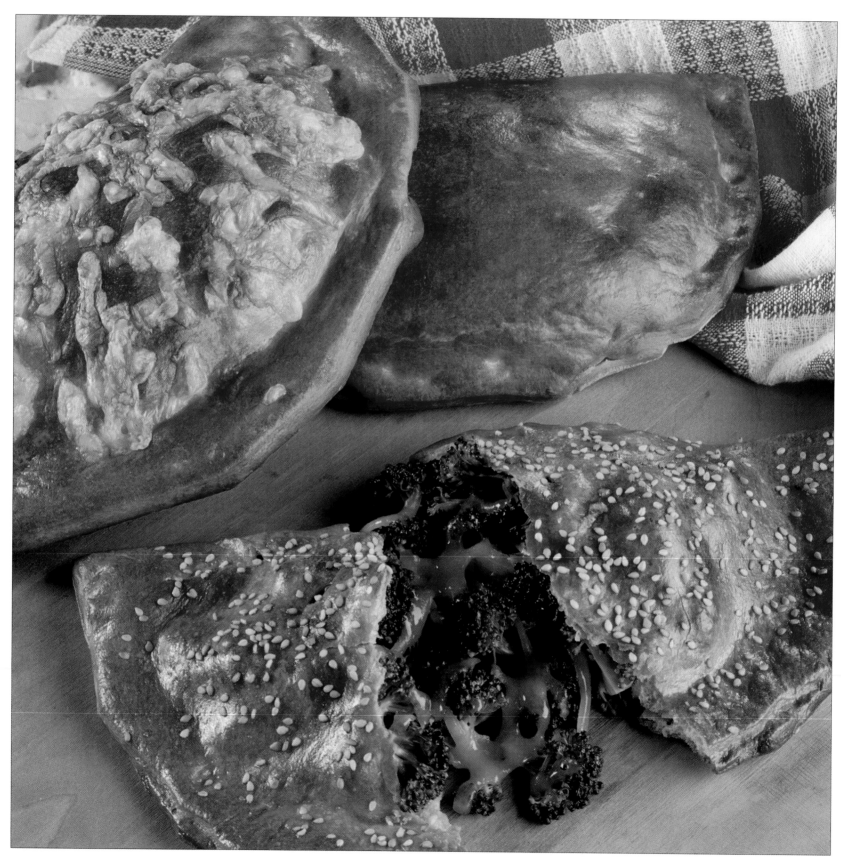

Spicy Sausage Calzones

Calzone is a pizza "sandwich." Here are some fantastic fillings.

12 ounces hot Italian sausage, casings removed
1 tablespoon olive oil
1 small yellow onion, finely chopped (½ cup)
1 stalk celery, finely chopped (½ cup)
½ teaspoon dried rosemary leaves, crumbled
1 6-ounce can tomato paste
½ cup hot water
⅛ teaspoon salt, or to taste
Freshly ground black pepper
Yellow cornmeal
1 10-ounce package pizza dough
4 ounces shredded Fontina cheese (1 cup)
1 large egg, lightly beaten

1 In a large skillet over moderately high heat, cook sausage, breaking it up with a wooden spoon and stirring frequently, for 5 minutes, or until no pink color remains. Using a slotted spoon, transfer sausage to a plate lined with paper towels to drain. Wipe out the skillet.

2 Heat oil in skillet over moderate heat for 1 minute. Add onion and celery and sauté for 5 minutes, or until onion is translucent. Add rosemary and cook for 2 minutes. Add tomato paste and water and cook, stirring continuously, for 3 minutes, or until well combined. Remove the skillet from the heat. Stir in the sausage. Season to taste.

3 Preheat oven to 425° F. Dust 2 baking sheets with cornmeal. Divide the dough in half. Set 1 piece aside. Lightly dust a work surface with cornmeal. Lightly flour a rolling pin and roll dough evenly, from the center outward, to a 10″ circle. Place half the sausage mixture on 1 side of dough circle. Sprinkle one-third of the cheese over the filling. Brush dough edges with water and fold over to enclose filling. Press edges firmly to seal. Transfer the calzone to a baking sheet. Repeat as directed with the second dough piece, the remaining filling, and one-third of the cheese. Transfer the calzone to second baking sheet.

4 Brush the calzones with the beaten egg. Sprinkle with remaining cheese. Bake for 18 to 20 minutes, or until golden brown. Remove from the oven. Cool for 5 minutes. Cut each calzone into 3 wedges, transfer to individual serving plates, and serve warm.

6 SERVINGS OR 2 CALZONES
PREP TIME: 30 MINUTES
COOKING TIME: 20 MINUTES

EQUIPMENT LIST

Utility knife
Pepper mill
Grater
Small bowl
Wire whisk
Large skillet
Wooden spoon
Slotted spoon
Plate
Paper towels
2 baking sheets
Rolling pin
Pastry brush

Mushroom-Ricotta Calzones

1 tablespoon unsalted butter
1 large clove garlic, chopped
1 pound mushrooms, finely chopped (4½ cups)
½ teaspoon dried sage leaves, crumbled
1 cup part-skim ricotta cheese
1 ounce grated Parmesan cheese (¼ cup)

1 In a large skillet over moderate heat, melt the butter. Add the garlic and sauté for 1 minute. Add mushrooms and cook for 10 minutes, stirring occasionally, until liquid has evaporated. Stir in sage. Remove skillet from the heat. Stir in the ricotta and Parmesan cheeses.

2 Roll out 2 dough circles as directed. Fill each with half of the mushroom mixture. Brush the dough edges with water, fold over, and press to seal. Brush with the egg. Bake as directed.

6 SERVINGS OR 2 CALZONES
PREP TIME: 30 MINUTES
COOKING TIME: 20 MINUTES

EQUIPMENT LIST FOR FILLING

Utility knife
Large skillet
Kitchen spoon

Broccoli-Cheddar Calzones

2 teaspoons olive oil
1 small yellow onion, chopped (½ cup)
1 large clove garlic, chopped
¼ teaspoon red pepper flakes
3 cups chopped broccoli florets
2 ounces shredded Cheddar cheese (¼ cup)
1 teaspoon sesame seeds (optional)

1 In a large skillet, heat the oil over moderate heat for 1 minute. Add the onion and garlic, and sauté for 5 minutes, or until onion is translucent. Stir in the red pepper flakes and broccoli.

2 Roll out 2 dough circles as directed. Fill each with half of the broccoli mixture. Sprinkle the cheese over filling. Brush the dough edges with water, fold over, and press to seal. Brush with the egg. Sprinkle with the sesame seeds, if desired. Bake as directed.

6 SERVINGS OR 2 CALZONES
PREP TIME: 30 MINUTES
COOKING TIME: 20 MINUTES

EQUIPMENT LIST FOR FILLING

Utility knife
Grater
Large skillet
Kitchen spoon

Cinnamon-Spiced French Toast

3 large eggs
2 cups milk
3 tablespoons granulated sugar
½ teaspoon ground cinnamon
4 tablespoons unsalted butter
8 day-old slices French bread,
    cut ½" thick
Fresh fruit (optional)
Maple syrup (optional)

HONEY-BUTTER BALLS (½ CUP)

¼ cup honey
¼ cup (½ stick) unsalted butter,
    softened
½ teaspoon grated orange rind

Treat someone to breakfast with French toast topped with a mixture of honey and butter. Serve it with freshly squeezed orange juice.

Make 2 batches of French toast and freeze one for a busy weekday morning. To freeze: Cool the toast slices on a wire rack. Place them on a baking sheet and freeze in a single layer for 1 to 2 hours. Wrap the slices individually in plastic wrap, then in aluminum foil, and freeze for up to 1 month. Unwrap the slices and reheat in a toaster oven, or bake at 375° F. for 8 to 10 minutes, or until heated through.

1 To make Honey-Butter Balls: In a medium-size bowl, using an electric mixer set on medium speed, beat the honey, ¼ cup of butter, and orange rind until well blended. Transfer the butter mixture to a small bowl, cover the bowl with plastic wrap, and chill in the refrigerator for 1 hour. Dip a melon-ball cutter into warm water and scoop the butter into balls.

2 To make the Cinnamon-Spiced French Toast: In a medium-size, shallow bowl, whisk together the eggs, milk, sugar, and cinnamon.

3 In a large skillet over moderate heat, melt 2 tablespoons of the butter. Dip 4 bread slices into the egg mixture, soaking both sides. Place slices in the skillet and cook for 2 to 3 minutes on each side, or until golden brown. Transfer the toast to a serving platter and keep warm. Melt the remaining 2 tablespoons of butter in the skillet. Dip and cook the remaining bread slices as directed.

4 Transfer the French toast slices to individual serving plates. Garnish with fresh fruit and serve with the Honey-Butter Balls and maple syrup, if desired.

This favorite breakfast dish is enhanced by honey and butter balls.

4 SERVINGS
PREP TIME: 15 MINUTES PLUS
1 HOUR TO CHILL
COOKING TIME: 12 MINUTES

EQUIPMENT LIST

Serrated knife
Grater
Medium-size bowl
Small bowl
Medium-size, shallow bowl
Electric mixer
Plastic wrap
Melon-ball cutter
Wire whisk
Large skillet
Large, metal spatula

Cheese and Onion Pie

The combination of Swiss and Parmesan cheeses gives this simply prepared quiche an excellent flavor and creamy texture.

1⅓ cups all-purpose flour
⅛ teaspoon salt
½ cup (1 stick) unsalted butter, chilled and cut in pieces
2-3 tablespoons ice water

SAVORY FILLING

1 tablespoon unsalted butter
1 medium-size yellow onion, thinly sliced (1½ cups)
4 green onions (including tops), sliced (½ cup)
1 shallot, sliced (2 tablespoons)
4 large eggs
1¼ cups half-and-half
¼ teaspoon ground nutmeg
⅛ teaspoon salt, or to taste
⅛ teaspoon ground white pepper
¼ teaspoon dry mustard
8 ounces shredded Swiss cheese (2 cups)
2 ounces grated Parmesan cheese (½ cup)
1 tablespoon cornstarch

1 To make the pastry crust: In a medium-size bowl, mix the flour and salt. Using a pastry blender or 2 knives, cut the butter into the flour until mixture resembles coarse crumbs. Sprinkle 2 tablespoons of ice water over the flour mixture. Gently toss with a fork, then add as much of the remaining ice water as needed to gather the pastry into a ball. Flatten slightly, wrap in wax paper, and chill for 30 minutes.

2 Preheat the oven to 400° F. Lightly flour a work surface and a rolling pin. Roll dough evenly, from the center outward, and line a 9″ pie pan or baking dish. Fit loosely and press pastry to fit the side. Trim edge ¼″ above rim of the pan, fold this edge under, and press in place with your fingers. Crimp pastry edges. Prick bottom of pastry shell with a fork, line with aluminum foil, and fill with pie weights or dried beans. Bake, uncovered, for 6 to 7 minutes. Remove weights and foil and bake pastry shell for 2 to 4 minutes more, or until golden.

3 To make the Savory Filling: In a large, heavy skillet over moderate heat, melt the butter. Add the yellow and green onions and the shallot and sauté for 10 minutes, or until transparent. Remove the pan from the heat.

4 In a medium-size bowl, beat the eggs. Brush a little egg over the pastry shell. Add the half-and-half, nutmeg, salt, pepper, and mustard to the bowl with the eggs and beat well.

5 In another medium-size bowl, mix the Swiss and Parmesan cheeses and the cornstarch with a fork. Place half of the cheese in the baked pastry shell and cover with the onion mixture. Sprinkle with the remaining cheese and gently pour the egg mixture over the top.

6 Bake for 35 to 40 minutes, or until well risen and firmly set. Remove the pie from the oven and transfer to a wire rack to cool slightly. Cut the pie into wedges and serve warm.

This luscious pie makes the most of the ever-popular cheese and egg combination.

8 SERVINGS
PREP TIME: 35 MINUTES PLUS
30 MINUTES TO CHILL
COOKING TIME: 50 MINUTES

EQUIPMENT LIST

Utility knife
Grater
3 medium-size bowls
Pastry blender or 2 knives
Fork
Wax paper
Aluminum foil
Rolling pin
9″ pie pan or baking dish
Pie weights or dried beans
Large, heavy skillet
Kitchen spoon
Pastry brush
Wire rack

Cheddar-Rice Griddle Cakes

1½ cups water
¾ cup long-grain white rice
4 ounces shredded sharp Cheddar cheese (1 cup)
1 small yellow onion, finely chopped (½ cup)
3 tablespoons all-purpose flour
3 large eggs, separated
½ teaspoon salt, or to taste
¼ teaspoon coarsely ground black pepper
⅛ teaspoon cream of tartar
2-3 tablespoons vegetable oil
Fresh strawberries (optional)
Sour cream (optional)
Sprigs of fresh mint (optional)

These griddle cakes are tremendously versatile. They can be served at any meal, any time of day. They will delight weekend guests for a late brunch or add flair to a luncheon. They are also a marvelous accompaniment to any kind of meat, poultry, or fish.

The rice can be prepared and combined with the other ingredients several hours ahead. Beat and fold in the egg whites just before cooking. This recipe can be halved or doubled depending on the number of people needed to serve.

1 In a medium-size saucepan, bring the water to a boil over high heat. Stir in the rice. Reduce the heat to low and cook, covered, for 20 minutes, or until the rice is tender and the liquid is absorbed. Fluff the rice with a fork and cool slightly.

2 Preheat the oven to 200° F. In a large bowl, mix together the rice, cheese, onion, flour, egg yolks, salt, and pepper.

3 In a medium-size bowl, using an electric mixer set on high speed, beat the egg whites with the cream of tartar to stiff peaks. Gently fold the egg whites into the rice mixture.

4 In a large, nonstick skillet, heat 1 tablespoon of the oil over moderate heat for 1 minute. Drop the rice mixture into the skillet, using about 2 tablespoons of the mixture for each cake.

5 Cook the griddle cakes for 1 to 2 minutes on each side, or until golden brown. Transfer the cooked griddle cakes to a baking pan, cover with aluminum foil, and keep warm in the oven. Repeat cooking the remaining mixture as directed, adding more oil to the skillet if needed.

6 Transfer the griddle cakes to a serving plate. Garnish with strawberries, sour cream, and sprigs of fresh mint, if desired, and serve warm.

These griddle cakes make a welcome change from the standard recipe.

6 SERVINGS
PREP TIME: 25 MINUTES
COOKING TIME: 20 MINUTES

EQUIPMENT LIST

Grater
Utility knife
2 small bowls
Large bowl
Medium-size bowl
Medium-size saucepan with lid
Fork
Kitchen spoon
Electric mixer
Rubber spatula
Large, nonstick skillet
Large, metal spatula
Baking pan
Aluminum foil

Cheese Strata
with Pesto and Vegetables

4 large eggs
2¾ cups milk
1½ tablespoons pesto sauce
2 tablespoons salted butter or margarine
8 ounces mushrooms, trimmed, cleaned, and sliced (2¼ cups)
4 green onions (including tops), finely chopped (½ cup)
1 loaf Italian bread, cut ½" thick
8 ounces sliced Swiss or American cheese

Pesto is a vivid green Italian sauce made from fresh basil leaves, garlic, pine nuts (pignoli), olive oil, and often Parmesan cheese. Homemade pesto is best, but bottled pesto, available in larger supermarkets, can be used in this recipe. This strata can be prepared up to 24 hours ahead and refrigerated until ready to bake. Serve it with grilled sausages and a fruit salad for an easy brunch.

1 Grease a 9" square baking pan. In a medium-size bowl, whisk together the eggs, milk, and pesto sauce.

2 In a medium-size skillet over moderate heat, melt the butter. Add the mushrooms and green onions and sauté for 5 minutes, or until the vegetables are softened. Remove the skillet from the heat.

3 Preheat the oven to 325° F. Arrange half of the bread slices in the prepared pan. Spoon half of the mushrooms and green onions over the bread slices, then pour half of the egg mixture over them. Cover with half of the cheese slices. Repeat layers with the remaining bread slices, mushrooms and green onions, egg mixture, and a final layer of cheese. Cover the pan with plastic wrap and chill in the refrigerator for 1 hour. Remove and discard plastic wrap.

4 Bake the strata, uncovered, for 30 to 35 minutes, or until a knife inserted in the center comes out clean. Serve immediately.

6 SERVINGS
PREP TIME: 15 MINUTES PLUS
1 HOUR TO CHILL
COOKING TIME: 35 MINUTES

EQUIPMENT LIST

Utility knife
Serrated knife
9" baking pan
Medium-size bowl
Wire whisk
Medium-size skillet
Kitchen spoon
Plastic wrap

Mediterranean Meatballs
in Pita Pockets

12 ounces lean ground beef
½ cup fresh bread crumbs
1 large egg, lightly beaten
1 medium-size yellow onion, finely chopped (1 cup)
2 large cloves garlic, finely chopped
2 teaspoons dried mint leaves, crumbled
1 teaspoon ground cumin
¼ teaspoon ground cinnamon
Freshly ground black pepper
⅛ teaspoon ground red pepper (cayenne)
1 4½-ounce can tomato sauce
1 14½-ounce can stewed tomatoes
4 large whole-wheat pita pockets

These easy-to-make meatballs are full of flavor and they are great to serve when a warm lunch is wanted. Accompany the meatballs with a Greek salad for a light lunch.

1 Preheat oven to 400° F. In a large bowl, combine the beef, bread crumbs, egg, onion, garlic, mint, cumin, cinnamon, and black and ground red peppers until well blended.

2 Divide the mixture into 12 equal portions, roll into balls, and place in a shallow baking pan. Bake, uncovered, turning occasionally, for 15 minutes, or until the meatballs begin to brown.

3 Meanwhile, in a medium-size bowl, combine the tomato sauce and stewed tomatoes and pour over the meatballs. Reduce the oven temperature to 350° F.

4 Bake, uncovered, brushing with sauce, for 30 minutes more, or until the meatballs are cooked through and sauce has thickened slightly. Remove the pan from the oven. Fill the pita pockets with some of the meatballs and sauce and serve immediately.

4 SERVINGS
PREP TIME: 10 MINUTES
COOKING TIME: 45 MINUTES

EQUIPMENT LIST

Small bowl
Large bowl
Medium-size bowl
Wire whisk
Utility knife
Pepper mill
Kitchen spoon
Shallow baking pan
Large, metal spatula
Pastry brush

Eggs Creole with Hash Browns

For a savory Sunday breakfast for two, serve these eggs and hash browns with croissants and fresh fruit. To serve four, simply double the quantities.

1 tablespoon salted butter or margarine
2 large eggs
Chopped fresh parsley (optional)

HASH BROWNS

1 tablespoon vegetable oil
2 teaspoons salted butter or margarine
1 small yellow onion, finely chopped (½ cup)
3 medium-size new potatoes, peeled and finely chopped (3 cups)
⅛ teaspoon salt, or to taste
Freshly ground black pepper

CREOLE SAUCE (1½ CUPS)

1 tablespoon salted butter or margarine
¼ cup finely chopped yellow onion
1 large clove garlic, finely chopped
¼ cup chopped celery
¼ cup chopped green or red bell pepper
1 14½-ounce can stewed tomatoes or tomato sauce
1 teaspoon chili powder
4 drops hot pepper sauce

1 To make the Hash Browns: In a large skillet, heat the oil and 2 teaspoons of butter over moderate heat for 1 minute. Add the ½ cup of onion and sauté for 5 minutes, or until translucent. Add the potatoes and season to taste with the salt and pepper. Cook, uncovered, stirring frequently, for 25 minutes, or until the vegetables are browned.

2 Meanwhile, make the Creole Sauce. In a medium-size saucepan over moderate heat, melt the 1 tablespoon of butter. Add the ¼ cup of onion, garlic, celery, and bell pepper and sauté for 5 minutes, or until the vegetables are softened. Add tomatoes, chili powder, and hot pepper sauce. Cook, covered, over low, stirring occasionally, heat for 10 minutes, or until thickened slightly.

3 In a medium-size skillet over moderate heat, melt the 1 tablespoon of butter. Gently break the eggs into the pan. Reduce the heat to moderately low and cook the eggs, uncovered, basting frequently with the butter, for 4 to 5 minutes, or until the whites are set and the yolks are covered with a pale film.

4 Transfer the potatoes to a serving platter. Using a large, metal spatula, place the eggs on top. Spoon some Creole Sauce over them. Garnish with chopped fresh parsley, if desired, and serve immediately.

2 SERVINGS
PREP TIME: 15 MINUTES
COOKING TIME: 31 MINUTES

EQUIPMENT LIST

Utility knife
Vegetable peeler
Pepper mill
Large skillet
Medium-size skillet
Kitchen spoon
Medium-size saucepan with lid
Large, metal spatula

Eggs with hash browns will be a real eye opener on a lazy weekend morning.

Scandinavian Picnic Loaf

Great for a picnic or a party, the loaf and filling can be prepared ahead and combined just before serving. Because the Danish Blue cheese is crumbly, it's best to add the cubes at the end, after the loaf is filled, instead of combining them with the other filling ingredients.

4   tablespoons unsalted butter
1   7½″ round crusty white loaf
1   medium-size tomato, seeded and chopped (1 cup)
1   small red or green bell pepper, cored, seeded, and cut in ¾″ pieces (½ cup)
¼   cup chopped red onion
½   cup whole pitted black olives
Ground white pepper
4   ounces Danish Blue cheese, cut in 1″ pieces (1 cup)
Leafy green lettuce leaves (optional)
Black grapes (optional)

1 Preheat the oven to 400° F. In a small saucepan over moderate heat, melt the butter.

2 Using a large, serrated knife, slice the top from the loaf and reserve. Scoop out and reserve the bread from the inside of the loaf, leaving a ½″ thick shell.

3 Place the hollowed-out loaf and the lid, cut-side up, on a large baking sheet. Brush the inside of the loaf and the cut-side of the lid with 2 tablespoons of the butter.

4 Cut the reserved bread into ¾″ cubes. Arrange 1 cup of the bread cubes in a single layer on a second baking sheet. (Store the remainder in a plastic bag in the refrigerator for another use, such as bread crumbs.) Brush the bread cubes with the remaining 2 tablespoons of butter. Bake for 5 minutes.

5 Remove the baking sheets from the oven. Transfer the lid to a wire rack. Turn the bread cubes and bake, with the loaf, for 5 to 6 minutes more.

6 In a medium-size bowl, combine the tomato, bell pepper, onion, olives, and the 1 cup of bread cubes. Season to taste with the pepper.

7 Transfer the loaf to a serving plate. Spoon the mixture into the loaf, adding the pieces of Danish Blue cheese at random. Garnish with the lettuce leaves and the black grapes, if desired. Cut the loaf into wedges and serve immediately.

Fun to eat, this picnic loaf is a wonderful centerpiece for entertaining. And it's a snap to make!

6 SERVINGS
PREP TIME: 20 MINUTES
COOKING TIME: 11 MINUTES

EQUIPMENT LIST

Utility knife
Large, serrated knife
Small saucepan
Kitchen spoon
2 baking sheets
Pastry brush
Wire rack
Medium-size bowl

MEATS

*P*ot roasts, meat pies, chili, meatloaf, and meat and vegetable stir-fries always receive high praise from family members. The dishes in this chapter provide a varied selection of meats to choose from, and old favorites are given a new twist that will be sure to appeal to everyone.

Lattice-Topped Meat Pie.

Lattice-Topped Meat Pie

3 tablespoons olive oil
1¼ pounds chuck or other stewing beef, cut in 1" cubes
1 medium-size yellow onion, chopped (1 cup)
1 large clove garlic, chopped
3 medium-size carrots, peeled and thinly slice (2¼ cups)
2 8-ounce cans tomato sauce
⅓ cup chopped fresh parsley
½ teaspoon dried marjoram leaves crumbled
¼ teaspoon dry mustard
⅛ teaspoon hot pepper sauce
½ teaspoon salt, or to taste
Sprigs of fresh parsley (optional)

POTATO TOPPING
2 large California white or other boiling potatoes, peeled and quartered (1½ pounds)
¼ cup milk
3 tablespoons unsalted butter

The appeal of this meat pie is its crusty lattice of potatoes. Serve it as a wintertime main dish with whole-wheat bread and mugs of apple cider.

1 Preheat the oven to 350° F. In a 6-quart Dutch oven, heat 2 tablespoons of oil over moderate heat for 1 minute. Add half the meat and sauté for 2 minutes, or until browned. Using a slotted spoon, transfer the meat to a plate. Repeat with the remaining meat.

2 Add the remaining 1 tablespoon of oil to the pan. Add onion and garlic and sauté for 5 minutes, or until onion is translucent. Add the carrots, tomato sauce, herbs, mustard, hot pepper sauce, and meat and stir well. Season to taste with the salt. Bring to a boil. Transfer the mixture to a 2-quart casserole and bake, covered, for 50 minutes.

3 Meanwhile place the potatoes in a large saucepan, with enough cold water to cover. Bring to a boil over high heat. Reduce the heat to low and cook, uncovered, for 20 minutes, or until tender when tested with a fork. Drain potatoes, add milk and butter, and mash well.

4 Remove the casserole from the oven. Spoon the potatoes into a pastry bag fitted with a ½" star tip. Pipe the potatoes around the edge of the casserole and across in a lattice pattern. Return the casserole to the oven and bake, uncovered, for 15 minutes, or until the potatoes are browned. Garnish with the sprigs of fresh parsley, if desired, and serve immediately.

4 SERVINGS
PREP TIME: 40 MINUTES
COOKING TIME: 1 HOUR 15 MINUTES

EQUIPMENT LIST
Chef's knife
Utility knife
Vegetable peeler
6-quart Dutch oven
2-quart casserole with lid
Kitchen spoon
Slotted spoon
Plate
Large saucepan
Fork
Colander
Potato masher
Pastry bag with ½" star tip

Texas-Style Beef Brisket

¼ cup finely chopped yellow onion
¾ teaspoon paprika
½ teaspoon coarsely ground black pepper
1 2-2½ pound boneless brisket of beef
½ cup water
½ cup prepared steak sauce

TEXAS-STYLE-SAUCE (⅔ CUP)
1 teaspoon unsalted butter
2 tablespoons finely chopped yellow onion
½ cup tomato ketchup
1 tablespoon dark brown sugar
¼ teaspoon crushed red pepper flakes

Serve this spicy brisket with potatoes and coleslaw.

1 Preheat the oven to 250° F. In a small bowl, mix the ¼ cup of onion, the paprika, and pepper. Rub mixture over the surface of the meat. Place the meat in a 5-quart Dutch oven and add the water. Cover tightly with aluminum foil, then with a lid. Cook for 1¼ hours.

2 Remove pan from the oven. Turn meat over. Pour off pan juices. Replace foil and lid and cook for 1¼ hours more. Remove pan from oven. Pour off pan juices and reserve ½ cup. Discard remainder.

3 In a medium-size bowl, mix the reserved ½ cup of pan juices with the steak sauce. Pour half the steak sauce mixture over meat and reserve the remaining mixture. Turn the meat to coat with the sauce. Cook the meat, covered, on top of the stove, over very low heat, for 2 hours, turning it and brushing with sauce in the pan every 15 minutes.

4 Meanwhile, make Texas-Style Sauce. In a small saucepan over moderate heat, melt the butter. Add 2 tablespoons onion and sauté for 1 minute, or until softened. Add reserved sauce mixture, ketchup, sugar, and red pepper flakes. Bring to a boil over moderately high heat. Reduce heat to moderately low and simmer, uncovered, stirring frequently, for 10 minutes. Remove the pan from the heat.

5 Transfer meat to a carving board and cut in thin slices across the grain. Warm the sauce over low heat and serve with the brisket.

6 SERVINGS
PREP TIME: 20 MINUTES
COOKING TIME: 4 HOURS 30 MINUTES

EQUIPMENT LIST
Utility knife
Carving knife
Small bowl
Medium-size bowl
Kitchen spoon
5-quart Dutch oven
Pastry brush
Aluminum foil
Small saucepan
Carving board

Rio Grande Chili

4 tablespoons olive oil
1½ pounds beef chuck, cut in ½" cubes
2 large yellow onions, finely chopped (3 cups)
4 large cloves garlic, finely chopped
1 28-ounce can whole tomatoes, chopped
1 medium-size green or red bell pepper, cored, seeded, and chopped (1 cup)
3 medium-size Anaheim or other mild chili peppers, cored, seeded, and chopped (1 cup)
¼ cup tomato paste
3 tablespoons chili powder
2 teaspoons dried oregano leaves, crumbled
1 teaspoon ground cumin
¼ teaspoon ground red pepper (cayenne)
¼ teaspoon salt, or to taste
Freshly ground black pepper
2 16-ounce cans pinto beans, drained and rinsed

CHILI ACCOMPANIMENTS

Boiled white rice
Sour cream
Chopped avocado
Shredded Cheddar cheese
Chopped red and green bell peppers
Chopped jalapeño peppers

Though it is usually served with rice, chili can also be a change of pace sauce on spaghetti (a Cincinnati special), a topping for potatoes, and a filling for omelets. Accompaniments add variety to the meal and also cut the fiery taste of the chili. Mexican beer or a pitcher of sangría, with or without alcohol, is a fine choice of beverage.

1 In a 5-quart Dutch oven, heat 2 tablespoons of the oil over moderately high heat for 1 minute. Add the meat and cook, stirring frequently, for 5 minutes, or until browned. Using a slotted spoon, transfer the meat to a plate.

2 Heat the remaining 2 tablespoons of oil over moderate heat for 1 minute. Add the onions and sauté for 5 minutes, or until translucent. Add the garlic and sauté for 30 seconds, or until fragrant. Return the beef, with any accumulated juices, to the pan.

3 Stir in the tomatoes with their juices, the bell and chili peppers, tomato paste, chili powder, oregano, cumin, and ground red pepper. Season to taste. Bring the mixture to a boil. Reduce the heat to moderately low and cook, covered, for 1½ hours, or until the meat is tender. (If the chili is too thick, stir in a little water.)

4 Just before serving, skim off the fat from the chili. Stir in the beans and cook, stirring occasionally, for 10 to 12 minutes, or until heated through. Ladle the chili into individual serving bowls and serve with some or all of the Chili Accompaniments, if desired.

8 SERVINGS
PREP TIME: 15 MINUTES
COOKING TIME: 2 HOURS

EQUIPMENT LIST

Chef's knife
Utility knife
Pepper mill
Colander
5-quart Dutch oven
Kitchen spoon
Slotted spoon
Plate

Spanish Beef Casserole

2 pound bottom round steak, cut in thin strips
¼ teaspoon salt, or to taste
Freshly ground black pepper
3 tablespoons vegetable oil
1 small yellow onion, finely chopped (½ cup)
8 ounces mushrooms, trimmed, cleaned, and thinly sliced (2¼ cups)
1 medium-size red or green bell pepper, cored, seeded, and chopped (1 cup)
1 large garlic clove, chopped
1 14½-ounce can crushed tomatoes
1 tablespoon chopped pimento-stuffed green olives
1 tablespoon chopped pepperoncini (optional)
2 tablespoons chopped fresh parsley
4 ounces shredded Monterey Jack cheese (1 cup)

1 Preheat the oven to 350° F. Sprinkle the round steak with the salt and pepper.

2 In a large skillet, heat 1 tablespoon of the oil over moderately high heat for one minute. Add half the beef to the skillet and cook, stirring frequently, for 3 minutes, or until browned. Using a slotted spoon, transfer the round steak to a plate. Add 1 tablespoon of the oil to the skillet and heat over moderately high heat for 1 minute. Cook the remaining round steak as directed and transfer to a plate.

3 In the same skillet, heat the remaining 1 tablespoon of oil over moderate heat for 1 minute. Add the onion and sauté for 5 minutes, or until translucent. Add the mushrooms and bell pepper and sauté for 3 minutes, or until the vegetables are softened. Add the garlic and sauté for 30 seconds, or until fragrant. Stir in the tomatoes with their juices, olives, and pepperoncini, if desired. Bring to a boil over moderately high heat. Reduce the heat to low and cook, uncovered, stirring occasionally, for 5 to 6 minutes, or until thickened slightly. Remove the skillet from the heat and stir in the round steak, with any accumulated juices, and the parsley.

4 Spoon the mixture into a 2-quart casserole and sprinkle with the cheese. Cover with aluminum foil and bake for 15 to 20 minutes, or until the cheese is melted. Remove the casserole from the oven and serve immediately.

6 SERVINGS
PREP TIME: 15 MINUTES
COOKING TIME: 45 MINUTES

EQUIPMENT LIST

Chef's knife
Utility knife
Pepper mill
Grater
Large skillet
Kitchen spoon
Slotted spoon
Plate
2-quart casserole
Aluminum foil

Herb-Stuffed Flank Steak

1½ pounds flank steak
¼ teaspoon salt, or to taste
3 tablespoons chopped fresh parsley
1 tablespoon dried thyme leaves, crumbled
2 teaspoons dried sage leaves, crumbled
1 medium-size carrot, peeled and cut lengthwise in thin strips (¾ cup)
1 medium-size leek (white and some green parts), trimmed, rinsed, and thinly sliced (½ cup)
⅓ cup all-purpose flour
2 tablespoons vegetable oil
1 cup beef stock or canned broth
1 cup dry red wine or water
1 small yellow onion, quartered

Accompany this flank steak with steamed vegetables such as asparagus or green beans and red-skinned potatoes.

1 Place the flank steak in a sheet of wax paper, cover with a second sheet and, using a meat mallet or a rolling pin, flatten the meat to 1¼" thick. Remove the wax paper.

2 Lay the flank steak on a work surface. Sprinkle the meat with salt and pepper and then with the herbs. Cover the herbs with the carrot and then with the leek. Starting with a short end, roll up the flank steak and tie securely with kitchen twine.

3 Place the flour on a sheet of wax paper. Dredge the flank steak in the flour, coating it completely and shaking off the excess.

4 In a 5-quart Dutch oven, heat the oil over moderately high heat for 1 minute. Add the flank steak and cook, turning frequently, for 10 minutes, or until browned on all sides. Add the stock, wine, and onion to the pan. Reduce the heat to moderately low and cook, covered, for 40 minutes, or until the meat is tender.

5 Transfer the flank steak to a carving board and let stand for 5 minutes. Strain the pan juices though a fine sieve into a small bowl and discard the solids. Slice the flank steak and arrange the slices on a serving platter. Serve immediately with the pan juices.

4 SERVINGS
PREP TIME: 25 MINUTES PLUS
5 MINUTES TO STAND
COOKING TIME: 50 MINUTES

EQUIPMENT LIST

Utility knife
Carving knife
Vegetable peeler
Wax paper
Meat mallet or rolling pin
Kitchen twine
5-quart Dutch oven
Kitchen spoon
Carving board
Fine sieve
Small bowl

Home-Style Pot Roast

1   3-pound bottom round or chuck roast
¼   cup all-purpose flour
½   teaspoon salt
½   teaspoon coarsely ground black pepper
2   tablespoons unsalted butter or margarine
2   tablespoons vegetable oil
1½   cups beef stock or canned broth
1   cup dry red wine or water
3   sprigs fresh thyme, or 2 teaspoons dried thyme leaves, crumbled
3   fresh sage leaves, or 2 teaspoons dried sage leaves, crumbled
3   parsley stems
8   small California white or other boiling potatoes, peeled (1½ pounds)
8   small carrots, peeled and halved (4 cups)
4   small white onions, peeled
1   tablespoon cornstarch
1   tablespoon water
Curly endive leaves (chicory) (optional)

The beauty of pot roast is that less expensive cuts of meat can be made to taste as good as their high-priced cousins. Long, slow cooking in liquid—in this case red wine and beef stock—tenderizes the meat, and the addition of fresh herbs and vegetables makes for a deliciously robust presentation.

Chuck, shoulder, top or bottom round, brisket, blade, or rump of beef can be used with equally good results.

1 Pat the roast dry with paper towels. On a sheet of wax paper, combine the flour, salt, and pepper. Dredge the meat in the flour, coating it completely and shaking off the excess.

2 In a 6-quart Dutch oven, heat the butter and oil over moderately high heat for 1 minute. Add the meat and cook, turning frequently, for 10 minutes, or until browned on all sides.

3 Add the stock, wine, thyme, sage, and parsley. Reduce the heat to low and cook, covered, for 2 hours.

4 Add the potatoes, carrots, and onions. Cook, covered, for 40 minutes more, or until the meat and vegetables are tender.

5 In a small bowl, dissolve the cornstarch in the water.

6 Transfer the roast to a serving platter and arrange the vegetables around it.

7 Strain the pan juices through a fine sieve into a medium-size saucepan and discard the solids. Stir in the cornstarch mixture and cook over moderately high heat, stirring continuously, for 1 minute, or until thickened slightly. Pour the sauce into a serving bowl.

8 Garnish the pot roast with curly endive leaves, if desired. Serve immediately with the sauce.

What dish could be homier than a delicious pot roast surrounded by perfectly cooked vegetables?

8 SERVINGS
PREP TIME: 10 MINUTES
COOKING TIME: 3 HOURS

EQUIPMENT LIST

Vegetable peeler
Utility knife
Paring knife
Paper towels
Wax paper
Kitchen spoons
6-quart Dutch oven
Small bowl
Fine sieve
Medium-size saucepan

Southwestern Meatloaf

½ cup sun-dried tomatoes, finely chopped

¼ cup plus 1 tablespoon yellow cornmeal

3 large cloves garlic, chopped

⅔ cup boiling water

1½ pounds lean ground beef

6 green onions (including tops), finely chopped (¾ cup)

1 4-ounce can chopped green chilies

2 medium-size jalapeño peppers, cored, seeded, and chopped (2 tablespoons)

½ cup dry unseasoned bread crumbs

2 large eggs

⅓ cup chopped fresh cilantro (coriander leaves) or fresh parsley

¼ teaspoon salt, or to taste

Freshly ground black pepper

Here's a meatloaf that will very quickly become a family favorite. A contemporary version of the classic recipe, it features the flavors of the Southwest with its zesty green chiles, jalapeño peppers, and cilantro. Sun-dried tomatoes are added for extra color and flavor.

This meatloaf can be prepared ahead and baked for dinner the next night. Serve it with steamed brown rice, a chilled green bean salad, and guacamole. Leftovers make a great luncheon dish—a crisp green salad will provide a quick and easy meal. Alternatively, use the leftovers as a sandwich filling for a packed lunch.

1 Preheat the oven to 375° F. In a large bowl, combine the sun-dried tomatoes, ¼ cup of the cornmeal, the garlic, and water and let stand for 10 minutes, or until the tomatoes are softened.

2 Add beef, green onions, chilies, jalapeño peppers, bread crumbs, eggs, cilantro, salt, and pepper and mix until well blended.

3 In a shallow baking pan, shape the mixture into a 12″ x 4″ loaf. Sprinkle the top with the remaining 1 tablespoon of cornmeal.

4 Bake, uncovered, for 50 minutes to 1 hour, or until the juices run clear when the meat is pierced with a knife. Remove pan from the oven and let the meatloaf stand for 10 minutes before slicing.

6 SERVINGS
PREP TIME: 15 MINUTES PLUS
20 MINUTES TO STAND
COOKING TIME: 1 HOUR

EQUIPMENT LIST

Utility knife
Pepper mill
Large bowl
Kitchen spoon
Shallow baking pan

Boiled Brisket with Vegetables

1 2½ pound boneless brisket of beef

1 medium-size yellow onion, peeled and stuck with 3 cloves

1 medium-size carrot, peeled and halved

3 large cloves garlic

4 sprigs fresh parsley

1 bay leaf

2 teaspoons coarse salt, or to taste

½ teaspoon black peppercorns

AROMATIC VEGETABLES

4 small leeks (including some green tops), trimmed and rinsed

2 small celeriacs (celery root), peeled and cut in 2″ pieces (1½ cups)

4 medium-size carrots, peeled and cut in 2″ pieces (3 cups)

A favorite "comfort food," boiled brisket is a dish that may stir memories. The best things about it are the relatively low cost of the meat, and the fact that is can be cooked slowly with little attention. This recipe provides a complete meal and is delicious the next day. If desired, accompany the brisket with a little bottled horseradish and Dijon-style mustard.

1 Place the brisket of beef in a 5-quart Dutch oven and add cold water to cover by 2″. Transfer the beef to a plate. Bring the water to a boil over high heat.

2 Gently lower the beef into pan and allow the water to return to a boil. Reduce the heat to moderate. Add the onion, carrot, garlic, parsley, bay leaf, salt, and peppercorns. Cook, covered, for 2 hours, occasionally skimming the fat.

3 Using a slotted spoon, remove and discard the vegetables and herbs. Add the Aromatic Vegetables and simmer, covered, for 45 minutes more, or until the beef is tender.

4 Transfer the beef to a carving board and cut in thin slices across the grain. Arrange the slices on a serving platter. Using a slotted spoon, transfer the Aromatic Vegetables to the platter and ladle some broth over the top. Serve immediately.

6 SERVINGS
PREP TIME: 15 MINUTES PLUS
COOKING TIME: 2 HOURS 45 MINUTES

EQUIPMENT LIST

Utility knife
Vegetable peeler
5-quart Dutch oven
Kitchen spoon
Slotted spoon
Ladle
Carving board
Carving knife

Pork and Mixed Vegetable Stir-Fry

1   10-ounce package frozen sliced okra, thawed and drained
1   pound pork tenderloin, trimmed
1   tablespoon chopped fresh thyme, or 1 teaspoon dried thyme leaves, crumbled
¼   teaspoon salt, or to taste
⅛   teaspoon coarsely ground black pepper
1   tablespoon vegetable oil
1   large clove garlic, finely chopped
1   small yellow onion, thinly sliced (1 cup)
1   medium-size red or green bell pepper, cored, seeded, and thinly sliced (1 cup)
1   8-ounce package frozen baby corn, thawed and drained
1   tablespoon chopped fresh parsley
1-2   drops hot pepper sauce
Sprigs of fresh thyme (optional)
Red chili peppers (optional)
Celery heart leaves (optional)

Pork tenderloin's mild flavor combines beautifully with okra, corn, bell pepper, and onion in this quick and healthful stir-fry. Accompany it with boiled white rice for an easy mid-week supper.

1   Bring a medium-size saucepan of water to a boil over high heat. Cook the okra in the boiling water for 3 to 5 minutes, or until tender. Drain well.

2   Cut the pork tenderloin lengthwise into quarters, then cut each quarter crosswise into ¾″ thick slices. In a small bowl, combine the chopped thyme, salt, and pepper. Sprinkle the mixture over the pork slices.

3   In a wok or large, heavy skillet, heat the oil over high heat for 1 minute, or until very hot. Add pork slices and garlic and stir-fry for 3 to 4 minutes, or until pork is lightly browned. Add the onion, bell pepper, and corn and stir-fry for 3 to 4 minutes, or until vegetables are crisp-tender. Stir in okra, parsley, and hot pepper sauce and stir-fry for 1 minute more, or until heated through. Remove wok from the heat.

4   Transfer the pork stir-fry to individual serving plates. Garnish with sprigs of fresh thyme, chili peppers, and celery heart leaves, if desired. Serve immediately.

4 SERVINGS
PREP TIME: 10 MINUTES
COOKING TIME: 15 MINUTES

Equipment List

Colander
Utility knife
Medium-size saucepan
Small bowl
Kitchen spoons
Wok or large, heavy skillet

When time is short, use this colorful stir-fry to make a tantalizing dish.

Choucroute Garni

This deliciously warming one-pot meal will fill the house with a wonderful aroma as it cooks. Originally from the Alsace region, the recipe combines the cuisines of France and Germany. It is best served with plain boiled potatoes and pumpernickel bread...and don't forget the grainy German-style mustard.

1 bay leaf
5 black peppercorns
5 juniper berries
2 whole cloves
4 strips lean bacon, chopped
1 large carrot, peeled and sliced (1 cup)
1 large yellow onion, chopped (1½ cups)
1¼ cups chicken stock or canned broth
1 cup Riesling or other fruity white wine
2 pounds chilled sauerkraut, or 2 16-ounce cans sauerkraut, drained and rinsed (3 cups)
8 ounces boneless pork loin chops, cut in 1½" cubes
4 ounces Virginia ham, cut in 1" cubes
8 ounces smoked sausage, cut in ½" slices
4 ounces bratwurst, cut in ½" slices
1 small Granny Smith or other tart apple, cored and cut in ½" cubes (1 cup)
Sprigs of fresh thyme (optional)

8 SERVINGS
PREP TIME: 15 MINUTES
COOKING TIME: 1 HOUR 25 MINUTES

EQUIPMENT LIST

Utility knife
Chef's knife
Vegetable peeler
Colander
Cheesecloth
Kitchen twine
6-quart Dutch oven
Kitchen spoon

1 On a work surface, place a small square of cheesecloth. In the center of the square, place the bay leaf, peppercorns, juniper berries, and cloves. Using kitchen twine, tie the 4 corners of the cheesecloth together to form a bag. Set aside.

2 In a 6-quart Dutch oven, cook the bacon over moderate heat for 8 to 10 minutes, or until crisp. Add the carrot and onion and sauté for 5 minutes, or until the onion is translucent. Add the cheesecloth bag containing the spice mixture.

3 Stir in the stock and the wine. Bring to a boil over high heat and add the sauerkraut, pork chops, ham, and smoked sausage. Reduce heat to low and simmer, covered, for 30 minutes.

4 Add the bratwurst and apple and stir well. Cook, uncovered, stirring occasionally, for 40 minutes to reduce the cooking liquid. Remove and discard the cheesecloth bag.

5 Garnish the Chocroute Garni with sprigs of fresh thyme, if desired, and serve immediately.

For a specialty of Alsace, try this hearty supper dish.

Pork Piccata

1   pound pork tenderloin, cut in
      8 slices
3   tablespoons all-purpose flour
2   teaspoons lemon pepper, or 1
      teaspoon coarsely ground
      black pepper and 1 teaspoon
      grated lemon rind
2   tablespoons unsalted butter
¼   cup dry sherry or dry white
      wine
¼   cup fresh lemon juice
4   tablespoons capers, drained
      and rinsed
Lemon slices (optional)
Sprigs of fresh parsley (optional)

*Light, lemony, and lovely to the eye—
a pork dish without compare.*

*Here's a dish that's easy to prepare for a weeknight meal or party entrée.
Serve it with steamed broccoli. This recipe works equally well when
4 boneless veal cutlets (4 ounces each) are substituted for the pork. Proceed
as directed, but reduce the cooking time to 1 to 2 minutes on each side.*

1 Place 1 slice of pork on a sheet of wax paper, cover with a second
sheet and, using a meat mallet or a rolling pin, flatten to ⅛" thick.
Flatten remaining pork slices as directed. Remove the wax paper.

2 On a sheet of wax paper, combine the flour and lemon pepper.
Dredge the pork slices in the flour mixture, coating them
completely and shaking off the excess.

3 In a large skillet over moderate heat, melt 1 tablespoon of the
butter. Add half the pork slices and cook for 2 to 3 minutes on
each side, or until golden brown. Using a slotted spoon, transfer the
pork slices to a plate and keep warm. Add the remaining 1 tablespoon
of butter to the skillet and melt over moderate heat. Cook the
remaining pork slices as directed. Return the cooked pork slices, with
any accumulated juices, to the skillet.

4 Add the sherry, lemon juice, and capers to the skillet and cook,
shaking the pan occasionally, for 2 minutes, or until the sauce has
thickened slightly.

5 Transfer the pork slices to a serving platter and spoon the sauce
over them. Garnish with lemon slices and sprigs of fresh parsley, if
desired. Serve immediately.

4 SERVINGS
PREP TIME: 15 MINUTES
COOKING TIME: 14 MINUTES

EQUIPMENT LIST

Chef's knife
Citrus juicer
Strainer
Wax paper
Meat mallet or rolling pin
Large skillet
Large, metal spatula
Slotted spoon
Plate

Cajun Pork Roast

Make this pork roast the centerpiece of a Sunday dinner or other family gathering. The Cajun Spice Mix is a snap to prepare and it can be used to give a lift to grilled or barbecued meat such as steak or chops. Accompany this dish with steamed green beans and roasted potatoes.

1   2-pound boneless pork loin
    roast
Sprigs of fresh herbs, such as sage
    or parsley (optional)

CAJUN SPICE MIX (6 TABLESPOONS)

3   tablespoons paprika
1   tablespoon garlic powder
1   tablespoon dried thyme leaves,
    crumbled
½   teaspoon ground red pepper
    (cayenne)
½   teaspoon ground cumin
¼   teaspoon ground nutmeg
½   teaspoon salt, or to taste
½   teaspoon coarsely ground
    black pepper

1 Preheat the oven to 350° F. Pat the pork dry with paper towels and place in a shallow roasting pan.

2 To make the Cajun Spice Mix: In a small bowl, combine the paprika, garlic powder, thyme, ground red pepper, cumin, nutmeg, salt, and pepper. Rub the spice mixture well into the surface of the pork.

3 Roast the pork for 45 minutes, or until the juices run clear when the meat is pierced with a knife, or a meat thermometer registers 155°-160° F. Transfer the pork to a serving platter, cover with aluminum foil, and let stand for 10 minutes.

4 Remove the foil. Garnish the pork roast with sprigs of fresh herbs, if desired. Slice the roast and serve immediately.

6 SERVINGS
PREP TIME: 5 MINUTES PLUS
10 MINUTES TO STAND
COOKING TIME: 45 MINUTES

EQUIPMENT LIST

Paper towels
Aluminum foil
Shallow roasting pan
Small bowl
Kitchen spoon
Utility knife or meat thermometer
Carving knife

Garden Hash

This hash recipe incorporates ham and the best summer produce. It's just right for a speedy supper, substantial lunch, or even brunch, and it can also be enhanced with poached eggs.

2   medium-size California white
    or other boiling potatoes,
    peeled (1 pound)
12 ounces cooked ham, chopped
1   16½-ounce can corn kernels,
    drained
1   medium-size tomato, seeded
    and chopped (1 cup)
1   medium-size green or red bell
    pepper, cored, seeded, and
    chopped (¾ cup)
1   small yellow onion, finely
    chopped (½ cup)
½   teaspoon coarsely ground
    black pepper
3   tablespoons unsalted butter
2   ounces shredded sharp
    Cheddar cheese (½ cup)
2   tablespoons chopped fresh
    parsley

1 Place the potatoes in a small saucepan with enough water to cover. Bring to a boil over high heat. Reduce the heat to moderately low and cook, uncovered, for 20 minutes, or until the potatoes are tender when tested with a fork. Drain well and set aside to cool.

2 In a large bowl, mix together the ham, corn, tomato, bell pepper, onion, and pepper. Cut the potatoes into ½" cubes and add to the ham and vegetable mixture.

3 In a large, nonstick skillet over moderate heat, melt the butter. Spoon the mixture into the skillet and flatten with a large, metal spatula. Increase the heat to moderately high and cook, without stirring, for 5 minutes, or until the bottom begins to brown.

4 Using the spatula, turn the mixture over in stages, scraping up the browned bits from the bottom of the pan. When all the mixture has been turned, flatten again with the spatula. Cook for 5 minutes more, or until the bottom begins to brown.

5 Turn the hash out onto a serving platter and sprinkle with grated Cheddar cheese and chopped fresh parsley. Serve immediately.

4 SERVINGS
PREP TIME: 10 MINUTES PLUS
10 MINUTES TO COOL
COOKING TIME: 30 MINUTES

EQUIPMENT LIST

Vegetable peeler
Utility knife
Colander
Grater
Small saucepan
Fork
Large bowl
Kitchen spoon
Large, nonstick skillet
Large, metal spatula

Lancashire Hot Pot

One of the best-known recipes of northern England, Lancashire Hot Pot takes its name from the deep brown and white pottery dish in which it is traditionally cooked. The county of Lancashire is also famous for its sheep—hence the use of lamb. This delicious and warming stew is often served with pickled red cabbage.

2	tablespoons vegetable oil
6	shoulder lamb chops (8 ounces each)
6	small California white or other boiling potatoes, peeled and thinly sliced (3 cups)
⅛	teaspoon salt, or to taste
	Freshly ground black pepper
2	small yellow onions, thinly sliced (2 cups)
8	ounces mushrooms, trimmed, cleaned, and sliced (2½ cups)
1½	cups beef stock or canned broth
2	tablespoons all-purpose flour
2	teaspoons unsalted butter
1	teaspoon chopped fresh parsley

6 SERVINGS
PREP TIME: 20 MINUTES
COOKING TIME: 2 HOURS

EQUIPMENT LIST

Vegetable peeler
Utility knife
Pepper mill
Large skillet
Kitchen spoon
Plate
6-quart casserole with lid
2 small saucepans
Pastry brush

1 Preheat the oven to 400° F. In a large skillet, heat 1 tablespoon of the oil over moderate heat for 1 minute. Cook 3 lamb chops for 1 to 2 minutes on each side, or until browned. Transfer the chops to a plate. Add the remaining 1 tablespoon of oil to the skillet and heat over moderate heat. Cook the remaining lamb chops as directed and transfer to the plate.

2 Arrange one-third of the potatoes in a layer on the bottom of a 6-quart casserole or Dutch oven. Season with the salt and pepper. Place 3 chops on top of the potatoes. Top with half of the onions and mushrooms. Repeat the layers as directed, ending with a layer of potatoes.

3 In a small saucepan, gradually add the stock to the flour, stirring until well blended. Cook, stirring continuously, over moderate heat for 5 minutes, or until thickened slightly. Pour the mixture over the layers in the casserole. Add enough water so the liquid comes halfway up the sides.

4 Bake, covered, for 30 minutes. Reduce the oven temperature to 325° F. and bake for 1 hour more.

5 In a small saucepan over low heat, melt the butter. Uncover the casserole, brush the butter over the potatoes, and bake, uncovered, for 30 minutes, or until the potatoes are browned and the chops are tender.

6 Remove the casserole from the oven, garnish with the chopped fresh parsley, if desired, and serve immediately.

This English one-pot dinner is just right for wet, cold, windy nights.

Grilled Lamb Steaks
with Barbecue Sauce

3   center-cut lamb steaks
     (1 pound each), cut 1″ thick,
     or 6 blade or shoulder lamb
     chops (4 ounces each), cut
     ¾″ thick
⅛   teaspoon salt, or to taste
Freshly ground black pepper
Celery leaves (optional)
Orange slices (optional)

BARBECUE SAUCE (1¾ CUPS)

2   teaspoons olive oil
¼   cup finely chopped yellow
     onion
¼   cup finely chopped green or
     red bell pepper
¾   cup bottled chili sauce or
     tomato ketchup
¼   cup orange juice
2   tablespoons firmly packed
     dark brown sugar
2   teaspoons Dijon-style
     mustard
2   teaspoons grated orange rind
5   drops hot pepper sauce

Lamb steaks, which are cut from the center of the leg, are becoming increasingly popular and more widely available in supermarkets. However, if lamb steaks are not available, ask the butcher to cut them or use blade or shoulder lamb chops instead.

Serve the steaks with traditional barbecue accompaniments, such as coleslaw, Boston baked beans, and freshly baked corn sticks.

1 Prepare a charcoal grill until the coals form white ash, preheat a gas grill to high, or preheat the broiler.

2 Meanwhile, prepare the Barbecue Sauce. In a medium-size skillet, heat the oil over moderately low heat for 1 minute. Add the onion and bell pepper and sauté for 5 minutes, or until the onion is translucent. Add the chili sauce, orange juice, sugar, mustard, orange rind, and hot pepper sauce. Cook, covered, over low heat, for 10 minutes. Remove the skillet from the heat and set aside.

3 Season the lamb steaks on both sides with the salt and pepper. Place the steaks on the grill or under the broiler 4″ from the heat source. Grill or broil, brushing frequently with the sauce, for 5 to 6 minutes on each side for medium-rare meat.

4 Transfer the lamb steaks to a serving platter. Garnish with celery leaves and orange slices, if desired. Warm the remaining sauce over low heat and serve with the lamb steaks.

6 SERVINGS
PREP TIME: 20 MINUTES
COOKING TIME: 28 MINUTES

EQUIPMENT LIST

Pepper mill
Utility knife
Grater
Charcoal or gas grill or broiler pan
Medium-size skillet with lid
Kitchen spoon
Large, metal spatula
Pastry brush

This dish makes a wonderful addition to barbecue repertoires.

Shoulder Lamb Chops
with Triple Apricot Sauce

A quick-to-prepare apricot-based sauce provides the right accent to grilled lamb chops. Accompany this dish with shiitake mushrooms, steamed snow peas, and saffron rice for a marvelous mid-week meal.

¼ cup olive oil

3 tablespoons low-sodium soy sauce

3 tablespoons rice wine vinegar or cider vinegar

2 large cloves garlic, finely chopped

¼ teaspoon coarsely ground black pepper

4 shoulder lamb chops (6-8 ounces each), cut ¾″ thick

Red onion rings (optional)

TRIPLE APRICOT SAUCE (⅔ CUP)

¼ cup apricot jam

¼ cup apricot nectar

1 ounce dried apricots, chopped (¼ cup)

1 tablespoon fresh lemon juice

¼ teaspoon curry powder

1 In a large, shallow glass dish, combine the oil, soy sauce, vinegar, garlic, and pepper. Add the lamb chops, turning to coat. Cover the dish with plastic wrap and marinate at room temperature for 1 hour, turning the lamb chops occasionally.

2 Prepare a charcoal grill until the coals form white ash, preheat a gas grill to high, or preheat the broiler.

3 To make the Triple Apricot Sauce: In a small saucepan, combine the apricot jam, apricot nectar, and dried apricots. Stir in the lemon juice and curry powder. Cook the sauce over moderately low heat, stirring occasionally, for 5 minutes, or until the jam is melted and the mixture is heated through. Remove pan from heat and keep warm.

4 Remove the lamb chops from the marinade and discard the liquid. Place the lamb chops on the grill or under the broiler 4″ from the heat source. Grill or broil, brushing occasionally with the sauce, for 5 to 6 minutes on each side for medium-rare meat.

5 Transfer the lamb chops to individual serving plates and spoon the remaining sauce over them. Garnish with the red onion rings, if desired, and serve immediately.

4 SERVINGS
PREP TIME: 20 MINUTES PLUS
1 HOUR TO MARINATE
COOKING TIME: 17 MINUTES

EQUIPMENT LIST

Utility knife
Citrus juicer
Large, shallow glass dish
Kitchen spoons
Plastic wrap
Charcoal or gas grill or broiler pan
Small saucepan
Pastry brush
Large, metal spatula

Lift lamb chops to new heights with a tangy sauce that is chock-full of apricots.

Pastitsio

Try this Greek lamb and macaroni casserole, with its thick and thin sauces, for an inexpensive party dish—all amounts can easily be doubled .

2   tablespoons olive oil
1   small yellow onion, finely chopped (½ cup)
1   large garlic clove, finely chopped
1   pound lean ground lamb
1   28-ounce can whole tomatoes in purée
¼   cup chopped, pitted black olives
1   teaspoon dried oregano leaves, crumbled
1   teaspoon dried basil leaves, crumbled
¼   teaspoon ground allspice
Freshly ground black pepper
1   pound whole-wheat elbow macaroni or ziti (4 cups)
½   cup dry unseasoned bread crumbs

Cream Sauce (3 cups)

¼   cup (½ stick) unsalted butter
⅓   cup all-purpose flour
2¼ cups milk
4   ounces grated Romano cheese (1 cup)
2   egg yolks

1 In a large skillet, heat the oil over moderate heat for 1 minute. Add onion and sauté for 5 minutes, or until translucent. Add garlic and sauté for 30 seconds, or until fragrant. Add the lamb and cook, stirring frequently, for 10 minutes, or until no pink color remains. Add the tomatoes with purée and, using the back of a spoon, break tomatoes into small pieces. Stir in the olives, oregano, basil, and allspice. Season to taste. Cook, covered, stirring occasionally, over low heat for 30 minutes.

2 Meanwhile, bring a large saucepan of water to a boil over high heat. Cook macaroni in the boiling water for 8 to 10 minutes, or until al dente. Drain well, rinse under cold running water, and drain again.

3 Preheat the oven to 350° F. Grease a shallow 4-quart casserole. To make the Cream Sauce: In a medium-size saucepan over moderate heat, melt the butter. Stir in flour and cook, stirring continuously, for 1 minute, or until a pale straw color. Slowly stir in 1¾ cups of the milk until well blended. Cook, stirring continuously, for 3 to 5 minutes, or until the sauce has thickened slightly. Stir in the Romano cheese. Pour 1¼ cups of the sauce into a small bowl. Stir in remaining ½ cup of milk to make a thin sauce. In a separate small bowl, lightly beat egg yolks. Add remaining sauce and mix well to make a thick sauce.

4 Skim off any fat from the meat sauce and stir in bread crumbs. Spread half the macaroni over the bottom of the prepared dish and cover with the meat sauce. Pour thin cream sauce over meat mixture. Top with remaining macaroni. Spread thick cream sauce evenly over surface.

5 Bake for 35 to 40 minutes, or until the top is lightly browned. Remove from the oven and let stand for 5 minutes before serving.

8 SERVINGS
PREP TIME: 20 MINUTES PLUS
5 MINUTES TO STAND
COOKING TIME: 1 HOUR 30 MINUTES

EQUIPMENT LIST

Utility knife
Pepper mill
2 small bowls
Large skillet with lid
Kitchen spoon
Large saucepan
Medium-size saucepan
Colander
Shallow 4-quart casserole

Herbed Leg of Lamb

For the holidays and special family occasions, serve this leg of lamb with a white bean casserole and grilled tomatoes.

1   5-pound leg of lamb
3   large cloves garlic, chopped
2   teaspoons dried rosemary leaves, crumbled
1   teaspoon dried sage leaves, crumbled
1   teaspoon dried thyme leaves, crumbled
½   teaspoon coarsely ground black pepper
1   pound baby carrots, peeled
1   pound pearl onions, peeled
Sprigs of fresh sage (optional)

1 Preheat the oven to 325° F. Pat the leg of lamb dry with paper towels. In a small bowl, combine garlic, rosemary, dried sage, thyme, and pepper. Rub mixture well into the surface of the lamb.

2 Place the lamb, fat-side up, on a rack in a roasting pan. Roast, uncovered, for 1 hour and 20 minutes. Add carrots and onions to roasting pan. Roast, uncovered, for 1 hour more for medium meat, or until a meat thermometer registers 150° F. Stir vegetables occasionally.

3 Remove the pan from the oven. Transfer the leg of lamb and the vegetables to a serving platter, cover loosely with aluminum foil, and let stand for 15 minutes.

4 Remove the foil. Garnish the leg of lamb with sprigs of fresh sage, if desired. Slice the leg of lamb and serve immediately.

8 SERVINGS
PREP TIME: 10 MINUTES PLUS
15 MINUTES TO STAND
COOKING TIME: 2 HOURS 20 MINUTES

EQUIPMENT LIST

Paring knife
Carving knife
Vegetable peeler
Paper towels
Aluminum foil
Small bowl
Roasting pan with rack
Meat thermometer

Lemon Veal with Artichokes

3 pounds boneless veal shoulder or other stewing veal, cut in 1½″ cubes
2 tablespoons unsalted butter
2-3 tablespoons vegetable oil
1 tablespoon peeled, grated fresh ginger, or 1½ teaspoons ground ginger
3 large cloves garlic, finely chopped
2 cups chicken stock or canned broth
1 small lemon, cut in 8 wedges
¼ teaspoon salt, or to taste
Freshly ground black pepper
1 14-ounce can artichoke hearts, drained and quartered
8 ounces snow peas, trimmed and strings removed
⅓ cup light cream or half-and-half
2 tablespoons all-purpose flour

Because veal is a lean meat, it must be cooked carefully to produce perfect results. Braising, a gentle method of cooking, helps retain the meat's delicate texture, yet allows other flavors to be absorbed. Serve this casserole with buttered noodles and crusty French bread to mop up the sauce.

1 In a 5-quart Dutch oven, heat the butter and 2 tablespoons of the oil over moderately high heat for 1 minute. Add one-third of the veal and sauté for 2 to 3 minutes, or until brown on all sides. Using a slotted spoon, transfer the veal to a plate. Repeat as directed with the remaining meat, adding more oil to the pan if needed.

2 Add the ginger and garlic to the pan and sauté for 1 minute. Return the veal, with any accumulated juices, to the pan and add the stock and lemon wedges. Season to taste with the salt and pepper. Reduce the heat to low and simmer, covered, stirring occasionally, for 1 to 1¼ hours, or until the veal is tender.

3 Add the artichoke hearts and snow peas and simmer, uncovered, for 10 minutes.

4 In a small bowl, mix together the cream and flour until smooth. Reduce the heat to very low, add the cream mixture to the pan, and stir gently to combine. Cook, stirring frequently, for 1 to 2 minutes, taking care not to let the sauce boil. Using a slotted spoon, remove and discard the lemon wedges.

5 Transfer the veal to individual serving plates and serve immediately.

8 SERVINGS
PREP TIME: 20 MINUTES
COOKING TIME: 1 HOUR 30 MINUTES

EQUIPMENT LIST

Utility knife
Vegetable peeler
Grater
Pepper mill
Strainer
5-quart Dutch oven
Kitchen spoons
Slotted spoon
Plate
Small bowl

Make this dish the pièce de résistance of a party. Guests will love it!

Veal Parmigiana

Fresh basil, bell pepper, and mushrooms accent the tomato sauce in this popular veal dish. Serve it with a mixed green salad and a side dish of spaghetti tossed with olive oil and sautéed garlic slices.

½ cup dry seasoned bread crumbs

2 ounces grated Parmesan cheese (½ cup)

4 boneless veal cutlets (4 ounces each)

1 tablespoon olive oil

1 tablespoon salted butter or margarine

4 slices mozzarella cheese (4 ounces)

Sprigs of fresh basil (optional)

TOMATO SAUCE (4 CUPS)

¼ cup chicken stock or canned broth or water

1 large clove garlic, finely chopped

1 small green or red bell pepper, cored, seeded, and finely chopped (½ cup)

4 ounces mushrooms, trimmed, cleaned, and sliced (1¼ cups)

1 tablespoon tomato paste

1 28-ounce can whole tomatoes, chopped

2 tablespoons chopped fresh basil, or 2 teaspoons dried basil leaves, crumbled

1 In a shallow bowl, combine the bread crumbs and Parmesan cheese. Dredge the cutlets in the bread crumb mixture, coating them completely and shaking off the excess.

2 In a large skillet, heat the oil and butter over moderately high heat for 1 minute. Add the veal cutlets and cook for 2 minutes on each side, or until lightly browned. Transfer the veal cutlets to a plate.

3 To make the Tomato Sauce: Add the stock to the skillet, stirring to scrape up the browned bits from the bottom of the pan. Add the garlic, bell pepper, and mushrooms and cook over moderate heat, stirring continuously, for 5 minutes, or until the vegetables are softened. Stir in the tomato paste and the tomatoes with their juices. Cook, uncovered, over moderately low heat, stirring frequently, for 30 minutes, or until the sauce has thickened slightly. Sprinkle with the chopped basil.

4 Preheat the broiler. Spoon ½ cup of the sauce into each of 4 individual ovenproof dishes and place the veal cutlets on top. Spoon the remaining sauce over the cutlets and top each one with a slice of the mozzarella cheese.

5 Place the dishes under the broiler 4″ from the heat source. Broil for 2 to 3 minutes, or until the cheese is melted and bubbling slightly. Remove the dishes from the broiler. Garnish each with a sprig of fresh basil, if desired, and serve immediately.

An Italian specialty—well loved and with good reason. This version is a knockout!

EQUIPMENT LIST

Utility knife
Shallow bowl
Kitchen spoons
Large skillet
Large, metal spatula
Plate
4 ovenproof dishes

FISH AND SHELLFISH

*F*ish dishes make main courses that are speedy and easy on the budget. Featured in this chapter are a cod and potato pie, grilled halibut with a flavorful vegetable sauce, and a creamy fish lasagne that's just right for cooking and freezing in quantity.

Grilled Tuna with Tarragon Marinade.

Grilled Tuna
with Tarragon Marinade

4 tuna steaks (8 ounces each), rinsed and patted dry
Lemon wedges (optional)
Sprigs of fresh tarragon (optional)

TARRAGON MARINADE (2 CUPS)

¾ cup plain lowfat yogurt
¾ cup mayonnaise
1 shallot, finely chopped (1 tablespoon)
1 tablespoon chopped fresh tarragon, or 1 teaspoon dried tarragon leaves, crumbled
½ teaspoon coarsely ground black pepper
¼ cup fresh lemon juice
¼ cup milk

Tuna, a member of the mackerel family, has a rich-flavored flesh. When buying fresh tuna, remember that the lighter the color of the flesh, the more delicate the flavor and texture.

1 Prepare a charcoal grill until the coals form white ash, preheat a gas grill to high, or preheat the broiler.

2 To make the Tarragon Marinade: In a large, shallow glass dish, combine the yogurt, mayonnaise, shallot, chopped tarragon, pepper, lemon juice, and milk. Add the tuna, turning to coat. Cover with plastic wrap and marinate at room temperature for 20 minutes or for up to 2 hours in the refrigerator. (After 2 hours the acid in the marinade will begin to "cook" the fish.)

3 Remove the tuna steaks from the marinade and place on the grill or under the broiler 4″ from the heat source. Grill or broil, brushing frequently with marinade, for 4 minutes on each side, or until the fish flakes easily when tested with a fork.

4 Using a large, metal spatula, transfer the tuna steaks to individual serving plates. Garnish with lemon wedges and sprigs of fresh tarragon, if desired, and serve immediately.

4 SERVINGS
PREP TIME: 5 MINUTES PLUS
20 MINUTES TO MARINATE
COOKING TIME: 8 MINUTES

EQUIPMENT LIST

Paper towels
Plastic wrap
Paring knife
Citrus juicer
Charcoal or gas grill or broiler pan
Large, shallow glass dish
Kitchen spoon
Pastry brush
Large, metal spatula
Fork

Swordfish
with Chive-Mustard Butter

4 swordfish steaks (8 ounces each), ¾″ thick, rinsed and patted dry

LEMON MARINADE (½ CUP)

¼ cup fresh lemon juice
¼ cup olive oil
⅛ teaspoon salt, or to taste
Freshly ground black pepper

CHIVE-MUSTARD BUTTER (½ CUP)

6 tablespoons unsalted butter, softened
2 teaspoons snipped fresh chives or chopped green onion tops
2 teaspoons Dijon-style mustard
2 teaspoons fresh lemon juice
Freshly ground black pepper

Serve these grilled swordfish steaks with a cold rice salad and marinated yellow and red cherry tomatoes.

1 Prepare a charcoal grill until coals form white ash, preheat a gas grill to high, or preheat the broiler.

2 To make the Lemon Marinade: In a large, shallow glass dish, combine the lemon juice, oil, salt, and pepper. Add the swordfish, turning to coat. Cover with plastic wrap and marinate at room temperature for 15 minutes, or for up to 2 hours in the refrigerator. (After 2 hours the acid in the marinade will begin to "cook" the fish.)

3 Meanwhile, prepare the Chive-Mustard Butter. In a small bowl, using a fork, blend the butter with the chives, mustard, and lemon juice until smooth. Season to taste with the pepper.

4 Lightly oil the preheated grill or a broiler pan. Place the swordfish steaks on the grill or under the broiler 4″ from the heat source. Grill or broil for 5 minutes on each side, or until the fish flakes easily when tested with a fork.

5 Using a large, metal spatula, transfer the swordfish to individual serving plates. Top the swordfish with a spoonful of the butter and serve immediately.

4 SERVINGS
PREP TIME: 15 MINUTES PLUS
15 MINUTES TO MARINATE
COOKING TIME: 10 MINUTES

EQUIPMENT LIST

Paper towels
Citrus juicer
Pepper mill
Kitchen scissors
Charcoal or gas grill or broiler pan
Large, shallow glass dish
Kitchen spoon
Plastic wrap
Small bowl
Large, metal spatula
Fork

Baked Cod
with Potatoes and Garlic

2　medium-size California white or other boiling potatoes, peeled (1 pound)

2　tablespoons salted butter or margarine

2　tablespoons olive oil

1　large clove garlic, finely chopped

1　teaspoon grated lemon rind

¼　teaspoon dried oregano leaves or dried thyme leaves, crumbled

½　teaspoon salt, or to taste

¼　teaspoon coarsely ground black pepper

1½　pounds cod fillet, rinsed, patted dry, and cut in 4 pieces

1　tablespoon chopped fresh parsley

Sprigs of fresh thyme (optional)

Lemon wedges (optional)

Cod is one of the most popular salt-water fish. Its delicately sweet flavor lends itself to many combinations. There are various species of cod, such as hake, haddock, and pollack. If none of these is available, substitute halibut or flounder. Serve this economical dish with a tomato and onion salad.

1　Preheat the oven to 400° F. Grease an 8″ square baking dish. Place the potatoes in a medium-size saucepan with enough cold water to cover. Bring to a boil over high heat. Reduce the heat to moderately low and cook, uncovered, for 20 minutes, or until the potatoes are tender when tested with a fork. Drain well, rinse under cold running water, and drain again.

2　Meanwhile, in a small saucepan over moderately low heat, melt the butter. Whisk in the oil, garlic, lemon rind, and oregano. Season to taste with the salt and pepper.

3　Slice the potatoes ½″ thick and arrange over the bottom of the prepared dish. Pour half of the butter mixture evenly over the potatoes. Place the pieces of cod on top of the potatoes and pour the remaining butter mixture over the fish. Sprinkle with chopped parsley.

4　Bake the cod, uncovered, for 30 minutes, or until the fish flakes easily when tested with a fork. Remove the baking dish from the oven. Garnish with sprigs of fresh thyme and lemon wedges, if desired, and serve immediately.

4 SERVINGS
PREP TIME: 35 MINUTES
COOKING TIME: 30 MINUTES

EQUIPMENT LIST

Vegetable peeler
Paring knife
Chef's knife
Grater
Paper towels
8″ square baking dish
Medium-size saucepan
Small saucepan
Fork
Colander
Wire whisk

Simple and satisfying, this cod and potato combination will get everyone's approval.

Vegetable- and Fruit-Stuffed Flounder

Flounder is a mild-flavored fish that is well-suited for stuffing and rolling. Serve this dish with an aromatic rice such as Texmati.

4   flounder fillets (6 ounces
     each), rinsed and patted dry
Lemon wedges (optional)

VEGETABLE AND FRUIT STUFFING

2   slices toasted white bread
2   tablespoons unsalted butter
1   large clove garlic, chopped
1   small carrot, peeled and
     shredded (½ cup)
1   small zucchini, trimmed and
     shredded (1 cup)
1   small tomato, chopped
     (½ cup)
1   medium-size orange, peeled,
     seeded, and chopped (½ cup)
1   tablespoon snipped fresh
     chives
¾   teaspoon dried tarragon
     leaves, crumbled
⅛   teaspoon salt, or to taste
Freshly ground black pepper

1   Preheat the oven to 350° F. Lightly grease an 8″ x 12″ baking dish. To make the Vegetable and Fruit Stuffing: Tear the toast in pieces and place in a blender or food processor fitted with the metal blade. Blend or process for 30 seconds, or until the bread becomes coarse crumbs. Transfer the bread crumbs to a medium-size bowl.

2   In a large skillet over moderate heat, melt the butter. Add the garlic, carrot, and zucchini and sauté for 3 minutes, or until the vegetables are slightly softened. Add the vegetables to the bread crumbs. Stir in the tomato, orange, chives, and tarragon. Season to taste with the salt and pepper.

3   Lay the flounder fillets on a work surface. Spoon one-fourth of the stuffing down the center of each flounder fillet. Roll up the flounder fillets, secure with toothpicks, and arrange, seam-side down, in the prepared baking dish. Bake, uncovered, for 20 to 25 minutes, or until the fish flakes easily when tested with a fork.

4   Using a large, metal spatula, transfer the stuffed flounder to individual serving plates. Remove and discard the toothpicks. Garnish with the lemon wedges, if desired, and serve immediately.

4 SERVINGS
PREP TIME: 20 MINUTES
COOKING TIME: 30 MINUTES

EQUIPMENT LIST

Paper towels
Utility knife
Vegetable peeler
Grater
Kitchen scissors
Pepper mill
8″ x 12″ baking dish
Blender or food processor with
    metal blade
Medium-size bowl
Large skillet
Kitchen spoon
Toothpicks
Fork

Pan-Fried Brook Trout

A light coating of cornmeal gives this trout extra crispness. If time is short, ask the fishmonger to remove the head and bones, but keep the fillets attached to the skin. Serve this dish with home-fries and tomato slices.

¼   cup yellow cornmeal
2   teaspoons chopped fresh
     parsley
⅛   teaspoon salt, or to taste
⅛   teaspoon coarsely ground
     black pepper
4   brook trout (10 ounces each),
     cleaned, heads and bones
     removed, rinsed and patted
     dry
2   tablespoons vegetable oil
¼   cup fresh lemon juice
1   tablespoon unsalted butter
Sprigs of fresh parsley (optional)

1   Preheat the oven to 200° F. In a large, shallow dish, combine the cornmeal, parsley, salt, and pepper. Open a trout and lay the flesh side in the cornmeal mixture, pressing gently so the cornmeal adheres. Place the trout on a plate, breaded-side up. Repeat as directed with the remaining trout.

2   In a large skillet, heat 2 teaspoons of the oil over moderate heat for 1 minute. Place 1 trout, flesh-side down, in the skillet. Cook for 3 minutes, or until the cornmeal coating is browned and the flesh is firm. Using a large, metal spatula, turn the trout and cook for 2 minutes more, or until the skin side is crisp.

3   Transfer the trout to a plate lined with paper towels to drain, and then to a serving platter. Cover loosely with aluminum foil and keep warm in the oven. Cook the remaining trout as directed, adding more oil to the skillet if needed.

4   When trout are cooked, add lemon juice to skillet. Bring to a boil over high heat and stir in butter until melted. Spoon sauce over trout. Garnish with sprigs of fresh parsley, if desired. Serve immediately.

4 SERVINGS
PREP TIME: 10 MINUTES
COOKING TIME: 20 MINUTES

EQUIPMENT LIST

Utility knife
Paper towels
Aluminum foil
Citrus juicer
Large, shallow dish
Kitchen spoon
2 plates
Large skillet
Large, metal spatula

Salmon and Dill Croquettes with Cucumber-Yogurt Sauce

2	medium-size California or other boiling potatoes, peeled and cut in 1″ pieces (2 cups)
2	tablespoons milk
1	pound fresh salmon fillet, skinned, boned, rinsed, and patted dry
2	large eggs
2	tablespoons chopped fresh dill, or 2 teaspoons dried dill weed
1	tablespoon chopped fresh parsley
⅛	teaspoon salt, or to taste

Freshly ground black pepper

1½	cups dry unseasoned bread crumbs
1	tablespoon all-purpose flour
4	tablespoons unsalted butter

Sprigs of fresh dill (optional)
Lemon slices (optional)
Cucumber slices (optional)

Cucumber-Yogurt Sauce (2 cups)

1	medium-size cucumber, peeled, halved, seeded, and thinly sliced (1 cup)
1	8-ounce container plain lowfat yogurt (1 cup)
2	tablespoon chopped fresh dill, or 2 teaspoons dried dill weed
1	small clove garlic, finely chopped

Salmon is a delicious but costly fish. In this recipe, a pound of fish is stretched to four servings by combining it with mashed potatoes. For a decorative presentation, cut the rim of 4 large lemons in a zigzag pattern, remove the pulp, and fill the shell with the sauce.

1 Preheat the oven to 375° F. Grease a small baking dish. To make the croquettes: Place the potatoes in a medium-size saucepan with enough cold water to cover. Bring to a boil over high heat. Reduce the heat to moderately low and cook, uncovered, for 20 minutes, or until the potatoes are tender when tested with a fork. Drain well. Transfer potatoes to a medium-size bowl and stir in the milk. Using a potato masher or fork, mash the potatoes. Let cool.

2 Meanwhile, place the salmon in the prepared dish and bake for 12 to 15 minutes, or until the fish flakes easily when tested with a fork. Remove the dish from the oven. In a large bowl, flake the salmon. Add the potatoes, eggs, 2 tablespoons of dill, and parsley and stir until well blended. Season to taste with the salt and pepper.

3 Place bread crumbs on a sheet of wax paper. Dip your fingers in a little flour and shape salmon mixture into sixteen 2½″ croquettes. Roll the croquettes in bread crumbs to coat completely. Transfer the croquettes to a plate and chill in the refrigerator for 30 minutes.

4 Meanwhile, make the sauce. In a medium-size bowl, combine the cucumber, yogurt, 2 tablespoons of dill, and garlic. Cover the bowl with plastic wrap and refrigerate until ready to use.

5 Preheat the oven to 200° F. In a large skillet over moderate heat, melt 2 tablespoons of the butter. Cook half of the croquettes, turning frequently, for 8 to 10 minutes, or until crisp and golden. Transfer the croquettes to a plate lined with paper towels to drain, and then to a baking pan. Keep warm in the oven. Melt remaining 2 tablespoons of butter over moderate heat and cook remaining croquettes as directed.

6 Transfer the croquettes to a serving platter. Garnish with sprigs of fresh dill and lemon and cucumber slices, if desired. Serve immediately with the sauce.

4 SERVINGS OR 16 CROQUETTES
PREP TIME: 25 MINUTES PLUS
30 MINUTES TO CHILL
COOKING TIME: 37 MINUTES

Equipment List

Vegetable peeler
Utility knife
Paper towels
Wax paper
Plastic wrap
Pepper mill
Small baking dish
Medium-size saucepan
Fork
Colander
2 medium-size bowls
Large bowl
Potato masher
Kitchen spoon
2 plates
Large skillet
Large, metal spatula

Rainbow Trout
with Vegetable Salsa

4   rainbow trout fillets
     (4 ounces each), rinsed and
     patted dry
¼   cup fresh lemon juice
1   tablespoon olive oil

VEGETABLE SALSA (2 CUPS)

1   small eggplant, trimmed,
     peeled, and thickly sliced
1   small green bell pepper,
     cored, seeded and halved
1   small red bell pepper, cored,
     seeded, and halved
5   green onions (including
     tops), trimmed
4   tablespoons olive oil
½   cup chopped, pitted black
     olives
2   tablespoons fresh lemon juice
¼   teaspoon salt, or to taste
Freshly ground black pepper

The term "salsa" often conjures up images of a fiery tomato and chili pepper sauce. This recipe goes easy on the heat but doesn't skimp on flavor.

1   Prepare a charcoal grill until the coals form white ash, preheat a gas grill to high, or preheat the broiler.

2   Place fish in a large, shallow glass dish. In a small bowl, whisk together the ¼ cup of lemon juice and 1 tablespoon of oil. Pour mixture over trout fillets, cover with plastic wrap, and set aside.

3   To make the Vegetable Salsa: Brush the eggplant, bell peppers, and green onions with 3 tablespoons of the oil. Place the vegetables on the grill or under the broiler 4″ from heat source. Grill or broil, turning occasionally, for 10 to 12 minutes, or until the vegetables are tender and lightly charred. Cool the vegetables slightly.

4   Finely chop the vegetables and combine in a medium-size bowl with the remaining 1 tablespoon of oil, the olives, and the 2 tablespoons of lemon juice. Season to taste and set aside.

5   Place the fish on the grill or under the broiler 4″ from the heat source. Grill or broil for 3 to 4 minutes on each side, or until the fish flakes easily when tested with a fork. Transfer the fish to individual serving plates. Spoon the salsa over the fish. Serve immediately.

4 SERVINGS
PREP TIME: 20 MINUTES
COOKING TIME: 30 MINUTES

EQUIPMENT LIST
Paper towels
Plastic wrap
Citrus juicer
Utility knife
Vegetable peeler
Pepper mill
Charcoal or gas grill or broiler pan
Large, shallow glass dish
Small bowl
Medium-size bowl
Wire whisk
Pastry brush
Large, metal spatula
Kitchen spoon
Fork

Baked Sole Obispo

2   tablespoons unsalted butter
2   large carrots, peeled and cut
     in narrow strips (2 cups)
8   ounces jicama, peeled and cut
     in narrow strips (2 cups)
4   sole fillets (4 ounces each)
½   ripe avocado, peeled and cut
     in 8 slices
4   sprigs of fresh cilantro
     (coriander leaves)
1   cup chicken stock or canned
     broth
2   teaspoons fresh lime juice
2   green onions (including
     tops), cut in narrow strips
     (¼ cup)

SPICY SAUCE (¾ CUP)

1   small ripe tomato, seeded and
     chopped (½ cup)
¼   cup mild taco sauce

In this colorful fish dish, delicate sole fillets are placed on a bed of carrot and jicama (pronounced HEE-kay-mah) strips. Top with a spicy tomato sauce and serve with warm flour tortillas.

1   Preheat the oven to 350° F. In a large skillet over moderate heat, melt the butter. Add the carrots and jicama and sauté for 5 minutes, or until crisp-tender.

2   Meanwhile, rinse the sole fillets under cold running water and pat dry with paper towels. Lay 2 fillets on a work surface with long edges slightly overlapping. Lay 4 avocado slices and 2 sprigs of fresh cilantro across the middle of the sole fillets. Roll up the sole fillets to enclose the filling. Repeat filling and rolling as directed with the remaining sole fillets.

3   Transfer the carrots and jicama to a 1-quart baking dish. Add the stock, lime juice, and green onions. Arrange the fillets, seam-sides down, on top of the vegetables. Cover the dish with aluminum foil and bake for 12 to 15 minutes, or until the fish is opaque throughout and flakes easily when tested with a fork.

4   Meanwhile, make the Spicy Sauce. In a small bowl, combine the tomato and the taco sauce. Remove the baking dish from the oven. Spoon some sauce over the fillets and serve immediately.

4 SERVINGS
PREP TIME: 30 MINUTES
COOKING TIME: 20 MINUTES

EQUIPMENT LIST
Vegetable peeler
Utility knife
Paring knife
Citrus juicer
Large skillet
Kitchen spoons
Paper towels
Aluminum foil
1-quart baking dish
Fork
Small bowl

Haddock Fillets
with Pears Jardinière

So simple and fresh tasting, this healthy dish can be prepared with ease. Ripe pears must be used to ensure good flavor and to release enough liquid for cooking. If haddock fillets are not available, substitute salmon or sea bass fillets and proceed as directed.

4	haddock fillets (6 ounces each)
1	tablespoon vegetable oil
1	medium-size yellow onion, thinly sliced (1½ cups)
2	medium-size carrots, peeled and cut in ¼″ thick strips (1½ cups)
½	teaspoon dry mustard
1½	teaspoons chopped fresh oregano, or ½ teaspoon dried oregano leaves, crumbled
¾	teaspoon chopped fresh rosemary, or ¼ teaspoon dried rosemary leaves, crumbled
⅛	teaspoon salt, or to taste
	Freshly ground black pepper
2	medium-size ripe Bartlett or other ripe pears, peeled, cored, and quartered lengthwise (1½ cups)
	Tomato slices (optional)
	Lemon slices (optional)
	Sprigs of fresh oregano (optional)
	Sprigs of fresh rosemary (optional)

1 Rinse the haddock fillets under cold running water and pat dry with paper towels.

2 In a large skillet, heat the oil over moderate heat for 1 minute. Add the onion and carrots and cook, covered, stirring occasionally, for 8 minutes, or until the vegetables are softened.

3 Meanwhile, in a medium-size bowl, combine the mustard, the chopped oregano and rosemary, the salt, and pepper. Add the pears, tossing to coat.

4 Arrange the pears and haddock fillets in a single layer on top of the vegetables. Cook, covered, over moderate heat for 10 minutes, or until the fish flakes easily when tested with a fork. Remove skillet from the heat.

5 Transfer 1 haddock fillet and 2 pear quarters to each of 4 individual serving plates. Top each haddock fillet with some of the vegetables. Garnish with tomato and lemon slices and sprigs of fresh oregano and rosemary, if desired, and serve immediately.

4 SERVINGS
PREP TIME: 10 MINUTES
COOKING TIME: 20 MINUTES

EQUIPMENT LIST
Utility knife
Vegetable peeler
Pepper mill
Paper towels
Large skillet with lid
Kitchen spoon
Medium-size bowl
Fork

Haddock and pears make a stunning presentation—and the dish is easy to prepare.

Baked Bluefish
with Tomato-Cream Sauce

2 bluefish fillets, skin removed, rinsed and patted dry (1 pound each)

1 small yellow onion, finely chopped (½ cup)

½ cup fish stock or bottled clam juice

½ cup dry white wine or water

Snipped fresh chives (optional)

TOMATO-CREAM SAUCE (2¼ CUPS)

1 cup light cream or half-and-half

2 medium-size tomatoes, peeled, seeded, and chopped (2 cups)

2 tablespoons snipped fresh chives

2 tablespoons fresh lemon juice

⅛ teaspoon salt, or to taste

Freshly ground black pepper

Bluefish is a feisty game fish found in Atlantic waters from Nova Scotia to Florida. Here, bluefish fillets are baked in fish stock and white wine, which is also the base for the sauce. Serve with baked potatoes and green beans.

1 Preheat the oven to 450° F. Grease a 9″ x 13″ baking dish. Cut each bluefish fillet into 3 pieces crosswise.

2 Sprinkle the onion over the bottom of the prepared dish, then place the fillets on top. Pour the stock and wine over the fillets. Cover the baking dish tightly with aluminum foil and bake for 15 minutes, or until the fish flakes easily when tested with a fork.

3 Remove the baking dish from the oven. Pour the cooking liquid from the baking dish into a medium-size saucepan. Re-cover the fillets with foil and keep warm.

4 To make the Tomato-Cream Sauce: Bring the cooking liquid to a boil over high heat. Boil for 10 to 12 minutes, or until reduced to ¼ cup. Add cream and cook, stirring frequently, for 10 minutes, or until reduced by one-third. Stir in the tomatoes and 2 tablespoons of chives. Cook, stirring continuously, for 1 minute more, or until heated through. Remove pan from the heat. Stir in the lemon juice and season to taste.

5 Transfer fillets to a serving platter and spoon the sauce over them. Garnish with snipped fresh chives, if desired. Serve immediately.

6 SERVINGS
PREP TIME: 10 MINUTES
COOKING TIME: 40 MINUTES

EQUIPMENT LIST
Paper towels
Aluminum foil
Utility knife
Paring knife
Kitchen scissors
Citrus juicer
Pepper mill
9″ x 13″ baking dish
Fork
Medium-size saucepan
Kitchen spoon

Grilled Halibut Steaks Provençale

4 halibut or salmon steaks (8 ounces each), cut ½″ thick, rinsed and patted dry

3 tablespoons olive oil

1 medium-size yellow onion, thinly sliced (1½ cups)

1 medium-size ripe tomato, peeled, seeded, and chopped (1 cup)

2 tablespoons chopped, pitted black olives

1 tablespoon capers, drained and rinsed

1 large clove garlic, chopped

1 tablespoon chopped fresh parsley

⅛ teaspoon salt, or to taste

Freshly ground black pepper

Lemon wedges (optional)

Sprigs of fresh parsley (optional)

Scents reminiscent of the South of France—garlic, tomatoes, and olives—perfume these halibut steaks. Serve with a mixture of brown and wild rice.

1 Prepare a charcoal grill until the coals form white ash, preheat a gas grill to high, or preheat the broiler.

2 Lightly brush both sides of the halibut steaks with 1 tablespoon of the oil. Set aside.

3 In a medium-size skillet, heat the remaining 2 tablespoons of oil over moderately high heat for 1 minute. Add the onion and sauté for 5 minutes, or until translucent. Add the garlic and sauté for 30 seconds, or until fragrant. Add the tomatoes, olives, and capers. Cook, stirring frequently, over moderate heat for 10 minutes, or until the tomatoes are softened. Stir in the chopped parsley. Season to taste. Remove skillet from heat and keep warm.

4 Place the halibut steaks on the grill or under the broiler 4″ from the heat source. Grill or broil for 3 or 4 minutes on each side, or until the fish flakes easily when tested with a fork.

5 Transfer the halibut steaks to individual serving plates. Spoon some of the tomato mixture over the fish. Garnish with the lemon wedges and sprigs of fresh parsley, if desired, and serve immediately.

4 SERVINGS
PREP TIME: 10 MINUTES
COOKING TIME: 25 MINUTES

EQUIPMENT LIST
Paper towels
Utility knife
Paring knife
Strainer
Pepper mill
Charcoal or gas grill or broiler pan
Pastry brush
Medium-size skillet
Kitchen spoon
Large, metal spatula
Fork

Mixed Fish Paella

A traditional Spanish dish, paella is usually served at family gatherings and celebrations. This adaptation captures the authentic flavor with saffron, which also gives a yellow tint to the rice.

1 cup chicken stock or canned broth

¼ teaspoon saffron threads

1 cup water

4 ounces chorizo or other hard spicy sausage, sliced

1 tablespoon olive oil

1 small yellow onion, finely chopped (½ cup)

1 large clove garlic, finely chopped

1 medium-size green or red bell pepper, cored, seeded, and cut in strips (1 cup)

1 medium-size tomato, chopped (1 cup)

1 cup long-grain white rice

¼ teaspoon salt, or to taste

¼ teaspoon ground red pepper (cayenne)

8 ounces mussels, cleaned

8 ounces medium-size uncooked shrimp, peeled and deveined, tails intact (12-16 shrimp)

1 catfish fillet (8 ounces), rinsed, patted dry, and cut in 1½" pieces

1 9-ounce package frozen artichoke hearts, thawed and drained (optional)

½ cup frozen peas, thawed and drained

1 In a small saucepan, combine the stock, saffron, and water. Bring to a simmer over moderate heat, then remove the pan from the heat. Set aside and keep warm.

2 In a large, ovenproof skillet or paella pan, cook the sausages over moderate heat, turning frequently, for 3 minutes, or until lightly browned. Using a slotted spoon, transfer the sausages to a plate lined with paper towels to drain. Wipe out the skillet with paper towels.

3 Heat the oil in the skillet over moderate heat for 1 minute. Add onion and sauté for 5 minutes, or until translucent. Add garlic, bell pepper, tomato, and rice, stirring to coat with the oil. Add stock mixture and sausages. Season to taste with the salt and ground red pepper. Increase heat to high and bring to a boil. Reduce heat to moderate and simmer, covered, for 10 minutes. Preheat the oven to 375° F.

4 Remove the skillet from the heat. Arrange the mussels, shrimp, catfish, and artichoke hearts, if desired, on top of the rice, pressing them in well. Sprinkle the peas over the top. Cover with aluminum foil and bake for 20 minutes, or until the fish is opaque and the mussels have opened. Serve the paella immediately, straight from the skillet.

6 SERVINGS
PREP TIME: 45 MINUTES
COOKING TIME: 40 MINUTES

EQUIPMENT LIST

Utility knife
Vegetable brush
Paper towels
Aluminum foil
Colander
Small saucepan
Kitchen spoon
Slotted spoon
Large, ovenproof skillet or paella pan with lid
Plate

Seafood Lasagne

8 ounces dried lasagne noodles

8 ounces shredded mozzarella cheese (2 cups)

SHRIMP SAUCE (3 CUPS)

1 tablespoon olive oil

1 large clove garlic, finely chopped

½ teaspoon crushed red pepper flakes

1 14½-ounce can crushed tomatoes

2 tablespoons chopped fresh parsley

2 tablespoons chopped fresh basil, or 2 teaspoons dried basil leaves, crumbled

8 ounces medium-size uncooked shrimp (12-16 shrimp), shelled, deveined, and chopped

¼ cup milk

2 teaspoons tomato paste

⅛ teaspoon salt, or to taste

⅛ teaspoon coarsely ground black pepper

SEAFOOD FILLING

1 tablespoon olive oil

1 tablespoon salted butter or margarine

1 pound monkfish fillets, rinsed, patted dry, and cut in ½" slices

1 15-ounce container part-skim ricotta cheese

2 tablespoons grated Parmesan cheese

¼ teaspoon ground nutmeg

2 tablespoons chopped fresh parsley

1 large egg

¼ teaspoon salt, or to taste

⅛ teaspoon coarsely ground black pepper

This recipe is a pleasant change from traditional lasagne. The creamy filling is flavored with monkfish, also known as angler fish. This firm-textured fish has a mild, sweet flavor that is similar to lobster, and indeed has often been referred to as "poor man's lobster" because it is less expensive.

This lasagne is an easy and delicious dish for entertaining. Assemble and refrigerate the dish up to 6 hours in advance and bake as directed 1 hour before serving. Or, make a double batch and freeze the second one for later. To freeze: Wrap the assembled and unbaked lasagne tightly with plastic wrap and then with aluminum foil. Freeze for up to 3 weeks. Defrost overnight in the refrigerator and bake as directed.

Serve this dish accompanied by a salad of mixed greens and crusty Italian bread for supper. For a more colorful dish, try using spinach lasagne noodles in place of the egg noodles.

1 To make the Shrimp Sauce: In a medium-size saucepan, heat the 1 tablespoon of oil over moderate heat for 1 minute. Add garlic and red pepper flakes and sauté for 30 seconds, or until fragrant. Add the tomatoes with their juices, the parsley, and basil and cook, uncovered, for 10 minutes, stirring frequently. Add the shrimp and cook, stirring occasionally, for 3 minutes more. Remove the pan from the heat. Stir in the milk and tomato paste. Season to taste with the salt and the ⅛ teaspoon of pepper and set aside.

2 To make the Seafood Filling: In a large skillet, heat the 1 tablespoon of oil and the butter over moderate heat for 1 minute. Add the monkfish slices and cook for 2 minutes on each side, or until golden. Remove the skillet from the heat and set aside.

3 In a medium-size bowl, combine the ricotta and Parmesan cheeses, nutmeg, parsley, and egg. Season to taste with the salt and the ⅛ teaspoon of pepper. Stir in the monkfish slices and set aside.

4 Preheat the oven to 375° F. Bring a large stockpot of water to a boil over high heat. Cook the lasagne noodles in the boiling water for 9 minutes, or until al dente. Drain the lasagne noodles well, rinse under cold running water, and drain again.

5 To assemble: Spoon ¼ cup of the Shrimp Sauce into a 9" square baking dish. Cut the lasagne noodles to fit the dish and place one-third of the noodles over the sauce, overlapping slightly. Gently spread one-half of the Seafood Filling over the noodles and top with 1 cup of the sauce and one-third of the mozzarella cheese. Repeat the layers once as directed. Top with the remaining one-third of the noodles, one-half cup of the sauce, and one-third of the mozzarella cheese.

6 Cover the dish with aluminum foil and bake for 30 minutes. Remove the foil and bake for 15 minutes more, or until the edges are lightly browned and the sauce is bubbling. Remove the baking dish from the oven and cool for 15 minutes before serving.

6 SERVINGS
PREP TIME: 45 MINUTES PLUS
15 MINUTES TO COOL
COOKING TIME: 45 MINUTES

EQUIPMENT LIST

Utility knife
Paper towels
Aluminum foil
Medium-size saucepan
Large stockpot
Kitchen spoons
Large skillet
Medium-size bowl
Colander
9" square baking dish

POULTRY

*F*amily meals using poultry are extremely popular. This chapter features recipes that are high on flavor, healthful, and economical. Select from a spicy chicken pot pie, classic coq au vin, roast turkey with a Spanish stuffing, and turkey ragoût, just to name a few.

Hearty Broiled Chicken and Potatoes.

Hearty Broiled Chicken and Potatoes

Here's a chicken recipe that's both tasty and easy to prepare.

1   1   3-3½ pound chicken, cut in serving pieces

1¼   pounds small new potatoes, peeled (6-8 potatoes)

1   small green or red bell pepper, cored, seeded, and cut in thin strips (¾ cup)

HERB COATING (¾ CUP)

⅓   cup fresh lemon juice

2   ounces grated Parmesan cheese (½ cup)

3   tablespoons chopped fresh parsley

1   large clove garlic, finely chopped

2   teaspoons dried rosemary leaves, crumbled

⅛   teaspoon salt, or to taste

½   teaspoon coarsely ground black pepper

1 Preheat the broiler. Rinse the chicken pieces under cold running water and pat dry with paper towels.

2 To make the Herb Coating: In a shallow dish, combine the lemon juice, Parmesan cheese, parsley, garlic, rosemary, salt, and pepper. Transfer one-third of the mixture to a plate and reserve.

3 Dredge the chicken, 1 piece at a time, in the coating and transfer to a broiler pan. Place chicken under the broiler 6″ from the heat source. Broil, turning chicken occasionally, for 30 minutes, or until the juices run clear when the meat is pierced with a knife.

4 Meanwhile, place the potatoes in a large saucepan with enough cold water to cover. Bring to a boil over high heat. Reduce the heat to moderately low and cook, uncovered, for 15 minutes. Add the bell pepper and cook, uncovered, for 5 minutes more, or until the potatoes are tender when tested with a fork. Drain the vegetables well and cool slightly.

5 Add the potatoes and peppers to the plate with the reserved coating, turning to coat. Remove the chicken from the broiler and arrange in a serving dish with the vegetables. Serve immediately.

4 SERVINGS
PREP TIME: 25 MINUTES
COOKING TIME: 30 MINUTES

EQUIPMENT LIST

Vegetable peeler
Utility knife
Citrus juicer
Paper towels
Shallow dish
Kitchen spoon
Plate
Broiler pan
Kitchen tongs
Large saucepan
Fork
Colander

Crusty Baked Chicken Strips

These spicy chicken strips are a light alternative to fried chicken. Serve them with corn on the cob and a tomato and red onion salad.

2   whole chicken breasts (4 halves), skinned and boned (1½ pounds)

3   tablespoons plain lowfat yogurt

3   tablespoons milk

2   teaspoons Dijon-style mustard

CRUMB COATING (2¼ CUPS)

½   small yellow onion, cut in half

2   large cloves garlic

3   tablespoons chopped fresh cilantro (coriander leaves) or fresh parsley

2   cups fresh bread crumbs

1   tablespoon yellow cornmeal

¼   teaspoon salt, or to taste

1 Preheat the oven to 400° F. Lightly grease a baking sheet. Rinse the chicken breasts under cold running water and pat dry with paper towels. Cut the chicken breasts into 1″ strips.

3 In a medium-size bowl, whisk together the yogurt, milk, and mustard until well blended.

4 To make the Crumb Coating: Place the onion, garlic, and cilantro in a blender or food processor fitted with the metal blade. Blend or process for 30 seconds, or until finely chopped. Transfer the onion mixture to a large bowl. Add the bread crumbs, cornmeal, and salt and stir until well blended.

5 Dip a strip of chicken into the yogurt mixture and coat lightly. Use a pastry brush to remove any excess. Dip the chicken strip into the crumb mixture and coat lightly, then transfer to the baking sheet. Repeat dipping and coating the remaining chicken as directed, arranging the strips on the baking sheet so that they do not touch.

6 Bake the chicken for 30 to 35 minutes, turning once, until crisp on the outside and cooked through. Transfer the chicken strips to individual serving plates. Serve hot or cold.

4 SERVINGS
PREP TIME: 15 MINUTES
COOKING TIME: 35 MINUTES

EQUIPMENT LIST

Utility knife
Baking sheet
Paper towels
Medium-size bowl
Large bowl
Wire whisk
Blender or food processor with metal blade
Kitchen spoon
Fork
Pastry brush
Large, metal spatula

Chicken Stew with Dumplings

1 tablespoon salted butter or margarine
2 tablespoons all-purpose flour
1 medium-size leek (including some green tops), trimmed, rinsed, and thinly sliced (½ cup)
2 medium-size carrots, peeled and sliced ½″ thick (1 cup)
1 medium-size turnip, trimmed, peeled, and cut in 1″ pieces (¾ cup)

CHICKEN STOCK

1 3-3½ pound chicken, skinned and cut in serving pieces
1 small yellow onion, thickly sliced (1 cup)
1 large carrot, peeled and coarsely chopped (1 cup)
1 stalk celery with leaves intact, coarsely chopped (½ cup)
5 cups water
¼ teaspoon dried thyme leaves, crumbled
4 stems fresh parsley
5 black peppercorns
⅛ teaspoon salt, or to taste

DUMPLINGS

1 tablespoon salted butter or margarine
1¼ cups all-purpose flour
2 teaspoons baking powder
⅛ teaspoon salt, or to taste
1 large egg
½ cup milk

Old-fashioned chicken and dumplings makes a satisfying meal in one pot. The stew can be made up to 2 days ahead and kept, covered with plastic wrap, in the refrigerator. The dumplings should be cooked just before serving so that they will remain soft and moist.

1 To make the Chicken Stock: In a 6-quart Dutch oven, combine the chicken, onion, the chopped carrot, celery, water, thyme, parsley, peppercorns, and ⅛ teaspoon of salt. Bring to a boil over high heat. Reduce the heat to low and cook, partially covered, for 30 minutes. Using a slotted spoon, transfer chicken pieces to a plate and cool slightly. Strain stock through a fine sieve into a large bowl and set aside. Discard vegetables.

2 To make the stew: Return the pan to moderately low heat and melt the 1 tablespoon of butter. Add the flour and cook, stirring continuously, for 2 minutes. Stir in the strained stock. Add the leek, the sliced carrots, and turnip and cook over moderately low heat for 15 minutes, or until the vegetables are slightly tender.

3 Meanwhile, remove and discard the bones from the chicken pieces. Cut the chicken meat into large chunks and add them to the pan with the vegetables. Simmer over low heat while preparing the Dumplings.

4 To make Dumplings: In a small saucepan over moderately low heat, melt the 1 tablespoon of butter. In a medium-size bowl, combine the flour, baking powder, and ⅛ teaspoon of salt. In a small bowl, combine the egg with the milk and melted butter and stir into the dry ingredients, mixing until just combined.

5 Drop heaping tablespoonfuls of the dumpling dough on top of the chicken mixture. Cook, covered, over low heat for 20 minutes, or until the dumplings are puffed and cooked through. Serve immediately.

This stew is a warm-up that's sure to please on a wintery evening.

4 SERVINGS
PREP TIME: 15 MINUTES
COOKING TIME: 1 HOUR 10 MINUTES

EQUIPMENT LIST

Utility knife
Vegetable peeler
6-quart Dutch oven
Slotted spoon
Kitchen spoons
Tablespoon
Plate
Fine sieve
Large bowl
Medium-size bowl
Small bowl
Small saucepan

Chicken Tango

The combination of ingredients in this recipe produces tangy results. Complete the menu with cornbread and a cucumber and red onion salad.

4	whole chicken legs, skinned (1½ pounds)
1	tablespoon salted butter or margarine
1	tablespoon vegetable oil
1	medium-size yellow onion, chopped (1 cup)
2	small cloves garlic, chopped
1½	cups orange juice
1	bay leaf
2	mild green chili peppers, cored, seeded, and thinly sliced (2 tablespoons)
1	large sweet potato, peeled and cut in chunks (2 cups)
1	14½-ounce can whole tomatoes
1	4-ounce jar chopped pimentos, drained and rinsed
2	tablespoons capers, drained and rinsed
½	teaspoon grated orange rind
1	medium-size orange, sliced (optional)

1 Rinse the chicken legs under cold running water and pat dry with paper towels. In a 4-quart Dutch oven, heat the butter with the oil over moderately high heat for 1 minute. Add the chicken and cook, turning occasionally, for 15 minutes, or until browned on all sides. Using a slotted spoon, transfer the chicken to a plate. Reduce the heat to moderate, add the onion and garlic to the pan, and sauté for 5 minutes, or until the onion is translucent.

2 Slowly add the orange juice, stirring to scrape up the browned bits from the bottom of the pan. Add the bay leaf. Return the chicken, with any accumulated juices, to the pan, cover, and reduce the heat to low. Cook the chicken, stirring occasionally, for 20 to 25 minutes. Add the chili peppers and sweet potato to the pan and cook for 20 minutes more, or until the sweet potato is tender.

3 Meanwhile, place the tomatoes, pimentos, and capers in a blender or food processor fitted with the metal blade. Blend or process for 30 seconds, or until smooth. With a slotted spoon, transfer the chicken to a serving platter and keep warm. Add the tomato mixture and the orange rind to the pan and cook for 5 minutes. Remove and discard the bay leaf. Spoon the sauce over the chicken. Garnish with the orange slices, if desired, and serve immediately.

4 SERVINGS
PREP TIME: 25 MINUTES
COOKING TIME: 1 HOUR 5 MINUTES

EQUIPMENT LIST

Utility knife
Vegetable peeler
Strainer
Grater
Paper towels
4-quart Dutch oven
Kitchen spoon
Slotted spoon
Plate
Blender or food processor with metal blade

Chutney-Glazed Chicken

For variety, try using other fruit chutneys, such as apple or peach, in place of mango. Serve this dish with wild rice.

1	3-3½ pound chicken, skinned and cut in serving pieces
2	tablespoons olive oil
1	large yellow onion, finely chopped (1½ cups)
3	large cloves garlic, finely chopped
¼	cup mango chutney
1	teaspoon ground cinnamon
1	teaspoon ground red pepper (cayenne)
½	teaspoon coarsely ground black pepper
½	cup dry vermouth or chicken stock or canned broth

1 Rinse the chicken under cold running water and pat dry with paper towels. In a large, nonstick skillet, heat 1 tablespoon of the oil over moderate heat for 1 minute. Add the onion and garlic and sauté for 5 minutes, or until the onion is translucent. Using a slotted spoon, transfer the onion and garlic to a plate.

2 In the same skillet, heat the remaining 1 tablespoon of oil over moderately high heat for 1 minute. Add the chicken. Cook, turning frequently, for 15 minutes, or until browned on all sides.

3 Spoon the chutney over the top of the chicken and sprinkle with the cinnamon and the ground red and black peppers. Pour ¼ cup of the vermouth into the skillet. Cook, uncovered, over moderately low heat for 15 minutes. Transfer the chicken to a plate.

4 Return the onion and garlic to the skillet. Add the remaining ¼ cup of vermouth, stirring to combine. Place the chicken on top of the onion, chutney-side down. Cook, stirring occasionally, over moderately low heat for 15 to 20 minutes, or until the chicken is tender and the juices run clear when the meat is pierced with a knife. Transfer the chicken to individual serving plates. Serve immediately.

4 SERVINGS
PREP TIME: 15 MINUTES
COOKING TIME: 55 MINUTES

EQUIPMENT LIST

Utility knife
Paper towels
Large, nonstick skillet
Kitchen spoon
Slotted spoon
2 plates

Southwestern Chicken Pot Pie

The filling for this pot pie can be prepared the night before. Prepare the biscuit topping and bake the assembled pie just before serving.

8	chicken thighs, skinned, boned, and cut in 1″ pieces (1½ pounds)
4	tablespoons vegetable oil
1	medium-size yellow onion, chopped (1 cup)
2	large cloves garlic, chopped
1	medium-size red or green bell pepper, cored, seeded, and chopped (1 cup)
2	small jalapeño peppers, cored, seeded, and finely chopped (2 tablespoons)
3	tablespoons all-purpose flour
1	16-ounce can whole tomatoes, drained and chopped
1½	cups chicken stock or canned broth
1	tablespoon chili powder
1	teaspoon ground cumin
1	16-ounce can pinto beans, drained and rinsed
1	11-ounce can corn kernels, drained
1	4-ounce can chopped green chilies
⅛	teaspoon salt, or to taste
	Freshly ground black pepper
1	small red chili pepper (optional)

BISCUIT TOPPING

1½	cups all-purpose flour
½	cup yellow cornmeal
1	tablespoon baking powder
1	tablespoon granulated sugar
1	teaspoon salt
6	tablespoons unsalted butter, chilled and cut in small pieces
⅔	cup milk

1 Rinse chicken under cold running water and pat dry with paper towels. In a 5-quart Dutch oven, heat 2 tablespoons of the oil over moderate heat for 1 minute. Add onion, garlic, and bell and jalapeño peppers and sauté for 5 minutes, or until the onion is translucent. Using a slotted spoon, transfer the vegetables to a large plate.

2 In the same pan, heat the remaining 2 tablespoons of oil over moderately high heat for 1 minute. Add the chicken and cook, stirring frequently, for 10 minutes, or until browned on all sides. Using a slotted spoon, transfer the chicken to the plate with vegetables.

3 Add the 3 tablespoons of flour to the pan and cook, stirring continuously, for 1 minute. Add tomatoes and stock, stirring to scrape up browned bits from the bottom of the pan. Add chili powder and cumin. Return the chicken and vegetables to pan. Cook, partially covered, over moderately low heat, for 30 minutes. Uncover and stir in the beans, corn, and green chilies. Season to taste with the ⅛ teaspoon of salt and the pepper. Cook, uncovered, stirring frequently, for 15 minutes, or until sauce has thickened slightly.

4 Meanwhile, make the Biscuit Topping: In a medium-size bowl, combine the 1½ cups flour, cornmeal, baking powder, sugar, and 1 teaspoon of salt. Using a pastry blender or 2 knives, cut the butter into the flour mixture until the mixture resembles coarse crumbs. Add the milk, stirring until just mixed.

5 Turn the dough out onto a lightly floured work surface and pat to ½″ thick. Using a 3″ round cookie cutter, cut the dough into 7 or 8 biscuits. Place biscuits on a plate and cover loosely with plastic wrap.

6 Preheat the oven to 400° F. Transfer chicken mixture to a shallow 3-quart casserole. Arrange the biscuits on top. Bake for 15 minutes, or until biscuits are lightly golden. Remove from the oven and let stand for 10 minutes. Garnish with a red chili pepper, if desired. Serve immediately.

6 SERVINGS
PREP TIME: 25 MINUTES PLUS
10 MINUTES TO STAND
COOKING TIME: 1 HOUR

EQUIPMENT LIST

Utility knife
Colander
Pepper mill
Paper towels
Plastic wrap
5-quart Dutch oven
Shallow 3-quart casserole
Kitchen spoons
Slotted spoon
2 plates
Medium-size bowl
Pastry blender or 2 knives
3″ round cookie cutter

Chicken-Potato Salad Mexicali

This main course salad can be prepared the night before and kept, covered with plastic wrap, in the refrigerator until ready to serve. Accompany it with warm corn tortillas for lunch or supper.

1 | pound small red-skinned potatoes, scrubbed (5-6 potatoes)
1 | whole chicken breast (2 halves), skinned and boned (12 ounces)
½ | cup reduced-calorie mayonnaise
¼ | cup plain lowfat yogurt
2 | tablespoons fresh lime juice
½ | teaspoon ground cumin
2 | medium-size ripe tomatoes, seeded and chopped (2 cups)
1 | medium-size yellow, red, or green bell pepper, cored, seeded, and chopped (¾ cup)
4 | green onions (including tops), finely chopped (½ cup)
2 | tablespoons chopped fresh cilantro (coriander leaves) or fresh parsley
1 | small jalapeño pepper, cored, seeded, and chopped (1 tablespoon)
¼ | teaspoon salt, or to taste
Ground white pepper
Leafy green lettuce leaves (optional)
Chopped green onion tops (optional)

1 Place the potatoes in a large saucepan with enough cold water to cover. Bring to a boil over high heat. Reduce heat to moderately low and cook, uncovered, for 20 minutes, or until potatoes are tender when tested with a fork. Drain well and let the potatoes cool slightly.

2 Meanwhile, bring a medium-size saucepan of water to a boil over high heat. Add the chicken breast. Reduce the heat to moderately low and cook, partially covered, for 10 minutes, or until tender. Drain well and let the chicken cool completely.

3 In a large bowl, whisk together the mayonnaise, yogurt, lime juice, and cumin. Add the tomatoes, bell pepper, the ½ cup of green onions, cilantro, and jalapeño pepper, tossing to coat. Season to taste with the salt and pepper.

4 Slice the potatoes ¼" thick. Using a sharp knife, shred the chicken breast. Add the potatoes and chicken to the salad, tossing to coat with the dressing. Cover with plastic wrap and chill in the refrigerator for 30 minutes.

5 Line a serving bowl with the lettuce leaves, if desired. Spoon the potato salad mixture into the bowl. Garnish with the chopped green onion tops, if desired, and serve chilled or at room temperature.

4 SERVINGS
PREP TIME: 15 MINUTES PLUS
45 MINUTES TO COOL AND CHILL
COOKING TIME: 20 MINUTES

EQUIPMENT LIST

Vegetable brush
Utility knife
Citrus juicer
Large saucepan
Medium-size saucepan with lid
Fork
Colander
Large bowl
Wire whisk
Kitchen spoon
Plastic wrap

Herbs and spices give this robust salad its south-of-the-border flavor.

Coq au Vin

Serve this classic dish with crusty French bread and steamed asparagus.

1 Rinse the chicken pieces under cold running water and pat dry with paper towels. Set aside.

2 Cook the bacon in a 5-quart Dutch oven over moderate heat for 8 to 10 minutes, or until crisp. Using a slotted spoon, transfer the bacon to a plate lined with paper towels to drain. Set aside.

3 Add the chicken and onions to bacon drippings in pan. Cook over moderate heat, turning occasionally, for 15 minutes, or until chicken and onions are browned. Using a slotted spoon, transfer them to a plate.

4 Add the mushrooms to the pan and cook, stirring frequently, for 5 minutes, or until softened. Transfer the mushrooms to the plate with the chicken and onions. Add the stock, wine, garlic, thyme, and sugar to the pan. Bring to a boil over high heat, stirring to scrape up the browned bits from the bottom of the pan. Return the chicken, onions, and mushrooms to the pan. Season to taste.

5 Reduce heat to low and cook, covered, for 30 to 35 minutes, or until chicken is tender and juices run clear when meat is pierced with a knife. Using a slotted spoon, transfer chicken and vegetables to a serving dish. Bring sauce in pan to a boil over high heat and cook, uncovered, for 3 minutes, or until thickened slightly. Pour sauce over chicken and vegetables. Garnish with the bacon and serve immediately.

Ingredients

1	3-3½ pound chicken, cut in serving pieces
5	strips lean bacon, chopped
1	pound pearl onions, peeled (3 cups)
8	ounces mushrooms, trimmed, cleaned, and quartered (2½ cups)
1½	cups chicken stock or canned broth
1	cup dry red wine
2	large cloves garlic, chopped
½	teaspoon dried thyme leaves, crumbled
¼	teaspoon granulated sugar
⅛	teaspoon salt, or to taste
	Freshly ground black pepper

4 SERVINGS
PREP TIME: 15 MINUTES
COOKING TIME: 1 HOUR 5 MINUTES

EQUIPMENT LIST

Utility knife
Paring knife
Pepper mill
Paper towels
5-quart Dutch oven
Slotted spoon
Kitchen spoon
2 plates

Herbed Chicken Stir-Fry

This recipe combines the Eastern technique of stir-frying with Western ingredients. Accompany the stir-fry with egg noodles or boiled rice.

1 Rinse the chicken breasts under cold running water and pat dry with paper towels. Cut the chicken into small pieces.

2 In a preheated wok or large, heavy skillet, heat 2 tablespoons of the oil over high heat for 2 minutes, or until very hot. Add the chicken pieces and stir-fry for 2 to 3 minutes, or until no pink color remains. Using a slotted spoon, transfer the chicken to a plate.

3 Add the remaining 2 tablespoons of oil to the wok and heat for 30 seconds over high heat. Add the onion and stir-fry for 1 minute. Add the garlic and basil and stir-fry for 10 seconds. Add the bell pepper and squash and stir-fry for 3 to 4 minutes, or until crisp-tender. Using a slotted spoon, transfer the vegetables to the plate.

4 In a small bowl, dissolve the cornstarch in the water. Add the tomatoes and stock to the wok. Bring the mixture to a boil over high heat and cook, stirring frequently, for 1 minute. Stir in the cornstarch mixture and cook, stirring continuously, for 30 seconds.

5 Return chicken, with any accumulated juices, and the vegetables to the wok, stirring to coat with the sauce. Season to taste. Cook, stirring frequently, for 3 minutes, or until heated through. Spoon the chicken mixture onto individual serving plates and serve immediately.

Ingredients

2	whole chicken breasts, (4 halves), skinned and boned (1½ pounds)
4	tablespoons olive oil
1	medium-size yellow onion, cut in wedges
1	large clove garlic, chopped
2	teaspoons dried basil leaves, crumbled
1	medium-size green bell pepper, cored, seeded, and cut in narrow strips (1 cup)
1	medium-size yellow squash, cut in ¼" slices (1 cup)
2	teaspoons cornstarch
2	teaspoons water
6	plum tomatoes, seeded and chopped (2 cups)
½	cup chicken stock or canned broth
¼	teaspoon salt, or to taste
	Freshly ground black pepper

4 SERVINGS
PREP TIME: 15 MINUTES
COOKING TIME: 15 MINUTES

EQUIPMENT LIST

Utility knife
Pepper mill
Paper towels
Wok or large, heavy skillet
Kitchen spoons
Slotted spoon
Plate
Small bowl

Turkey Swirls

4   **turkey thighs, skinned, boned, rinsed, and patted dry (1½ pounds)**
Green onions (optional)

APRICOT-RAISIN STUFFING (1½ CUPS)

2   ounces dried apricots, chopped (½ cup)
2   tablespoons dark raisins
1   tablespoon vegetable oil
1   large clove garlic, chopped
¼   cup chopped yellow onion
1   stalk celery, finely chopped (½ cup)
⅔   cup dry unseasoned bread crumbs
2   tablespoons water
⅛   teaspoon salt, or to taste
Freshly ground black pepper

CREAMY MUSTARD SAUCE (⅔ CUP)

1   teaspoon cornstarch
1   tablespoon water
⅔   cup chicken stock or canned broth
1½   teaspoons grainy mustard
1½   teaspoons honey
1   teaspoon fresh lemon juice
1   tablespoon reduced-calorie mayonnaise

1 To make the stuffing: In a small bowl, soak the apricots and raisins in hot water to cover for 5 minutes. Drain well. In a large skillet, heat the oil over moderate heat for 1 minute. Add garlic, onion, and celery. Sauté for 3 minutes, or until softened. Remove skillet from heat. Stir in fruit, bread crumbs, and 2 tablespoons of water. Season to taste.

2 Preheat the oven to 425° F. Place a turkey thigh on a sheet of wax paper, then cover with a second sheet of wax paper. Using a meat mallet or a rolling pin, flatten to ½″ thick. Flatten remaining turkey thighs as directed. Remove wax paper and place 1 turkey thigh on a work surface. Spread one-quarter of the stuffing over the surface to within ½″ of the edges. Roll into a cylinder and secure with kitchen twine. Repeat as directed with remaining turkey thighs.

3 Place turkey thighs, seam-sides down, on a lightly greased rack in a roasting pan. Cover with aluminum foil and place in oven. Reduce oven temperature to 325° F. Bake for 1 hour, or until a meat thermometer registers 180°-185° F.

4 Meanwhile, make the sauce. In a small bowl, mix cornstarch with 1 tablespoon of water until well blended. In a small saucepan, bring stock to a boil over moderately high heat. Whisk in mustard, honey, lemon juice, and cornstarch mixture. Cook over moderate heat, stirring continuously, for 1 minute, or until the sauce has thickened slightly. Remove pan from heat. Stir in the mayonnaise. Keep warm.

5 Remove the roasting pan from oven. Transfer the turkey thighs to a carving board. Let stand for 10 minutes. Remove and discard the kitchen twine. Slice turkey thighs ¾″ thick. Spoon the sauce onto individual serving plates. Arrange the slices over the sauce. Garnish with green onions, if desired, and serve immediately.

4 SERVINGS
PREP TIME: 20 MINUTES PLUS
15 MINUTES TO STAND
COOKING TIME: 1 HOUR

EQUIPMENT LIST

Utility knife
Carving knife
Paper towels
Wax paper
Aluminum foil
Pepper mill
Citrus juicer
2 small bowls
Strainer
Large skillet
Kitchen spoon
Meat mallet or rolling pin
Thin, metal spatula
Kitchen twine
Roasting pan with rack
Meat thermometer
Small saucepan
Wire whisk
Carving board

Turkey Ragoût with Mushrooms

2	pounds turkey tenderloins
⅓	cup all-purpose flour
¼	teaspoon salt
¼	teaspoon coarsely ground black pepper
3	tablespoons unsalted butter
3	tablespoons vegetable oil
1	small yellow onion, finely chopped (½ cup)
1	large clove garlic, chopped
8	ounces mushrooms, trimmed, cleaned, and quartered (2½ cups)
1	16-ounce can whole tomatoes, drained and chopped
½	cup dry white wine or water
1½	cups chicken stock or canned broth
2	teaspoons herbes de Provence
1	teaspoon fresh lemon juice

If herbes de Provence (a blend of herbs characteristic of Provençal cooking) are not available at the supermarket, substitute ½ teaspoon each of dried, crumbled rosemary, thyme, oregano, and tarragon leaves.

1 Rinse the turkey tenderloins under cold running water and pat dry with paper towels. Cut the turkey into 1″ pieces.

2 On a sheet of wax paper, combine the flour, salt, and pepper. Dredge the turkey pieces in the flour mixture, coating them completely and shaking off the excess.

3 In a large skillet, heat 2 tablespoons of the butter with the 2 tablespoons of the oil over moderately high heat for 1 minute. Add half of the turkey and sauté for 2 minutes, or until browned on all sides. Using a slotted spoon, transfer the turkey to a plate. Cook the remaining turkey as directed and transfer to the plate.

4 Add remaining 1 tablespoon of butter and 1 tablespoon of oil to skillet and heat over moderate heat for 1 minute. Add onion and sauté for 5 minutes, or until translucent. Add garlic and sauté for 30 seconds, or until fragrant. Add mushrooms and sauté for 3 minutes, or until softened. Add tomatoes, wine, stock, herbs, and lemon juice.

5 Return the turkey to the skillet. Bring the mixture to a boil over moderately high heat. Reduce heat to low and cook, uncovered, for 10 to 12 minutes, or until turkey is tender and sauce has thickened slightly. Transfer to individual serving plates and serve immediately.

4 SERVINGS
PREP TIME: 15 MINUTES
COOKING TIME: 32 MINUTES

EQUIPMENT LIST

Utility knife
Colander
Citrus juicer
Paper towels
Wax paper
Large skillet
Kitchen spoon
Slotted spoon
Plate

Paprika-Spiced Turkey Meatballs

1	pound ground turkey
2	tablespoons salted butter or margarine, softened
¼	cup fresh bread crumbs
2	teaspoons dried basil leaves, crumbled
¼	teaspoon ground nutmeg
1	large egg, lightly beaten

HUNGARIAN SAUCE (2 CUPS)

2	tablespoons olive oil
1	small red or green bell pepper, cored, seeded, and finely chopped (½ cup)
2	large cloves garlic, chopped
3	medium-size ripe tomatoes, finely chopped (3 cups)
1	tablespoon tomato paste
1	teaspoon paprika
⅛	teaspoon ground red pepper (cayenne)

This colorful entrée offers a new way to enjoy ground turkey, a healthful alternative to ground beef. For a complete meal, serve it over egg noodles and accompany it with a mixed vegetable salad.

1 In a medium-size bowl, combine the turkey, butter, bread crumbs, basil, nutmeg, and salt. Stir in the beaten egg to bind the mixture.

2 Using oiled hands, form the mixture into sixteen 1½″ balls. Arrange the meatballs, in a single layer, in a steamer set over boiling water in a large saucepan. Steam, covered, over moderately high heat, for 15 to 20 minutes, or until the meatballs are cooked through and no pink color remains.

3 Meanwhile, make the Hungarian Sauce. In a medium-size saucepan, heat oil over moderate heat for 1 minute. Add the bell pepper and garlic and sauté for 2 minutes, or until the bell pepper is softened. Add tomatoes, tomato paste, paprika, and ground red pepper. Increase the heat to moderately high and cook, uncovered, stirring occasionally, for 20 minutes, or until the sauce has thickened slightly.

4 Spoon some of the sauce onto individual serving plates. Arrange 4 meatballs on each plate and spoon more sauce on top. Serve the remaining sauce separately.

4 SERVINGS OR 16 MEATBALLS
PREP TIME: 25 MINUTES
COOKING TIME: 25 MINUTES

EQUIPMENT LIST

Small bowl
Medium-size bowl
Wire whisk
Utility knife
Kitchen spoons
Steamer
Large saucepan with lid
Medium-size saucepan

Turkey Picadillo with Brown Rice

Traditionally, picadillo is made with well-seasoned ground beef. This spicy version calls for ground turkey. While picadillo is perfect for spooning over fluffy brown rice, it also makes a tasty filling for savory pies.

2½   cups water
1½   tablespoons salted butter or margarine
⅛   teaspoon salt, or to taste
1   cup long-grain brown rice
2   tablespoons vegetable oil
1   small yellow onion, finely chopped (½ cup)
1   small green or red bell pepper, cored, seeded, and chopped (½ cup)
2   large cloves garlic, finely chopped
1   pound ground turkey
1   teaspoon granulated sugar
½   teaspoon ground cinnamon
½   teaspoon ground cumin
¼   teaspoon ground cloves
1   14½-ounce can stewed tomatoes
1   small Granny Smith or other tart apple, peeled, cored, and chopped (1 cup)
¼   cup dark raisins
2   tablespoons sliced pimento-stuffed green olives
Chopped fresh parsley (optional)

4 SERVINGS
PREP TIME: 20 MINUTES
COOKING TIME: 45 MINUTES

EQUIPMENT LIST

Utility knife
Vegetable peeler
Medium-size saucepan with lid
Large skillet with lid
Kitchen spoons
Fork

1 In a medium-size saucepan, bring the water, butter, and salt to a boil over high heat. Stir in the rice. Reduce the heat to low and cook, covered, for 45 to 50 minutes, or until the rice is tender and the liquid is absorbed.

2 Meanwhile, in a large skillet, heat the oil over moderately high heat for 1 minute. Add the onion, bell pepper, and garlic and sauté for 5 minutes, or until the onion is translucent.

3 Add the turkey to the skillet. Cook, stirring frequently, for 5 minutes, or until cooked through and no pink color remains.

4 Stir in the sugar, cinnamon, cumin, cloves, tomatoes, apple, raisins, and olives. Reduce the heat to low and cook, covered, stirring occasionally, for 15 to 20 minutes, or until the apple is tender. Keep the turkey mixture warm over low heat.

5 Fluff the rice with a fork and transfer to a serving platter. Spoon the picadillo over the rice, garnish with the chopped parsley, if desired, and serve immediately.

6 Alternatively, lightly grease a ring mold. Pack the rice tightly into the mold and invert onto a serving platter. Fill the center of the ring with picadillo and garnish with the chopped parsley, if desired.

Roast Turkey with Chorizo Stuffing

1 16-17 pound turkey
1 tablespoon salt
3 tablespoons unsalted butter
Assorted fresh chilies (optional)

CHORIZO STUFFING (6 CUPS)

1½ pounds chorizo sausage, casings removed, thinly sliced
2 large yellow onions, chopped (3 cups)
3 large cloves garlic, chopped
1 pound chicken livers, trimmed, rinsed, and finely chopped
1 15-ounce can chick peas, drained and rinsed
3 tablespoons chopped fresh cilantro (coriander leaves) or fresh parsley

1 To make the Chorizo Stuffing: In a large, nonstick skillet, cook the chorizo over moderately high heat, stirring occasionally, for 5 minutes, or until brown. Using a slotted spoon, transfer the chorizo to a plate lined with paper towels to drain.

2 Discard all but 2 tablespoons of fat. Add onions and garlic to the skillet and sauté for 5 minutes, or until onions are translucent. Add chicken livers to the skillet and sauté for 5 minutes, or until brown. Transfer chicken liver mixture to a large bowl. Add chorizo, chick peas, and cilantro. Mix well, cover with plastic wrap, and chill for 30 minutes.

3 Meanwhile, rinse turkey, inside and out, under cold running water and pat dry with paper towels. Sprinkle inside and out with salt. Preheat the oven to 400° F. In a small saucepan over moderate heat, melt the butter. Set aside.

4 Spoon some stuffing into the turkey neck cavity, bring the skin up over the stuffing, and secure to the backbone with a skewer. Fill the main cavity with the remaining stuffing and tie the drumsticks together with kitchen twine. Place turkey on a rack in a roasting pan.

5 Roast the turkey for 5 hours, or until golden brown and a meat thermometer inserted in the thigh registers 180°-185° F. Brush with melted butter every 15 minutes until juices collect in the roasting pan. Continue to brush frequently with the pan juices.

6 Remove from the oven and cover with aluminum foil. Let stand for 15 minutes. Using a large spoon, transfer stuffing to a serving dish. Transfer turkey to a serving platter and garnish with chilies, if desired.

16 SERVINGS
PREP TIME: 25 MINUTES PLUS
45 MINUTES TO CHILL AND STAND
COOKING TIME: 5 HOURS

EQUIPMENT LIST

Utility knife
Colander
Large, nonstick skillet
Kitchen spoon
Slotted spoon
Plate
Paper towels
Plastic wrap
Aluminum foil
Large bowl
Small saucepan
Skewer
Kitchen twine
Roasting pan with rack
Meat thermometer
Pastry brush

Make family celebrations especially festive with this imaginative roast turkey.

Turkey Patties
with Warm Fruit Compôtes

This turkey dish gains an autumnal flavor with its use of two fruit compôtes—one made with pears and figs and the other with cranberries, pears, and orange juice. Serve the patties with garlic mashed potatoes.

1   To make the Pear-Fig Compôte: In a medium-size saucepan, bring the water and honey to a boil over high heat. Stir in the pears, figs, lemon rind, and cinnamon. Reduce the heat to low. Cook, uncovered, stirring frequently, for 20 to 25 minutes, or until the mixture thickens. Remove the pan from the heat and set aside.

2   Meanwhile, make the Cranberry-Orange Compôte: In a medium-size saucepan, combine the sugar, ginger, and cornstarch. Slowly stir in the orange juice until well blended. Add cranberries and pears. Cook, uncovered, over moderate heat, stirring continuously, until the mixture comes to a boil. Cook for 2 minutes, or until the mixture has thickened slightly. Remove the pan from the heat and set aside.

3   To make the Turkey Patties: In a large bowl, combine the turkey, celery, onion, sage, hot pepper sauce, egg, bread crumbs, salt, and pepper. Mix until well blended. Form turkey mixture into 8 flattened patties about 3″ in diameter. Place the patties on a plate, cover with plastic wrap, and chill in the refrigerator for 15 minutes.

4   In a large skillet, heat the oil over moderate heat for 2 minutes. Cook the patties in 2 batches for 3 to 4 minutes on each side, or until the patties are golden brown. Using a large, metal spatula, transfer patties to a plate lined with paper towels to drain and then to a serving platter.

5   Meanwhile, warm the compôtes over low heat and transfer to serving bowls. Garnish the patties with celery leaves, if desired, and serve immediately.

---

1   pound ground turkey
1   stalk celery, finely chopped (½ cup)
1   small yellow onion, finely chopped (½ cup)
¼   teaspoon dried sage leaves or dried thyme leaves, crumbled
4-5   drops hot pepper sauce
1   large egg
½   cup dry unseasoned bread crumbs
¼   teaspoon salt, or to taste
Freshly ground black pepper
2-3   tablespoons vegetable oil
Celery leaves (optional)

PEAR-FIG COMPÔTE (3 CUPS)

¾   cup water
¼   cup honey
2   small ripe Anjou or other pears, peeled, cored, and chopped (1½ cups)
6   ounces dried figs, chopped (1½ cups)
1   teaspoon grated lemon rind
½   teaspoon ground cinnamon

CRANBERRY-ORANGE COMPÔTE (3 CUPS)

½   cup granulated sugar
1   teaspoon ground ginger
1   teaspoon cornstarch
½   cup orange juice
6   ounces fresh cranberries (1½ cups)
2   small ripe Anjou or other pears, peeled, cored, and chopped (1½ cups)

---

4 SERVINGS
PREP TIME: 35 MINUTES PLUS
15 MINUTES TO CHILL
COOKING TIME: 43 MINUTES

EQUIPMENT LIST

Utility knife
Pepper mill
Vegetable peeler
Grater
2 medium-size saucepans
Kitchen spoons
Large bowl
2 plates
Plastic wrap
Paper towels
Large skillet
Large, metal spatula

Transform turkey patties with delicate fruit compôtes.

Turkey and Spinach Casserole

1 Rinse the turkey steaks under cold running water and pat dry with paper towels. Cut the turkey into 1″ pieces.

2 In a large skillet over moderate heat, melt 1 tablespoon of the butter. Add the turkey and cook, stirring frequently, for 10 minutes, or until golden brown. Using a slotted spoon, transfer the turkey to a plate and set aside.

3 In the same skillet over moderately low heat, melt 1 tablespoon of the butter. Stir in flour, salt, and black and ground red peppers. Cook, stirring continuously, for 1 minute. Slowly stir in milk until well blended. Increase the heat to moderately high and bring mixture to a boil, stirring continuously. Stir in the cream and cheese and cook, stirring continuously, for 1 minute more, or until cheese is melted. Remove pan from the heat, stir in the turkey pieces, and set aside.

4 Preheat the broiler. Rinse spinach under cold running water. Shake it lightly and place in a large saucepan with water still clinging to the leaves. Cook, covered, over moderate heat for 2 to 3 minutes, or until wilted. Drain well, squeezing out the excess liquid.

5 Place the spinach in a 2-quart flameproof casserole. Pour the turkey mixture over spinach. Sprinkle with bread crumbs and dot with the remaining 1 tablespoon of butter. Place the casserole under the broiler 4″ from the heat source. Broil for 3 to 4 minutes, or until the top is lightly browned. Remove from the broiler and serve immediately.

1½ pounds turkey steaks
3 tablespoons unsalted butter
3 tablespoons all-purpose flour
¼ teaspoon salt, or to taste
Freshly ground black pepper
⅛ teaspoon ground red pepper (cayenne)
1½ cups milk
½ cup light cream or half-and-half
2 ounces shredded Monterey Jack cheese (½ cup)
1 pound fresh spinach, stemmed (4 cups)
¼ cup dry unseasoned bread crumbs

6 SERVINGS
PREP TIME: 15 MINUTES
COOKING TIME: 19 MINUTES

EQUIPMENT LIST

Pepper mill
Grater
Utility knife
Paper towels
Large skillet
Kitchen spoon
Slotted spoon
Plate
Large saucepan with lid
Colander
2-quart flameproof casserole

Turkey and Pasta Bake

1 Preheat the oven to 350° F. Lightly grease a 2-quart casserole. Rinse the turkey steaks under cold running water and pat dry with paper towels. Cut the turkey into 1″ pieces.

2 Bring a large saucepan of water to a boil over high heat. Cook the pasta in the boiling water for 8 to 10 minutes, or until al dente. Drain well and set aside.

3 Meanwhile, in a large skillet over moderate heat, melt 1 tablespoon of the butter. Add the turkey and cook, stirring frequently, for 10 minutes, or until golden brown. Using a slotted spoon, transfer the turkey to a plate and set aside.

4 In the same skillet over moderate heat, melt the remaining 1 tablespoon of butter. Add mushrooms, bell pepper, and green onions and sauté for 3 minutes, or until softened. Stir in the flour until well blended. Slowly stir in the stock and cream. Cook, stirring continuously, for 2 to 3 minutes, or until mixture boils and thickens slightly. Stir in the turkey pieces and thyme. Season to taste with the salt and pepper. Stir in the pasta and Parmesan cheese.

6 Spoon the turkey mixture into the prepared casserole. Bake for 30 minutes. Sprinkle Swiss cheese over the top. Bake for 3 to 4 minutes more, or until the cheese is bubbly and golden brown. Remove casserole from the oven and serve immediately.

1½ pounds turkey steaks
8 ounces dried rotelle pasta (twists) (2 cups)
2 tablespoons unsalted butter
4 ounces mushrooms, trimmed, cleaned, and sliced (1¼ cups)
1 medium-size red bell pepper, cored, seeded, and cut in narrow strips (1 cup)
4 green onions (including tops), thinly sliced (½ cup)
¼ cup all-purpose flour
1¾ cups chicken stock or canned broth
1 cup light cream
¼ teaspoon dried thyme leaves, crumbled
¼ teaspoon salt, or to taste
Freshly ground black pepper
1 ounce grated Parmesan cheese (¼ cup)
4 ounces shredded Swiss cheese (1 cup)

6 SERVINGS
PREP TIME: 20 MINUTES
COOKING TIME: 35 MINUTES

EQUIPMENT LIST

Utility knife
Pepper mill
Grater
2-quart casserole
Paper towels
Large saucepan
Colander
Large skillet
Kitchen spoon
Slotted spoon
Plate

VEGETABLES

*W*hether they are served as a light meal on their own or as accompaniments to a main course, vegetables are versatile. The selection included here transforms ordinary vegetables, such as peas, corn, carrots, and cauliflower, into purées, custards, and loaves.

Summer Pea Combo.

Summer Pea Combo

2 pounds fresh lima beans, shelled (2 cups)
3 strips lean bacon
½ cup fresh whole-wheat bread crumbs
2 pounds fresh peas, shelled (2 cups)
1 4-ounce jar chopped pimento, drained and rinsed
¼ teaspoon salt, or to taste
Freshly ground black pepper
1 large hard-cooked egg, peeled and chopped

The fresh pea season is short, but it is easy to recreate this dish using frozen peas. Fresh lima beans are sometimes available in supermarkets, but they may also be replaced by the frozen variety. Substitute a 10-ounce package of frozen lima beans for the fresh beans and reduce the cooking time to 10 minutes. For the fresh peas, substitute a 10-ounce package of frozen peas and reduce the cooking time to 3 minutes. Drain the vegetables well and proceed as directed.

1 Bring a large saucepan of water to a boil over high heat. Add the lima beans and cook, partially covered, over moderate heat for 25 minutes.

2 Meanwhile, in a medium-size skillet, cook the bacon over moderate heat for 8 to 10 minutes, or until crisp. Using a slotted spoon, transfer the bacon to a plate lined with paper towels to drain.

3 Add the bread crumbs to the bacon drippings in the skillet and cook over moderate heat, stirring frequently, for 2 minutes, or until browned. Remove the skillet from the heat and set aside.

4 Add the peas to the lima beans, and cook, stirring occasionally, for 8 to 10 minutes more, or until tender. Drain well and stir in the pimento. Season to taste with the salt and pepper.

5 Transfer the vegetables to a serving dish and sprinkle with the bread crumbs. Sprinkle the hard-cooked egg over the crumbs and crumble the bacon on top. Cool for 15 minutes. Serve at room temperature.

4 SERVINGS
PREP TIME: 20 MINUTES PLUS
15 MINUTES TO COOL
COOKING TIME: 35 MINUTES

EQUIPMENT LIST

Strainer
Pepper mill
Utility knife
Large saucepan with lid
Medium-size skillet
Slotted spoon
Kitchen spoon
Plate
Paper towels
Colander

Creamed Onions

1½ pounds pearl onions, unpeeled (4½ cups)
5 tablespoons unsalted butter
4 shallots, chopped (¼ cup)
¼ cup all-purpose flour
1¾ cups milk
1 tablespoon chopped fresh parsley
1 tablespoon snipped fresh chives or chopped green onion tops
1 teaspoon dried tarragon leaves, crumbled
⅛ teaspoon salt, or to taste
2 tablespoons dry unseasoned bread crumbs
2 tablespoons grated Parmesan cheese

These tiny onions are a tasty complement to roast turkey or chicken.

1 Preheat the oven to 350° F. Bring a large saucepan of water to a boil over high heat. Cook the onions for 2 to 3 minutes. Drain well, rinse under cold running water, and drain again. Peel the onions and trim off the root ends.

2 In a large skillet over moderate heat, melt 4 tablespoons of the butter. Add the shallots and sauté for 2 to 3 minutes, or until softened. Stir in the flour and cook, stirring continuously, for 1 minute. Add the milk, stirring until well blended. Cook, stirring continuously, for 2 minutes more, or until thickened slightly. Stir in the parsley, chives, tarragon, and onions. Season to taste with the salt.

3 Transfer the mixture to a 3-quart baking dish. In a small bowl, combine bread crumbs and cheese. Sprinkle the mixture over the onions. Dot with the remaining 1 tablespoon of butter. Bake for 30 minutes, or until golden brown. Serve immediately.

4 SERVINGS
PREP TIME: 20 MINUTES
COOKING TIME: 30 MINUTES

EQUIPMENT LIST

Paring knife
Kitchen scissors
Large saucepan
Colander
Large skillet
Kitchen spoons
3-quart baking dish
Small bowl

Spinach Puff

This flavorful and versatile dish makes an ideal luncheon or brunch entrée, or it can be served as a festive side dish for a Sunday dinner of pork roast or leg of lamb. Prepare it while the meat is roasting then pop it in the oven for the last 50 minutes of roasting time.

For variety, substitute a 10-ounce package of frozen chopped broccoli, thawed and drained, for the spinach and proceed as directed.

1	10-ounce package frozen chopped spinach, thawed and drained
3	tablespoons unsalted butter
1	tablespoon all-purpose flour
1¼	cups milk
3	large eggs, lightly beaten
2	ounces shredded Cheddar, Swiss, or Gruyère cheese (½ cup)
⅛	teaspoon ground nutmeg
¼	teaspoon salt, or to taste

Freshly ground black pepper

1 Preheat the oven to 375° F. Grease a 1½-quart round casserole or soufflé dish. Squeeze the excess liquid from the spinach.

2 In a medium-size saucepan over moderate heat, melt the butter. Stir in the flour and cook, stirring continuously, for 2 minutes, or until a pale straw color. Slowly add the milk and stir until well blended. Stir in the eggs. Cook, stirring continuously, over moderate heat for 3 to 5 minutes, or until thickened slightly. Stir in the spinach, cheese, and nutmeg and cook, stirring continuously, for 1 to 2 minutes more, or until the cheese is melted. Season to taste with the salt and pepper. Remove the pan from the heat.

3 Pour the spinach mixture into the prepared casserole. Place the dish in a 9″ deep-sided layer cake pan. Carefully pour enough hot water into the cake pan to come halfway up the side of the casserole. Bake, uncovered, for 45 to 50 minutes, or until puffed and a knife inserted in the center comes out clean.

4 Remove the dish from the oven and serve immediately.

6 SERVINGS
PREP TIME: 15 MINUTES
COOKING TIME: 1 HOUR 5 MINUTES

Equipment List

Colander
Small bowl
Wire whisk
Grater
Pepper mill
1½-quart round casserole or soufflé dish
Medium-size saucepan
Kitchen spoon
9″ deep-sided layer cake pan

This dish will convert the whole family to spinach lovers.

Double Potato Rosettes

The combination of white and sweet potatoes piped in rosettes elevates these everyday vegetables into an attractive side dish. Serve them with roast beef or chops.

2   large Idaho or other baking potatoes (11 ounces each), peeled and quartered

2   large sweet potatoes or yams, (11 ounces each), peeled and quartered

2   tablespoons salted butter or margarine

¼   cup milk

1   ounce grated Parmesan cheese (¼ cup)

4 SERVINGS
PREP TIME: 30 MINUTES
COOKING TIME: 40 MINUTES

Equipment List
Vegetable peeler
Utility knife
2 medium-size saucepans
Fork
Baking sheet
Aluminum foil
Colander
Potato masher
Large pastry bag with large star tip
Kitchen spoon

1 In separate medium-size saucepans, place the white potatoes and sweet potatoes with enough water to cover. Bring both to a boil over high heat. Reduce heat to moderately low and cook, uncovered, for 20 minutes, or until potatoes are tender when tested with a fork.

2 Preheat the oven to 375° F. Line a baking sheet with aluminum foil. Lightly grease the foil.

3 Drain the white and sweet potatoes separately and return them to their pans. Using a potato masher or fork, mash white potatoes until almost smooth. Add 1 tablespoon of butter and 2 tablespoons of milk and continue mashing until smooth. Mash the sweet potatoes as directed until light and fluffy, adding the remaining 1 tablespoon of butter and 2 tablespoons of milk.

4 Place a large pastry bag fitted with a large star tip on a work surface. Spoon the white potatoes into the bag along one side. Spoon the sweet potatoes along the other side of the bag. Close the bag and gently push mixtures along until they reach the tip.

5 To make a rosette: Holding the bag closed with one hand, and using the other hand to guide, pipe a 2½″ circle. Without lifting the tip, continue piping a spiral 2 layers high that finishes in the center. Lift off the tip firmly. Make the remaining 7 rosettes as directed.

6 Sprinkle the top of each rosette with some of the grated Parmesan cheese. Bake for 15 to 20 minutes, or until the rosettes are lightly golden. Using a large, metal spatula, transfer the rosettes to a serving platter. Serve immediately.

Sweet and Sour Red Cabbage

A mixture of vinegar and brown sugar adds a sweet and sour flavor to this traditional pairing of red cabbage and apple. The vinegar also helps to preserve the bright color of the vegetable. Serve this dish with roast turkey or duck, pot roast, or bratwurst.

1   tablespoon unsalted butter
1   small red onion, thinly sliced (1¼ cups)
¾   cup plus 1 tablespoon water
¼   cup red wine vinegar
1   tablespoon firmly packed light brown sugar
⅛   teaspoon ground cloves
¼   teaspoon salt, or to taste
¼   teaspoon coarsely ground black pepper
1   small head red cabbage, finely shredded (5 cups)
1   medium-size Granny Smith or other tart apple, peeled, cored, and thinly sliced (1½ cups)
1   tablespoon all-purpose flour
2   teaspoons light molasses
2   teaspoons fresh lemon juice
1   teaspoon chopped fresh parsley (optional)

1 In a large skillet over moderate heat, melt the butter. Add the red onion and sauté for 5 minutes, or until translucent. Add the ¾ cup of water, the vinegar, sugar, cloves, salt, and pepper. Bring the mixture to a boil over high heat.

2 Stir the cabbage into the onion mixture and return the mixture to a boil. Reduce the heat to moderately low and cook, covered, stirring occasionally, for 30 minutes. Stir in the apple and cook, covered, for 12 to 15 minutes more, or until the cabbage and apple are tender.

3 Meanwhile, in a small bowl, combine the flour with the remaining 1 tablespoon of water. Remove the skillet from the heat. Stir the flour mixture into the cabbage until well blended and thickened slightly. Stir in the molasses and lemon juice.

4 Transfer the cabbage to a serving bowl and garnish with chopped fresh parsley, if desired. Serve immediately.

4 SERVINGS
PREP TIME: 20 MINUTES
COOKING TIME: 50 MINUTES

EQUIPMENT LIST

Utility knife
Vegetable peeler
Citrus juicer
Large skillet with lid
Kitchen spoons
Small bowl

Carrot and Orange Purée

Vegetable purées make excellent accompaniments to roast meats and rich stews. They taste better if they are made a few hours in advance because the flavors have more time to blend. Reheat purées gently before serving. The combination of carrot and orange is refreshing, and the yogurt, stirred in at the end, adds creaminess without the fat of cream.

2   pounds carrots, peeled and thinly sliced (8 cups)
1½ cups water
2   tablespoons salted butter or margarine, softened
½   teaspoon ground nutmeg
2   tablespoons grated orange rind
¼   cup orange juice
¼   cup plain lowfat yogurt
⅛   teaspoon ground white pepper
Chopped fresh parsley (optional)

1 Place the carrots in a medium-size saucepan with the water and bring to a boil over high heat. Reduce the heat to moderately low and cook, covered, for 15 to 20 minutes, or until the carrots are tender.

2 Drain the carrots well and return them to the pan. Using a potato masher or fork, mash the carrots well.

3 Stir in the butter, nutmeg, and orange rind. Cook the carrot purée over low heat, stirring continuously, for 1 minute, or until any excess liquid has evaporated.

4 Stir the orange juice and yogurt into the carrot purée and season to taste with pepper. Cook over low heat, stirring continuously, for 1 minute, or until heated through.

5 Transfer the carrot purée to a serving dish and garnish with the chopped fresh parsley, if desired. Serve immediately.

4 SERVINGS
PREP TIME: 15 MINUTES
COOKING TIME: 22 MINUTES

EQUIPMENT LIST

Vegetable peeler
Utility knife
Grater
Medium-size saucepan with lid
Colander
Potato masher
Kitchen spoon

Mixed Vegetable Stuffed Eggplant

These colorful stuffed eggplants will perk up any meal, especially one centered around roast lamb or beef.

2   small eggplants (8 ounces each), cut in half lengthwise
2   tablespoons salt
4   tablespoons olive oil
1   medium-size yellow onion, finely chopped (1 cup)
2   large cloves garlic, finely chopped
3   medium-size ripe tomatoes, peeled, seeded, and chopped (3 cups)
2   tablespoons chopped fresh basil, or 2 teaspoons dried basil leaves, crumbled
2   tablespoons chopped fresh oregano, or 2 teaspoon dried oregano leaves, crumbled
2   tablespoons grated Parmesan cheese
Freshly ground black pepper
Chopped fresh parsley (optional)
Ripe cherry tomatoes (optional)

4 SERVINGS
PREP TIME: 20 MINUTES PLUS
30 MINUTES TO STAND
COOKING TIME: 1 HOUR 30 MINUTES

EQUIPMENT LIST

Utility knife
Paring knife
Pepper mill
Paper towels
Teaspoon or melon-ball cutter
Kitchen spoon
Large, shallow baking pan
Large skillet

1 Using a small, sharp knife, make several shallow slits in the cut surfaces of the eggplants. Sprinkle each half with some of the salt and let stand at room temperature for 30 minutes. Rinse the eggplants under cold running water and pat dry with paper towels. Using a teaspoon or melon-ball cutter, scoop out the flesh, leaving a ¼″ shell. Chop the eggplant flesh and set aside.

2 Preheat the oven to 350° F. Grease a large, shallow baking pan. In a large skillet, heat 2 tablespoons of the oil over moderately high heat for 1 minute. Add the onion and sauté for 5 minutes, or until translucent. Add the garlic and sauté for 30 seconds, or until fragrant. Add the chopped tomatoes and eggplant, basil, and oregano. Cook, uncovered, for 20 minutes, stirring occasionally. Stir in the Parmesan cheese and season to taste with the pepper.

3 Arrange eggplant shells, cut-side up, in the prepared baking pan. Spoon filling into shells, mounding it slightly. Drizzle remaining 2 tablespoons of oil over the filling. Bake, uncovered, for 1 hour, or until eggplants are tender. Remove the baking pan from the oven. Transfer the baked eggplants to a serving platter. Garnish with chopped fresh parsley and cherry tomatoes, if desired, and serve immediately.

Mediterranean flavors abound in this stuffed eggplant dish.

Vegetarian Baked Beans

1   pound dried small white beans, sorted and rinsed
2   tablespoons unsalted butter
2   large yellow onions, chopped (3 cups)
1   small green or red bell pepper, cored, seeded, and finely chopped (½ cup)
1   large clove garlic, finely chopped
2   tablespoons tomato paste
4   cups water
3   tablespoons red wine vinegar
⅓   cup molasses
½   cup firmly packed dark brown sugar
3   tablespoons Dijon-style mustard
1   bay leaf
¼   teaspoon dried thyme leaves, crumbled
¼   teaspoon salt, or to taste
Freshly ground black pepper
Chopped green or red bell pepper (optional)
Chopped green onion (white part only) (optional)

This recipe is similar to traditional baked beans, minus the pork and bacon. The result is a hearty and healthful dish that will be a welcome addition to a summer barbecue or a casual buffet.

1 In a large saucepan, soak the beans in cold water for 8 hours, or overnight. To quick soak beans: Bring the water and beans to a boil over high heat and boil for 2 minutes. Remove pan from heat, cover, and let stand for 1 hour.

2 Drain the soaking liquid and cover the beans with fresh cold water. Bring to a boil over high heat. Reduce heat to moderate and cook, uncovered, for 35 minutes, or until the beans are tender. Drain well. Preheat the oven to 350° F.

3 In a 4-quart Dutch oven over moderate heat, melt the butter. Add the onions and cook, stirring frequently, for 5 minutes, or until translucent. Add the ½ cup of bell pepper and the garlic and cook, stirring frequently, for 4 minutes, or until vegetables are softened. Stir in the tomato paste and cook, stirring continuously, for 1 minute. Stir in the beans, the 4 cups of water, vinegar, molasses, sugar, mustard, bay leaf, and thyme until well blended. Season to taste with the salt and pepper. Bring to a boil over moderately high heat, stirring frequently.

4 Transfer the pan to the oven and bake, uncovered, for 1¾ to 2 hours, or until the liquid has almost evaporated. (The onions and bell pepper will float to the top of the dish and form a crust during baking which protects the beans from drying out.)

5 Remove the pan from the oven and stir the mixture well. Remove and discard the bay leaf. Garnish with the chopped bell pepper and green onion, if desired, and serve immediately.

6 SERVINGS
PREP TIME: 15 MINUTES PLUS
8 HOURS TO SOAK
COOKING TIME: 2 HOURS 50 MINUTES

EQUIPMENT LIST

Colander
Utility knife
Pepper mill
Large saucepan with lid
4-quart Dutch oven
Kitchen spoon

Broccoli and Cauliflower Custard

This combination of vegetables is delicious on its own as a light entrée or as an accompaniment to roast meats or grilled chops and chicken.

1	small head broccoli, trimmed and cut in florets (4 cups)
1	small head cauliflower, trimmed and cut in florets (4 cups)
3	tablespoons unsalted butter
2	tablespoons grated Parmesan cheese
1	large clove garlic, finely chopped
½	cup fresh bread crumbs
1	teaspoon paprika
½	teaspoon dried basil leaves, crumbled
¼	teaspoon dried thyme leaves, crumbled
1	cup half-and-half
3	large eggs
1	tablespoon Dijon-style mustard

1 Preheat the oven to 350° F. Bring a large saucepan of water to a boil over high heat. Add the broccoli and cauliflower florets and cook, uncovered, for 2 to 3 minutes, or until the broccoli is bright green. Drain well and set aside.

2 In a large skillet over moderate heat, melt the butter. Remove skillet from the heat and brush the inside of a 2-quart round casserole or soufflé dish with a little of the butter. Sprinkle the cheese inside the dish, turning to coat.

3 Add the garlic to the skillet and sauté over moderate heat for 30 seconds, or until fragrant. Add the bread crumbs, paprika, basil, and thyme. Cook, stirring frequently, for 3 to 4 minutes, or until golden and crisp. Remove the skillet from the heat.

4 Arrange half the florets in the prepared dish and sprinkle with half the bread crumb mixture. Arrange the remaining florets over the top and sprinkle with the remaining bread crumbs.

5 To make the custard: In a medium-size bowl, whisk together half-and-half, eggs, and mustard. Slowly pour custard over vegetables.

6 Place soufflé dish in a 9″ deep-sided layer cake pan. Carefully pour enough hot water into the cake pan to come halfway up the side of soufflé dish. Bake, uncovered, for 1 hour, or until a knife inserted in the center comes out clean. Remove dish from the oven. Serve immediately.

4 TO 6 SERVINGS
PREP TIME: 20 MINUTES
COOKING TIME: 1 HOUR

EQUIPMENT LIST

Utility knife
Large saucepan
Colander
Large skillet
Pastry brush
2-quart round casserole or soufflé dish
9″ deep-sided layer cake pan
Kitchen spoon
Medium-size bowl
Wire whisk

Lemon-Dill Baked Beets

The beets are baked whole in this recipe to retain the sweet flavor, juices, and crisp texture of this vegetable. Beet greens are also edible and nutritious. If the beets have their greens intact, cut them off 1″ above the stem so they will not leach moisture from the beets. Wash the greens well, trim off and discard the stems, and sauté the greens in butter.

8	medium-size whole beets, rinsed and trimmed, leaving 1″ of stem intact (2 pounds)

LEMON-DILL VINAIGRETTE (1 CUP)

2	tablespoons fresh lemon juice
1	tablespoon balsamic vinegar or red wine vinegar
2	teaspoons Dijon-style mustard
1	teaspoon dried dill weed, crumbled
1	shallot, finely chopped (1 tablespoon)
⅓	cup olive oil
¼	teaspoon salt, or to taste
Freshly ground black pepper

1 Preheat the oven to 400° F. Wrap the beets in aluminum foil (2 to 3 beets in each package) and place on a baking sheet.

2 Bake for 1 hour, or until the beets are tender when tested with a fork. Remove the baking sheet from the oven, loosen the foil, and cool the beets for 20 minutes.

3 Meanwhile, make the Lemon-Dill Vinaigrette. In a small bowl, whisk together the lemon juice, vinegar, mustard, dill, and shallot. Slowly add the oil, whisking vigorously until well blended, or place the ingredients in a small jar with a tight-fitting lid and shake to blend. Season to taste with the salt and pepper and set aside.

4 Remove beets from the foil packages and, using a paper towel or a paring knife, slip off skins. Transfer beets to a cutting board, cut into ¼″ slices, and place in a large bowl. Whisk the vinaigrette, pour over beets, tossing to coat. Serve beets chilled or at room temperature.

4 SERVINGS
PREP TIME: 20 MINUTES PLUS 20 MINUTES TO COOL
COOKING TIME: 1 HOUR

EQUIPMENT LIST

Utility knife
Paring knife
Citrus juicer
Pepper mill
Aluminum foil
Paper towels
Baking sheet
Fork
Small bowl
Large bowl
Wire whisk
Cutting board
Kitchen spoon

Mixed Vegetable Gratinée

For a new way with some favorite vegetables, try this colorful gratinée. Experiment with using different cheeses for the topping, for instance Jarlsberg, Gruyère, or Cheddar. Serve the casserole as a vegetarian brunch entrée, or as an accompaniment to grilled meats.

4	tablespoons olive oil
1	large yellow onion, finely chopped (1½ cups)
3	large cloves garlic, finely chopped
1	28-ounce can whole tomatoes in purée
1½	teaspoons chopped fresh thyme, or ½ teaspoon dried thyme leaves, crumbled
2	large Idaho or other baking potatoes, peeled and cut in ¼″ cubes (3 cups)
¼	teaspoon salt, or to taste
Freshly ground black pepper	
3	small zucchini, trimmed and cut in narrow strips (3 cups)
1	large red or green bell pepper, cored, seeded, and cut in narrow strips (1½ cups)
3	green onions (including tops), sliced diagonally (6 tablespoons)
3	ounces shredded Swiss cheese (¾ cup)

1 In a large saucepan, heat 1 tablespoon of the oil over moderate heat for 1 minute. Add the onion and sauté for 5 minutes, or until translucent. Add the garlic and sauté for 30 seconds, or until fragrant. Add the tomatoes with the purée and the thyme and cook, uncovered, stirring occasionally, for 15 minutes, or until most of the liquid has evaporated and the sauce is reduced by one-quarter.

2 Meanwhile, in a large skillet, heat 1 tablespoon of the oil over moderate heat for 1 minute. Add the potatoes, salt, and pepper. Cook, uncovered, stirring occasionally, for 5 to 6 minutes, or until tender and lightly browned.

3 Preheat the oven to 350° F. Grease a large, oval casserole.

4 Transfer the potatoes to a large bowl and set aside. Wipe the skillet clean with paper towels. Add the remaining 2 tablespoons of oil to the skillet and heat over moderate heat for 1 minute. Add the zucchini, bell pepper, and green onions and sauté for 1 to 2 minutes, or until the vegetables are crisp-tender. Transfer the vegetables to the bowl with the potatoes, tossing gently to combine.

5 Spoon the tomato sauce over the bottom of the prepared casserole. Arrange the vegetables on top of the sauce. Sprinkle the cheese over the vegetables. Cover the casserole with aluminum foil and bake for 20 minutes. Remove the casserole from the oven. Serve warm or at room temperature.

4 TO 6 SERVINGS
PREP TIME: 20 MINUTES
COOKING TIME: 45 MINUTES

EQUIPMENT LIST

Utility knife
Vegetable peeler
Pepper mill
Grater
Large saucepan
Kitchen spoon
Large skillet
Large, oval casserole
Large bowl
Paper towels
Aluminum foil

Winter Vegetable Loaf
with Spicy Lentils

1 cup dried brown lentils
1 medium-size carrot, peeled and shredded (1 cup)
1 medium-size yellow onion, finely chopped (1 cup)
1 stalk celery, finely chopped (½ cup)
2 ounces chopped walnuts (½ cup)
1 large egg, beaten
½ cup dry seasoned bread crumbs
2 tablespoons tomato paste
1 teaspoon ground cumin
¾ teaspoon chopped fresh thyme, or ¼ teaspoon dried thyme leaves, crumbled
¼ teaspoon salt, or to taste
Freshly ground black pepper
Sprigs of fresh thyme (optional)

Here, protein-packed lentils are combined with nuts and vegetables to make a delicious, healthy, and economical alternative to meatloaf. Round out the meal with whole-grain bread and a spinach salad. The loaf also makes a great accompaniment to grilled lamb.

Because they require no presoaking, lentils are a good vegetable choice when time is short. They are available in a variety of shades, including green and pink, in addition to the familiar brown. Any shade can be used in this recipe, although the preliminary cooking time may vary slightly. Store dry lentils in an airtight container in a cool, dry place.

1 Bring a large saucepan of salted water to a boil over high heat. Stir in the dried lentils. Reduce the heat to low and cook, uncovered, for 30 minutes, or until tender. Drain the lentils well.

2 Preheat the oven to 350° F. Grease a 9″ x 5″ x 3″ loaf pan. In a large bowl, combine the lentils, carrot, onion, celery, walnuts, egg, bread crumbs, and tomato paste. Stir in the cumin and chopped thyme. Season to taste with the salt and pepper.

3 Spoon the lentil mixture into the prepared pan. Bake, uncovered, for 30 minutes, or until the center is firm to the touch. Cool slightly and invert the loaf onto a serving platter. Cut into slices and garnish with sprigs of fresh thyme, if desired. Serve immediately.

4 SERVINGS OR 1 LOAF
PREP TIME: 15 MINUTES
COOKING TIME: 1 HOUR

Equipment List

Vegetable peeler
Grater
Utility knife
Small bowl
Large bowl
Wire whisk
Pepper mill
Large saucepan
Colander
9″ x 5″ x 3″ loaf pan
Kitchen spoon

Curried Chick Peas

1 tablespoon vegetable oil
1 small yellow onion, finely chopped (½ cup)
2 tablespoons all-purpose flour
1 tablespoon curry powder
2 teaspoons granulated sugar
½ teaspoon dry mustard
1½ cups chicken stock or canned broth
2 16-ounce cans chick peas, drained and rinsed
1 cup frozen peas, thawed
2 ounces chopped unsalted peanuts (½ cup)
2 teaspoons fresh lemon juice
Freshly ground black pepper
½ cup plain lowfat yogurt

This spicy, Indian-style dish makes the most of store cupboard and freezer items, such as canned chick peas, frozen green peas, and peanuts. It's perfect to prepare when time is tight or unexpected guests arrive. Excellent as a meatless main dish, it can also be served with grilled chicken or fish.

1 In a large skillet, heat the oil over moderately low heat for 1 minute. Add the onion and sauté for 5 minutes, or until translucent. Remove the pan from the heat.

2 Stir in the flour, curry powder, sugar, and mustard. Return the pan to moderate heat and slowly add the stock, stirring continuously. Add the chick peas, green peas, peanuts, and lemon juice.

3 Cook over low heat, stirring occasionally, for 5 minutes, or until chick peas are heated through and mixture has thickened. Season to taste with the pepper. Serve immediately with the yogurt.

4 SERVINGS
PREP TIME: 5 MINUTES
COOKING TIME: 15 MINUTES

Equipment List

Utility knife
Colander
Citrus juicer
Pepper mill
Large skillet
Kitchen spoon

Chinese-Style Vegetables

2 tablespoons sesame seeds
3 tablespoons peanut oil
2 medium-size carrots, peeled and cut in narrow strips (1½ cups)
3 cups broccoli florets
3 stalks celery, cut in narrow strips (1½ cups)
4 ounces mushrooms, trimmed, cleaned, and sliced (1¼ cups)
3 green onions (including tops), cut in narrow strips (6 tablespoons)
1 8-ounce can sliced water chestnuts, drained

CHINESE SAUCE (½ CUP)

¼ cup chicken stock or canned broth
2 tablespoons soy sauce
2 tablespoons rice wine vinegar
1 tablespoon cornstarch
1 teaspoon granulated sugar
1 large clove garlic, finely chopped
¼ teaspoon crushed red pepper flakes

This versatile stir-fry dish lends itself to various vegetable combinations, depending on what vegetables are on hand and what is in season. For best results, before heating the wok, cut the vegetables into small uniform pieces and be sure to stir continuously while cooking.

1 To make the Chinese Sauce: In a small bowl, whisk together the stock, soy sauce, vinegar, cornstarch, sugar, garlic, and red pepper flakes, if desired, and set aside.

2 To toast the sesame seeds: In a small skillet over moderate heat, toast the sesame seeds, stirring frequently, for 2 minutes, or until fragrant and golden. Transfer to a small bowl and set aside.

3 Heat the oil in a preheated wok or large, heavy skillet over high heat for 1 minute, or until very hot. Add the carrots and stir-fry for 1 minute. Add the broccoli and celery and stir-fry for 1 minute. Add the mushrooms, green onions, and water chestnuts and stir-fry for 1 to 2 minutes more.

4 Whisk the sauce again and pour over the vegetables. Cook, covered, over high heat for 2 to 3 minutes, or until the vegetables are crisp-tender. Sprinkle the vegetables with the toasted sesame seeds and serve immediately.

4 SERVINGS
PREP TIME: 25 MINUTES
COOKING TIME: 10 MINUTES

EQUIPMENT LIST

Vegetable peeler
Utility knife
Strainer
2 small bowls
Wire whisk
Small skillet
Wok or large, heavy skillet with lid
Kitchen spoons

Serve this crunchy stir-fry over brown rice for a light meal.

Roasted Corn with Cilantro Butter

4 large ears of corn
2 tablespoons vegetable oil

CILANTRO BUTTER
(3 TABLESPOONS)

2 tablespoons unsalted butter
1 tablespoon chopped fresh cilantro (coriander leaves) or chopped fresh parsley
⅛ teaspoon ground red pepper (cayenne)
⅛ teaspoon salt, or to taste

Soaking corn on the cob (with the husk intact) before grilling prevents the husks from burning and keeps the corn kernels moist while cooking. The result is a sublime summertime treat.

1 Prepare a charcoal grill until the coals form white ash, preheat a gas grill to high, or preheat the oven to 375° F.

2 Gently peel the husks from the ears of corn, leaving them attached. Remove and discard the silk. Re-wrap the corn in the husks. Place the ears of corn in a large bowl with cold water to cover. Let stand for 15 minutes.

3 Drain the corn. Lightly brush the outer husks with the oil. Place the corn on the grill or on the rack in the oven. Grill or roast, turning frequently, for 20 to 25 minutes, or until the kernels are tender.

4 Meanwhile, make the Cilantro Butter. In a small saucepan over moderate heat, melt the butter. Stir in the cilantro and ground red pepper. Season to taste with the salt.

5 Remove the corn from the grill or oven, pull back the husks, and place on a serving platter. Brush the corn with the Cilantro Butter and serve immediately.

4 SERVINGS
PREP TIME: 10 MINUTES PLUS
15 MINUTES TO STAND
COOKING TIME: 25 MINUTES

EQUIPMENT LIST

Utility knife
Charcoal or gas grill
Large bowl
Colander
Pastry brush
Large, metal spatula
Small saucepan
Kitchen spoon
Kitchen tongs

Marinated Garden Vegetables

2 medium-size carrots, peeled and sliced diagonally in 1″ pieces (1½ cups)
1½ cups water
¾ cup fresh lemon juice
¾ cup white vinegar
½ olive oil
½ cup vegetable oil
6 large cloves garlic, peeled
½ cup fresh parsley sprigs
1 teaspoon dried rosemary leaves, crumbled
½ teaspoon granulated sugar
½ teaspoon salt, or to taste
Freshly ground black pepper
1 large zucchini, trimmed, halved lengthwise, and sliced ½″ thick (2½ cups)
1 medium-size green bell pepper, cored, seeded, and cut in 1″ pieces (¾ cup)
1 medium-size red bell pepper, cored, seeded and cut in 1″ pieces (¾ cup)
1 small yellow onion, chopped (½ cup)

A tart vinegar and lemon juice marinade can enhance crisp vegetables. Ideal for entertaining, these vegetables can be prepared ahead and the quantities can easily be doubled. Try them at a picnic or barbecue.

To prepare ahead: Transfer the drained vegetables to a plastic or glass container, cover with plastic wrap, and store in the refrigerator. One hour before serving, remove the vegetables form the refrigerator and let them stand, covered, at room temperature.

1 Bring a medium-size saucepan of water to a boil over high heat. Cook the carrots in the boiling water for 3 minutes, or until crisp-tender. Drain well.

2 In a large saucepan, combine the 1½ cups of water, lemon juice, vinegar, olive and vegetable oils, garlic, parsley, rosemary, sugar, salt, and pepper. Bring to a boil over high heat.

3 Meanwhile, in a large glass or stainless steel bowl, combine the zucchini, carrots, green and red bell peppers, and onion. Pour the hot liquid through a fine sieve over the vegetables. Set the sieve in the vegetables to allow further infusion of the herbs and garlic. Marinate at room temperature for 45 minutes.

4 Remove the sieve and discard the herbs and garlic. Drain the vegetables and discard the marinade. Transfer the vegetables to a serving dish. Serve at room temperature.

6 SERVINGS
PREP TIME: 20 MINUTES PLUS
45 MINUTES TO MARINATE
COOKING TIME: 3 MINUTES

EQUIPMENT LIST

Vegetable peeler
Utility knife
Citrus juicer
Pepper mill
Medium-size saucepan
Large saucepan
Kitchen spoon
Colander
Fine sieve
Large glass or stainless steel bowl

SALADS

*E*ye-catching, healthful, and crunchy, salads, as entrées or side dishes, provide vast scope for the family cook. The following recipes include new versions of such old favorites as chicken salad and coleslaw, up-to-date spinach and pasta salads, a classic salade Niçoise, and much more.

Coleslaw with Roquefort Dressing.

Coleslaw with Roquefort Dressing

Coleslaw, an all-time favorite, is given added zest and creaminess with Roquefort Dressing. The coleslaw is the perfect accompaniment to grilled hamburgers or steaks at a barbecue or picnic.

For a novel presentation, line a serving bowl with red cabbage leaves and use the coleslaw as a filling, or serve it in a large, hollowed out cabbage shell.

2 cups shredded green cabbage
2 cups shredded red cabbage
1 stalk celery, finely chopped (½ cup)
¼ cup finely chopped yellow onion
1 dill pickle, finely chopped
1 celery top (optional)

ROQUEFORT DRESSING (1 CUP)

½ cup mayonnaise
4 ounces Roquefort cheese, finely crumbled (1 cup)
1 tablespoon prepared horseradish
¼ teaspoon salt, or to taste
Ground white pepper

1 In a large bowl, mix together the red and green cabbage, celery, onion, and dill pickle.

2 To make the Roquefort Dressing: In a small bowl, combine the mayonnaise, cheese, and horseradish. Season to taste with the salt and pepper.

3 Pour the Roquefort Dressing over the vegetable mixture, tossing gently to coat. Garnish the coleslaw with the celery top, if desired, and serve immediately.

4 SERVINGS
PREP TIME: 15 MINUTES

EQUIPMENT LIST
Utility knife
Large bowl
Small bowl
Kitchen spoons
Salad servers

Curried Brown Rice Salad

Dried peaches and cashew nuts, enhanced by a curry flavor, make this salad special. It can be prepared ahead and chilled until ready to serve.

2½ cups water
1 cup long-grain brown rice
3 ounces dried peaches, chopped (½ cup)
½ cup boiling water
⅓ cup dark raisins
2 tablespoons vegetable oil
2 ounces unsalted cashew nuts (½ cup)
1 small yellow onion, finely chopped (½ cup)
1 tablespoon curry powder
1 teaspoon cumin seeds
⅓ cup orange juice
¼ teaspoon salt, or to taste
¼ teaspoon coarsely ground black pepper
Sprigs of fresh cilantro (coriander leaves) or fresh parsley (optional)

1 In a medium-size saucepan, bring the 2½ cups of water to a boil over high heat. Stir in the rice. Reduce the heat to low and cook, covered, for 45 to 50 minutes, or until the rice is tender and the liquid is absorbed. Transfer the rice to a colander, rinse under cold running water, and drain. Transfer the rice to a large bowl.

2 Meanwhile, in a small bowl, soak the dried peaches in the ½ cup of boiling water for 15 minutes. Drain the peaches well. Add the peaches and raisins to the rice, tossing to combine.

3 In a medium-size skillet, heat 1 tablespoon of the oil over moderate heat for 1 minute. Add the nuts and sauté for 2 to 3 minutes, or until golden. Using a slotted spoon, transfer the nuts to a plate lined with paper towels to drain.

4 Add the remaining 1 tablespoon of oil to the skillet and heat over moderate heat for 1 minute. Add the onion to the skillet and sauté for 5 minutes, or until translucent. Stir in the curry powder and cumin seeds and cook, stirring continuously, for 2 minutes, or until fragrant. Add the orange juice and cook, stirring continuously, for 1 minute more. Remove the skillet from the heat and set aside.

5 Add the nuts to the rice, then pour the curry mixture over the rice, tossing to coat. Season to taste with the salt and pepper.

6 Cover the bowl with plastic wrap and chill in the refrigerator for 2 hours. Remove the salad from the refrigerator 20 minutes before serving. Garnish with sprigs of fresh cilantro, if desired.

4 TO 6 SERVINGS
PREP TIME: 20 MINUTES PLUS
2 HOURS AND 20 MINUTES TO CHILL
AND STAND
COOKING TIME: 50 MINUTES

EQUIPMENT LIST
Utility knife
Medium-size saucepan with lid
Kitchen spoons
Slotted spoon
Colander
Strainer
Large bowl
Small bowl
Medium-size skillet
Plate
Paper towels
Plastic wrap

Thai Chicken Salad

The chili oil and rice wine vinegar used in this recipe can be found in Asian food stores and some large supermarkets.

2   whole chicken breasts (4 halves), skinned and boned (1 pound)

4   ounces green beans, trimmed and cut diagonally in 1″ pieces (1 cup)

4   ounces bean sprouts, rinsed (1 cup)

1   medium-size cucumber, halved lengthwise and sliced ¼″ thick (¾ cup)

1   11-ounce can mandarin oranges in natural juice

Lettuce or escarole leaves (optional)

Lime wedges (optional)

THAI MARINADE (½ CUP)

¼   cup fresh lime juice

¼   cup olive oil

1   large clove garlic, finely chopped

¼   teaspoon salt, or to taste

⅛   teaspoon coarsely ground black pepper

CHILI OIL DRESSING (⅓ CUP)

1   tablespoon rice wine vinegar

2   tablespoons vegetable oil

2   teaspoons chili oil

1   tablespoon chopped fresh cilantro (coriander leaves) or fresh parsley

2   tablespoons coarsely chopped unsalted peanuts

1 To make the Thai Marinade: In a large, shallow glass dish, combine the lime juice, olive oil, garlic, salt, and pepper. Add the chicken, turning to coat. Cover with plastic wrap and marinate at room temperature for 15 minutes.

2 Meanwhile, place the green beans in a steamer set over boiling water in a medium-size saucepan and cook, covered, over high heat for 4 to 6 minutes, or until crisp-tender. Rinse the green beans under cold running water and drain well.

3 In a large bowl, combine the green beans, bean sprouts, and cucumber. Drain the juice from the mandarin oranges and reserve 2 tablespoons. (Save remainder for another use.) Add the oranges to the green bean mixture. Preheat the broiler.

4 To make the Chili Oil Dressing: In a small bowl, whisk together the vinegar, vegetable and chili oils, cilantro, reserved orange juice, and peanuts, or place the ingredients in a small jar with a tight-fitting lid and shake to blend. Set aside.

5 Remove the chicken from the marinade and place on the broiler pan. Discard the marinade. Place the pan under the broiler 4″ from the heat source. Broil the chicken for 4 to 5 minutes on each side, or until the juices run clear when the meat is pierced with a knife. Transfer the chicken to a carving board, cover with aluminum foil, and let stand for 10 minutes.

6 Pour the dressing over the green bean mixture, tossing gently to coat. Line individual serving plates with lettuce leaves, if desired, and spoon the green bean mixture on top. Slice the chicken diagonally into ¼″ thick strips and arrange on top. Garnish the salad with lime wedges, if desired, and serve immediately.

A Thai marinade and dressing add an exotic flavor to chicken salad.

4 SERVINGS
PREP TIME: 30 MINUTES PLUS
10 MINUTES TO STAND
COOKING TIME: 16 MINUTES

EQUIPMENT LIST

Utility knife
Colander
Citrus juicer
Large, shallow glass dish
Kitchen spoons
Plastic wrap
Aluminum foil
Steamer
Medium-size saucepan with lid
Large bowl
Small bowl
Wire whisk
Broiler pan
Large, metal spatula
Carving board

Spinach, Radish, and Celery Salad with Sesame Vinaigrette

1 pound fresh spinach, stemmed, rinsed, and torn in small pieces (4 cups)
1 medium-size cucumber, peeled, seeded, and chopped (1 cup)
1 small bunch radishes, trimmed, rinsed, and sliced (1½ cups)
1 stalk celery, chopped (½ cup)
¼ cup chopped fresh parsley
¼ cup quartered, pitted green olives
¼ cup quartered, pitted black olives

SESAME VINAIGRETTE (½ CUP)

3 tablespoons sesame seeds
1 tablespoon rice wine vinegar or cider vinegar
1 shallot, finely chopped (1 tablespoon)
1 teaspoon Chinese sesame oil
½ teaspoon Dijon-style mustard
⅓ cup vegetable oil
¼ teaspoon salt, or to taste
Freshly ground black pepper

This salad provides a great contrast in textures and flavors. In it leafy green spinach (watercress can be substituted), crisp vegetables, and olives are tossed with a subtle, nutty Sesame Vinaigrette. Serve the salad with grilled cheese and tomato sandwiches for lunch, or with a creamy fish chowder for a Sunday supper.

1 To make the Sesame Vinaigrette: In a small skillet over moderate heat, toast the sesame seeds, stirring frequently, for 1 to 2 minutes, or until fragrant and golden. Transfer the sesame seeds to a small bowl and set aside.

2 In a small bowl, combine the vinegar, shallot, sesame oil, and mustard. Slowly add the vegetable oil, whisking vigorously until well blended, or place the ingredients in a small jar with a tight-fitting lid and shake to blend. Season to taste with the salt and pepper. Stir in 2 tablespoons of the sesame seeds.

3 In a large bowl, toss together the spinach, cucumber, radishes, celery, parsley, and green and black olives. Pour the Sesame Vinaigrette over the salad, tossing to coat. Sprinkle the remaining 1 tablespoon of sesame seeds over the salad. Serve immediately.

4 SERVINGS
PREP TIME: 20 MINUTES
COOKING TIME: 2 MINUTES

EQUIPMENT LIST

Colander
Vegetable peeler
Utility knife
Pepper mill
Small skillet
2 small bowls
Large bowl
Kitchen spoons
Wire whisk
Salad servers

East meets West in this crunchy salad.

Mid-Summer Vegetable Salad
with Herb Dressing

6   ripe plum tomatoes, peeled, seeded, and chopped (2 cups)

1   large cucumber, peeled, seeded, and chopped (1½ cups)

1   large green bell pepper, cored, seeded, and chopped (1½ cups)

1   large red bell pepper, cored, seeded, and chopped (1½ cups)

¼   cup finely chopped yellow onion

4   green onions (including tops), finely chopped (½ cup)

HERB DRESSING (⅔ CUP)

3   tablespoons red wine vinegar

1   teaspoon Dijon-style mustard

1   small clove garlic, finely chopped

1½   teaspoons chopped fresh thyme, or ½ teaspoon dried thyme leaves, crumbled

1½   teaspoons chopped fresh oregano, or ½ teaspoon dried oregano leaves, crumbled

½   cup extra virgin olive oil

⅛   teaspoon salt, or to taste

Freshly ground black pepper

A light dressing made with fresh herbs adds a refreshing lift to summer salads.

This salad is an excellent way to take advantage of summer's bounty of garden produce. Serve it with roast beef, poultry, or lamb, or use it as a relish with cold meats, cheese, and curries.

1   In a large bowl, combine the tomatoes, cucumber, green and red bell peppers, and yellow and green onions.

2   To make the Herb Dressing: In a small bowl, combine the vinegar, mustard, garlic, thyme, and oregano. Slowly add the oil, whisking vigorously until well blended, or place the ingredients in a small jar with a tight-fitting lid and shake to blend. Season to taste with the salt and pepper.

3   Pour the dressing over the vegetables, tossing gently to coat. Serve the salad immediately. Alternatively, cover the bowl with plastic wrap and chill in the refrigerator for up to 3 hours. Remove from the refrigerator 20 minutes before serving. Serve at room temperature.

4 SERVINGS (6 CUPS)
PREP TIME: 15 MINUTES

EQUIPMENT LIST

Paring knife
Pepper mill
Vegetable peeler
Large bowl
Small bowl
Kitchen spoon
Wire whisk

Tri-Colored Pasta Salad
with Mustard-Garlic Dressing

Serve this salad for a light lunch, or as a side dish to roast chicken or pork.

6 ounces fresh or dried small pasta shells (2½ cups)

1 15-ounce can red kidney beans, drained and rinsed, or 1½ cups cooked red kidney beans

1 10-ounce package frozen cut green beans, thawed and drained

1 medium-size tomato, seeded and chopped (1 cup)

4 green onions (green parts only), finely chopped (¼ cup)

MUSTARD-GARLIC DRESSING
(½ CUP)

3 tablespoons cider vinegar

1 tablespoon grainy mustard

1 large clove garlic, finely chopped

⅓ cup olive oil

¼ teaspoon salt, or to taste

¼ teaspoon coarsely ground black pepper

Pretty and pungent, this pasta salad is extremely simple to prepare.

1 Bring a large saucepan of water to a boil over high heat. Cook the pasta in the boiling water for 3 to 4 minutes for fresh and 8 to 10 minutes for dried, or until al dente. Drain the pasta well, rinse under cold running water, and drain again.

2 In a large bowl, combine the pasta, kidney beans, green beans, tomato, and green onions and mix well.

3 To make the Mustard-Garlic Dressing: In a small bowl, whisk together the vinegar, mustard, and garlic. Slowly add the oil, whisking vigorously until well blended, or place the ingredients in a small jar with a tight-fitting lid and shake to blend. Season to taste.

4 Pour dressing over salad, tossing gently to coat. Serve immediately or cover with plastic wrap and chill for up to 2 hours. Remove from refrigerator 20 minutes before serving. Serve at room temperature.

4 SERVINGS
PREP TIME: 10 MINUTES
COOKING TIME: 10 MINUTES

EQUIPMENT LIST

Strainer
Colander
Utility knife
Large saucepan
Large bowl
Small bowl
Kitchen spoons
Wire whisk

Double Rice and Bell Pepper Salad

½ cup wild rice
2½ cups water
½ cup long-grain white rice
1 large red bell pepper, cored, seeded, and chopped (1 cup)
1 large yellow bell pepper, cored, seeded, and chopped (1 cup)
4 green onions (including tops), cut in ½" pieces (½ cup)
¼ cup chopped fresh parsley
⅛ teaspoon salt, or to taste
Freshly ground black pepper

SPICED YOGURT DRESSING
(½ CUP)

¼ cup plain lowfat yogurt
2 tablespoons mayonnaise
1 tablespoon olive oil
1 tablespoon fresh lemon juice
¼ teaspoon grated lemon rind
½ teaspoon ground cardamom
¼ teaspoon peeled, grated fresh ginger, or ⅛ teaspoon ground ginger
⅛ teaspoon crushed red pepper flakes

Wild rice is often paired with white rice. Here, the two grains make a lively contrast to brightly colored bell peppers. Red and yellow are used, but different combinations are possible with orange, purple, and, of course, green. Serve the salad with grilled meats or poultry.

For variety, substitute ½ cup of quick-cooking couscous for the white rice. In a medium-size saucepan, bring 1 cup of water to a boil over high heat. Stir in the couscous. Cover the pan and remove from the heat. Let stand for 15 minutes, or until the couscous is tender and liquid is absorbed. Fluff the couscous with a fork and proceed as directed.

1 In a medium-size saucepan, combine the wild rice and 1½ cups of the water. Bring to a boil over high heat. Reduce the heat to moderately low and cook, covered, for 45 minutes, or until the rice is tender and the liquid is absorbed.

2 Meanwhile, in a small saucepan, bring the remaining 1 cup of water to a boil over high heat. Stir in the white rice. Reduce the heat to low and cook, covered, for 20 minutes, or until the rice is tender and the liquid is absorbed.

3 Transfer the wild rice and brown rice to a colander, rinse under cold running water, and drain. Transfer rice mixture to a large, shallow serving bowl.

4 To make the Spiced Yogurt Dressing: In a small bowl, stir together the yogurt, mayonnaise, oil, lemon juice and rind, cardamom, ginger, and red pepper flakes until well blended.

5 Add the red and yellow bell peppers, green onions, and parsley to the rice mixture, stirring to combine. Spoon the dressing over the rice mixture, tossing to coat. Season to taste with the salt and pepper. Serve the salad immediately, or cover the bowl with plastic wrap and chill in the refrigerator for 2 hours, or overnight. Serve chilled or remove the salad from the refrigerator 20 minutes before serving.

4 SERVINGS
PREP TIME: 20 MINUTES
COOKING TIME: 45 MINUTES

EQUIPMENT LIST

Utility knife
Pepper mill
Citrus juicer
Grater
Kitchen spoons
Vegetable peeler
Medium-size saucepan with lid
Small saucepan with lid
Colander
Large, shallow bowl
Small bowl

This brightly colored salad is full of bite.

Salade Niçoise

The French phrase "à la Niçoise," meaning "as prepared in Nice," refers to the cuisine of this famous city on the French Riviera. Characteristic ingredients include tomatoes, black olives, and garlic. Salade Niçoise also contains green beans, tuna, and hard-cooked eggs with an Herb Dressing.

12 ounces green beans, trimmed
1½ pounds small red-skinned potatoes, scrubbed and halved (8 potatoes)
1 small head leafy green lettuce, leaves separated and rinsed
2 6½-ounce cans chunk tuna packed in water, drained
2 medium-size ripe tomatoes, cut in wedges
2 large hard-cooked eggs, cut in wedges
12 small, pitted black olives

CAPER DRESSING (¾ CUP)
2 tablespoons white wine vinegar
¼ cup chopped fresh parsley
2 teaspoons snipped fresh chives
2 teaspoons capers, drained and rinsed
1 large clove garlic, chopped
¼ teaspoon dry mustard
½ cup olive oil
¼ teaspoon salt, or to taste
Freshly ground black pepper

1 To make the Caper Dressing: In a small bowl, whisk together the vinegar, parsley, chives, capers, garlic, and mustard. Slowly add the oil, whisking vigorously until well blended, or place the ingredients in a small jar with a tight-fitting lid and shake to blend. Season to taste with the salt and pepper.

2 To make the salad: Bring a large saucepan of water to a boil over high heat. Cook green beans in the boiling water for 5 minutes, or until crisp-tender. Using a slotted spoon, transfer the beans to a colander, rinse under running cold water, and drain well.

3 Return water to a boil over high heat. Cook potatoes in the water for 7 to 10 minutes, or until tender when tested with a fork. Drain well, rinse under cold running water and drain again. Transfer potatoes and beans to a shallow glass dish and pour ½ cup of the dressing over them, tossing gently to coat. Cover the dish with plastic wrap and marinate in the refrigerator for 30 minutes.

4 Line a large serving platter with the lettuce leaves. Remove the tuna from the cans and place in center of the platter. Using a fork, separate the tuna into small pieces. Spoon the potatoes and beans around the tuna. Arrange the tomatoes, egg wedges, and olives around the potato mixture. Whisk the remaining dressing and drizzle over the salad. Serve immediately.

4 SERVINGS
PREP TIME: 15 MINUTES PLUS
30 MINUTES TO MARINATE
COOKING TIME: 15 MINUTES

EQUIPMENT LIST

Utility knife
Vegetable brush
Colander
Strainer
Kitchen scissors
Pepper mill
Small bowl
Wire whisk
Large saucepan
Slotted spoon
Kitchen spoon
Shallow glass dish
Plastic wrap
Fork

Fresh Fruit Medley Melon Bowls

A bowl of colorful fruit makes an eye-catching salad or a healthful dessert. For a special treat, sprinkle the melon bowls with 2 tablespoons toasted coconut and 1 ounce (¼ cup) slivered almonds just before serving.

4 medium-size oranges, peeled, seeded, and sectioned
1 pint strawberries, hulled and sliced (2 cups)
2 cups seedless red or green grapes
2 medium-size ripe cantaloupes (1½ pounds each)

MINT DRESSING (½ CUP)
2 tablespoons orange juice
2 tablespoons fresh lime juice
2 tablespoons chopped fresh mint, or 2 teaspoons dried mint leaves, crumbled
2 teaspoons granulated sugar
⅛ teaspoon ground cinnamon
¼ cup vegetable oil

1 To make the Mint Dressing: In a small bowl, whisk together the orange and lime juices, the mint, sugar, and cinnamon. Slowly add the oil, whisking vigorously until well blended, or place the ingredients in a small jar with a tight-fitting lid and shake to blend.

2 In a large bowl, combine the oranges, strawberries, and grapes. Using a sharp knife, cut the melons in half, making a zigzag cut. Separate the halves and scoop out the seeds. Using a melon-ball cutter, remove the flesh and add the melon balls to the mixed fruit. If necessary, cut a thin slice from the bottom of each melon half so it will stand upright. Cover the melon halves with plastic wrap and chill in the refrigerator for 30 minutes, or until ready to use.

3 Pour the dressing over the fruit, tossing to coat. Cover with plastic wrap and chill in the refrigerator for 30 minutes.

4 Unwrap the melon bowls and transfer them to individual serving plates. Spoon the mixed fruit into them and serve immediately.

4 SERVINGS
PREP TIME: 20 MINUTES PLUS
30 MINUTES TO CHILL

EQUIPMENT LIST

Utility knife
Chef's knife
Citrus juicer
Small bowl
Large bowl
Wire whisk
Kitchen spoon
Melon-ball cutter
Plastic wrap

PASTA AND GRAINS

*P*asta and grain dishes receive high ratings for taste and nutrition. This chapter provides recipes that are sure to become household favorites. Choose from a three layer pasta bake, pasta with a hearty Bolognese sauce, fried rice, and a barley pilaf.

Fourth of July Triple-Layered Savory Casserole.

Fourth of July
Triple-Layered Savory Casserole

Here's a dish that's sure to be a crowd-pleaser at either a Fourth of July celebration or a pot luck supper. It has the added bonus of being easy on the budget, too. Ground turkey or veal can be substituted for the ground beef in the meat layer. For serving, use a clear, ovenproof dish to show off the layers of vegetables, beef, and macaroni.

This casserole can be assembled a day ahead and kept, covered with plastic wrap, in the refrigerator until ready to bake.

2 tablespoons unsalted butter
1 medium-size leek (white and some green part), trimmed, rinsed, and cut in ¼" slices (½ cup)
1 medium-size green bell pepper, cored, seeded, and cut in ½" pieces (¾ cup)
2 medium-size zucchini, trimmed and cut in ½" pieces (2 cups)
1 10-ounce package frozen leaf spinach, thawed and drained
⅛ teaspoon salt, or to taste
⅛ teaspoon coarsely ground black pepper

MEAT LAYER

1 tablespoon olive oil
1 medium-size yellow onion, chopped (1 cup)
1 stalk celery, chopped (½ cup)
1 pound lean ground beef
½ cup beef stock or canned broth
¼ cup tomato paste
1 teaspoon dried oregano leaves, crumbled
½ teaspoon dried thyme leaves, crumbled
½ teaspoon dried basil leaves, crumbled
⅛ teaspoon salt, or to taste
⅛ teaspoon coarsely ground black pepper

MACARONI-CHEESE LAYER

6 ounces elbow macaroni (2½ cups)
2 tablespoons unsalted butter
3 tablespoons all-purpose flour
1¼ cups milk
6 ounces shredded sharp Cheddar cheese (1½ cups)
⅛ teaspoon ground white pepper

6 SERVINGS
PREP TIME: 1 HOUR
COOKING TIME: 30 MINUTES

EQUIPMENT LIST

Utility knife
Colander
Grater
2 large skillets
Kitchen spoons
Slotted spoon
2½-quart casserole
Large saucepan
Medium-size saucepan

1 To make the Vegetable Layer: In a large skillet over moderate heat, melt the 2 tablespoons of butter. Add the leek and sauté for 2 to 3 minutes, or until softened. Add the bell pepper and sauté for 3 minutes more. Add the zucchini and spinach and sauté for 3 minutes more. Season to taste with the ⅛ teaspoon each of the salt and pepper. Using a slotted spoon, transfer the vegetable mixture to a 2½-quart casserole and set aside.

2 To make the Meat Layer: In a large skillet, heat the oil over moderate heat for 1 minute. Add the onion and celery and sauté for 5 minutes, or until the onion is translucent. Add the beef and cook, stirring continuously, for 5 minutes, or until no pink color remains. Stir in the stock, tomato paste, oregano, thyme, and basil. Cook, uncovered, stirring occasionally, for 5 minutes. Season to taste with the ⅛ teaspoon each of the salt and pepper. Remove the pan from the heat. Spoon the meat mixture evenly over the Vegetable Layer.

3 To make the Macaroni-Cheese Layer: Bring a large saucepan of water to a boil over high heat. Cook the macaroni in the boiling water for 10 minutes, or until al dente. Drain well, rinse under cold running water, and drain again.

4 Preheat the oven to 350° F. In a medium-size saucepan over moderate heat, melt the 2 tablespoons of butter. Slowly add the flour and cook, stirring continuously, for 2 minutes, or until a pale straw color. Gradually add the milk, stirring continuously, until the sauce is smooth. Bring to a boil, reduce the heat to low, and simmer, uncovered, for 2 minutes, or until thickened slightly.

5 Remove the pan from the heat and stir in 1¼ cups of the cheese. Season to taste with the white pepper. Stir in the macaroni. Spoon the macaroni mixture over the Meat Layer. Sprinkle with the remaining ¼ cup of cheese.

6 Bake for 25 to 30 minutes, or until the top is golden and the layers are heated through. Remove the casserole from the oven and serve immediately.

Pasta Nostra Italiano

- 1   pound dried orecchiette or other small dried pasta (4 cups)
- 2   tablespoons olive oil
- 4   ounces bean sprouts, rinsed (1 cup)
- 1   large clove garlic, finely chopped
- 1   medium-size zucchini, trimmed and chopped (2 cups)
- 1   14½-ounce can tomatoes, drained and chopped
- 12   sliced, pitted black olives (⅓ cup)
- ⅛   teaspoon salt, or to taste
- Freshly ground black pepper
- 8   ounces part-skim mozzarella cheese, cut in ¼″ pieces (1½ cups)
- 1   ounce grated Parmesan cheese (¼ cup) (optional)

Orecchiette (meaning ear-shaped) is a lesser-known form of pasta, but it is traditionally chosen for this simply prepared and tasty dish. The pieces of dough are shaped with the thumb to make a small cup, which holds the sauce. If this type of pasta is unavailable, other small pasta, such as shells, ditalini, or even elbow macaroni, can be used.

For a different flavor, try smoked mozzarella cheese. It is available at specialty food stores and Italian delicatessens. Serve this dish with a salad of Italian greens, such as arugula or radicchio in a light balsamic vinaigrette, and crusty Italian bread.

1 Bring a large stockpot of water to a boil over high heat. Cook the pasta in the boiling water for 8 to 10 minutes or until al dente.

2 Meanwhile, in a large skillet, heat the oil over moderately high heat for 1 minute. Add the garlic and sauté for 30 seconds, or until fragrant.

3 Add the zucchini to the skillet and sauté for 2 to 3 minutes, or until barely tender. Stir in the tomatoes and sauté for 3 minutes, or until the sauce has thickened slightly.

4 Stir in the olives and season to taste with the salt and pepper. Remove the skillet from the heat.

5 Drain the pasta well and return it to the pan. Pour the zucchini and tomato sauce over the pasta and sprinkle with the mozzarella cheese. Toss the pasta gently to coat with the sauce.

6 Spoon the pasta onto individual serving plates. Garnish with Parmesan cheese, if desired, and serve immediately.

4 SERVINGS
PREP TIME: 15 MINUTES PLUS
COOKING TIME: 10 MINUTES

EQUIPMENT LIST

Colander
Utility knife
Pepper mill
Large stockpot
Large skillet
Kitchen spoon

Orecchiette pasta captures chunks of tomato and mozzarella.

Pasta-Stuffed Peppers

Whole bell peppers make perfect containers for this flavorful stuffing of rice-shaped pasta. This dish can be served hot or cold, which makes it ideal for summertime eating. To serve cold: Let the peppers cool for 30 minutes, cover them with plastic wrap and chill in the refrigerator for up to 6 hours.

4 medium-size orange, yellow, red, or green bell peppers
½ cup hot water
Curly endive leaves (optional)
Sprigs of fresh dill (optional)

ORZO STUFFING (4 CUPS)

2 cups chicken stock or canned broth
⅔ cup orzo
2 tablespoons olive oil
8 ounces mushrooms, trimmed, cleaned, and thinly sliced (2½ cups)
4 green onions (including tops), finely chopped (½ cup)
1 stalk celery, finely chopped (½ cup)
2 large cloves garlic, finely chopped
8 ounces shredded Swiss cheese (2 cups)
3 tablespoons chopped fresh parsley
⅛ teaspoon salt, or to taste
Freshly ground black pepper

1 Preheat the oven to 350° F. Using a sharp knife, cut around the stem of each pepper. Remove the stems and scoop out the cores and the seeds. If necessary, remove a thin slice from the base of each pepper so that it will stand upright. Wash the peppers under cold running water, pat dry with paper towels, and place them, cut side up, in a small baking dish.

2 To make the Orzo Stuffing: In a medium-size saucepan, bring stock to a boil over high heat. Add the orzo, reduce the heat to moderately high, and cook, partially covered, for 7 to 8 minutes, or until al dente. Remove the pan from the heat. Drain the orzo, if necessary. Cool slightly.

3 In a large skillet, heat the oil over moderately high heat for 1 minute. Add the mushrooms and sauté for 3 minutes, or until softened. Add the green onions, celery, and garlic and sauté for 2 minutes, or until softened. Add the mushroom mixture, Swiss cheese, and parsley to the orzo, tossing gently to combine. Season to taste with the salt and pepper.

4 Spoon 1 cup of stuffing into each pepper. Pour the hot water into the bottom of the dish and cover tightly with aluminum foil. Bake for 25 to 30 minutes, or until peppers are tender.

5 Remove the baking dish from the oven. Remove and discard the foil. Line a serving platter with curly endive leaves, if desired. Using a large, metal spatula, transfer the peppers to the serving platter. Garnish with sprigs of fresh dill, if desired, and serve immediately.

4 SERVINGS
PREP TIME: 30 MINUTES
COOKING TIME: 30 MINUTES

EQUIPMENT LIST

Utility knife
Grater
Pepper mill
Paper towels
Aluminum foil
Small baking dish
Medium-size saucepan with lid
Colander
Large skillet
Kitchen spoon

Pasta with Bolognese Sauce

1 pound dried corkscrew pasta
(4 cups)
Celery leaves (optional)
Grated Parmesan cheese (optional)

BOLOGNESE SAUCE (6 CUPS)

6 ounces chicken livers, trimmed
1 tablespoon olive oil
1 large yellow onion, finely chopped (1½ cups)
3 large cloves garlic, finely chopped
2 stalks celery, finely chopped (1 cup)
1 pound lean ground beef
2 cups dry white wine or beef stock or canned broth
1 28-ounce can crushed tomatoes in purée
½ teaspoon ground nutmeg
½ teaspoon dried oregano leaves, crumbled
½ teaspoon dried thyme leaves, crumbled
¼ teaspoon salt, or to taste
¼ teaspoon coarsely ground black pepper

Bolognese Sauce, the classic Italian meat sauce, has many variations. This version will surely become a hit in any household. It features chicken livers, which add a distinct robustness. Serve this sauce with pasta or use it to make a memorable lasagne.

1 To make the Bolognese Sauce: Rinse the chicken livers under cold running water and pat dry with paper towels. Chop the chicken livers and set aside.

2 In a large saucepan, heat the oil over moderate heat for 1 minute. Add the onion and sauté for 5 minutes, or until translucent. Add the garlic and celery and sauté for 2 minutes, or until softened.

3 Add the beef and cook, stirring continuously, for 5 minutes, or until no pink color remains. Stir in the chicken livers, wine, tomatoes with the purée, nutmeg, oregano, and thyme. Season to taste with the salt and pepper. Increase the heat to high and bring the mixture to a boil. Reduce the heat to moderately low and simmer, covered, stirring occasionally, for 2 hours, or until the sauce has thickened.

4 Fifteen minutes before the sauce is finished, bring a large stockpot of water to a boil over high heat. Cook the pasta in the boiling water for 8 to 10 minutes, or until al dente. Drain well.

5 Transfer the pasta to individual serving plates and spoon some of the sauce on top. Garnish with celery leaves and serve immediately with the Parmesan cheese, if desired.

This Bolognese Sauce is richer than others because it contains chicken livers.

6 SERVINGS
PREP TIME: 30 MINUTES
COOKING TIME: 2 HOURS 15 MINUTES

EQUIPMENT LIST

Utility knife
Paper towels
Large saucepan with lid
Kitchen spoon
Large stockpot
Colander

Cinnamon Noodle Pudding

Think of this dish as a variation of bread pudding, but instead of day-old bread, it calls for egg noodles baked in a creamy blend of cottage cheese and yogurt. Top with a berry sauce made from heated jam.

Leftover portions are delicious cold or may be frozen for another occasion. To freeze: Cut cooled pudding into serving-size pieces and freeze, wrapped in aluminum foil and plastic wrap. Thaw, unwrap, then reheat, covered, in a 350° F. oven for 25 minutes, or until heated through.

4	ounces medium-width egg noodles (2 cups)
1	16-ounce container lowfat cottage cheese
1	8-ounce container plain lowfat yogurt (1 cup)
4	large eggs, lightly beaten
⅓	cup golden raisins
2	tablespoons granulated sugar
1	teaspoon ground cinnamon
¼	teaspoon salt
1	tablespoon unsalted butter
2	tablespoons toasted wheat germ

1 Preheat the oven to 375° F. Grease a 9″ square baking pan. Bring a large saucepan of water to a boil over high heat. Cook the noodles in the boiling water for 6 to 8 minutes, or until al dente. Drain the noodles well, rinse under cold running water, and drain again.

2 In a large bowl, mix together the cottage cheese, yogurt, eggs, raisins, sugar, cinnamon, and salt. Stir in the noodles. Spoon the mixture into the prepared pan.

3 In a small saucepan over low heat, melt the butter. Remove the pan from the heat and stir in the wheat germ. Sprinkle the wheat germ mixture over the noodles.

4 Bake the pudding, uncovered, for 25 minutes, or until firm. Remove pan from the oven and let stand for 10 minutes before serving. Transfer to individual serving plates and serve immediately.

6 SERVINGS
PREP TIME: 10 MINUTES PLUS
10 MINUTES TO STAND
COOKING TIME: 25 MINUTES

EQUIPMENT LIST

Small bowl
Large bowl
Fork
9″ square baking pan
Large saucepan
Small saucepan
Colander
Kitchen spoons

Savory Jumbo Shells

12	jumbo pasta shells
2	tablespoons unsalted butter
1	10-ounce package frozen chopped spinach, thawed
8	ounces baked or smoked ham, finely chopped
2	ounces grated Parmesan cheese (½ cup)
2	large eggs
3	green onions (white parts only), chopped (3 tablespoons)
¾	teaspoon dried oregano leaves, crumbled

Freshly ground black pepper

CHEESE SAUCE (2 CUPS)

3	tablespoons unsalted butter
1	large clove garlic, chopped
3	tablespoons all-purpose flour
2	cups milk
2	ounces grated Parmesan cheese (½ cup)

Freshly ground black pepper

1 Preheat the oven to 350° F. To prepare the pasta shells: Bring a large saucepan of water to a boil over high heat. Cook the shells in the boiling water for 15 minutes, or until al dente. Drain well, rinse under cold running water, and drain again.

2 Meanwhile, in a small saucepan over moderately low heat, melt the 2 tablespoons of butter. Squeeze the excess moisture from the spinach. In a large bowl, combine the spinach, ham, ½ cup of Parmesan cheese, eggs, onions, oregano, and butter. Season to taste.

3 Transfer the shells to a large plate. Using a teaspoon, generously fill the shells with spinach mixture. Set aside.

4 To prepare the Cheese Sauce: In a medium-size saucepan over moderately low heat, melt the 2 tablespoons of butter. Add garlic and sauté for 30 seconds, or until fragrant. Add flour and cook, stirring continuously, for 2 minutes, or until a pale straw color. Slowly stir in the milk. Cook over moderately high heat, stirring continuously, for 5 minutes, or until the sauce has thickened slightly. Reduce the heat to low and stir in the ½ cup of Parmesan cheese. Season to taste.

5 Pour 1 cup of sauce into a 9″ round baking dish. Transfer shells to the dish and arrange in a single layer. Pour remaining sauce over them. Cover with aluminum foil and bake for 20 minutes. Uncover the dish and bake for 5 to 10 minutes more, or until filling is heated through. Transfer shells to individual serving plates. Serve immediately.

4 SERVINGS
PREP TIME: 30 MINUTES
COOKING TIME: 30 MINUTES

EQUIPMENT LIST

Utility knife
Pepper mill
Large saucepan
Small saucepan
Medium-size saucepan
Colander
Large bowl
Kitchen spoons
Large plate
Teaspoon
9″ round baking dish
Aluminum foil

Vegetable and Rice Casserole

2 cups water
1 cup long-grain white rice
1 medium-size tomato, seeded and chopped (1 cup)
2 green onions (including tops), finely chopped (¼ cup)
1 small yellow onion, finely chopped (½ cup)
1 medium-size green bell pepper, cored, seeded, and chopped (¾ cup)
1 medium-size red bell pepper, cored, seeded, and chopped (¾ cup)
1 teaspoon dried basil leaves, crumbled
¼ teaspoon salt, or to taste
Ground white pepper
½ cup milk
3 large eggs, beaten
2 ounces shredded Cheddar cheese (½ cup)
2 ounces shredded mozzarella cheese (½ cup)

This colorful casserole is simple to prepare and healthful, too. The rice can be prepared ahead and kept, covered, in the refrigerator until ready to use. Round out the meal with a fruit salad and whole-grain bread.

1 In a medium-size saucepan, bring the water to a boil over high heat. Stir in the rice. Reduce the heat to low, and cook, covered, for 20 minutes, or until the rice is tender and the liquid is absorbed. Remove the pan from the heat. Fluff the rice with a fork and transfer to a large bowl.

2 Preheat the oven to 375° F. Lightly grease a 1½-quart baking dish. Add the tomato, onions, ½ cup each of the green and red bell peppers, and basil to the rice, stirring until well combined. Season to taste with the salt and pepper. Stir in the milk and eggs. Spoon the rice and vegetable mixture into the prepared dish. Sprinkle the Cheddar and mozzarella cheeses over the top.

3 Bake the casserole for 20 to 25 minutes, or until a knife inserted in the center comes out clean. Remove the casserole from the oven and garnish with the remaining ¼ cup each of the green and red bell peppers. Serve immediately.

4 SERVINGS
PREP TIME: 10 MINUTES
COOKING TIME: 45 MINUTES

EQUIPMENT LIST

Utility knife
Small bowl
Large bowl
Wire whisk
Grater
Medium-size saucepan with lid
Fork
1½-quart baking dish
Kitchen spoon

¾ cup dried black beans
½ teaspoon dried oregano leaves, crumbled
4 ounces hickory-smoked ham, chopped (optional)

YELLOW RICE

4 strips lean bacon, chopped
2 tablespoons olive oil
1 medium-size yellow onion, chopped (1 cup)
2 large cloves garlic, chopped
¾ cup long-grain white rice
½ teaspoon ground cumin
¼ teaspoon ground turmeric
¼ teaspoon salt, or to taste
1½ cups water
1 medium-size tomato, seeded and chopped (1 cup)
1 small green bell pepper, cored, seeded, and chopped (½ cup)

Black Beans and Yellow Rice

Black beans lend themselves to robust dishes such as this traditional Caribbean-style recipe. It makes a delicious and economical entrée.

1 To make the black beans: In a large saucepan, soak the beans in cold water to cover for 8 hours. Drain the liquid and cover the beans with fresh cold water and bring to a boil over high heat. Reduce the heat to moderately low and cook, partially covered, for 2 hours, or until the beans are tender.

2 Meanwhile, make the Yellow Rice. Cook the bacon in a medium-size skillet over moderate heat for 8 to 10 minutes, or until crisp. With a slotted spoon, transfer the bacon to a plate lined with paper towels to drain. Pour off the drippings from the skillet and wipe out with paper towels.

3 Heat the oil in the skillet over moderate heat for 1 minute. Add the onion and garlic and cook, stirring occasionally, for 2 minutes. Add the rice, cumin, turmeric, salt, and water. Bring to a boil over high heat. Reduce the heat to low and cook, covered, for 10 minutes. Add the tomato and bell pepper and cook, covered, for 10 minutes more, or until the rice is tender and the liquid is absorbed. Remove the pan from the heat and fluff the rice with a fork.

4 Add the bacon, oregano, and the smoked ham, if desired, to the black beans Spoon the rice into individual bowls, top with some of the black beans, and serve immediately.

4 SERVINGS
PREP TIME: 20 MINUTES PLUS
8 HOURS TO SOAK
COOKING TIME: 2 HOURS

EQUIPMENT LIST

Utility knife
Large saucepan with lid
Colander
Medium-size skillet with lid
Kitchen spoons
Slotted spoon
Plate
Paper towels
Fork

Barley Pilaf
with Mushrooms and Onions

Barley, probably the earliest grain known to humankind, was cultivated in ancient Egypt and throughout the Middle East as a bread grain where it is still an important food. In the United States, barley is used to make malt, which is made into beer and distilled in liquor; however, it is gaining popularity in cooking for health reasons as well as taste. In this dish it is combined with mushrooms and onions for a subtle tasting side dish that teams well with roast lamb.

1 tablespoon olive oil
1 tablespoon unsalted butter
6 ounces mushrooms, trimmed, cleaned, and sliced (1¾ cups)
1 small yellow onion, thinly sliced (1 cup)
1 cup small pearl barley
⅛ teaspoon salt, or to taste
Freshly ground black pepper
3 cups chicken stock or canned broth
2 tablespoons chopped fresh parsley
Sprigs of fresh parsley (optional)

4 SERVINGS
PREP TIME: 10 MINUTES
COOKING TIME: 1 HOUR

EQUIPMENT LIST

Utility knife
Pepper mill
Medium-size skillet
Kitchen spoon
2-quart casserole with lid

1 Preheat the oven to 350° F. In a medium-size skillet, heat the oil and butter over moderate heat for 1 minute. Add the mushrooms and onion and sauté for 5 minutes, or until the onion is translucent. Stir in the barley and cook, stirring frequently, for 3 minutes more. Season to taste with the salt and pepper.

2 Transfer the mixture to a 2-quart casserole. Stir in the stock. Bake, covered, for 1 hour, or until the barley is tender and the liquid is absorbed.

3 Remove the casserole from the oven. Stir in the chopped parsley. Garnish with sprigs of fresh parsley, if desired. Serve immediately.

This hearty and wholesome side dish offers an unusual twist to standard pilaf recipes.

Shrimp and Vegetable Fried Rice

3   cups water
1½   cups long-grain white rice
4   tablespoons vegetable oil
1   medium-size yellow onion, finely chopped (1 cup)
8   ounces baked ham, chopped
1   medium-size ripe tomato, peeled, seeded, and chopped (1 cup)
⅔   cup frozen peas, thawed and drained
1   pound medium-size uncooked shrimp, peeled and deveined (20-24 shrimp)
     Freshly ground black pepper
2   large eggs
1   tablespoon low-sodium soy sauce

Fried rice is a popular Chinese dish that is surprisingly simple to prepare. For the home cook, it is also a great way to combine a variety of on-hand ingredients, especially leftovers. Try chicken, beef, pork, ham, or shellfish and any sort of vegetable—whatever you like to make an appetizing entrée or accompaniment to a Chinese-style meal.

1 In a medium-size saucepan, bring the water to a boil over high heat. Stir in the rice. Reduce the heat to low and cook, covered, for 20 minutes, or until the rice is tender and the liquid is absorbed. Remove pan from the heat. Fluff the rice with a fork and set aside.

2 In a wok or large, heavy skillet, heat 3 tablespoons of the oil over high heat for 1 minute, or until very hot. Add the onion and stir-fry for 2 minutes. Add the ham, tomato, peas, and shrimp and stir-fry for 1 minute more.

3 Add cooked rice to wok and stir-fry for 2 minutes more. Season to taste with the pepper. Remove wok from the heat and keep warm.

4 In a small bowl, beat the eggs with the soy sauce until well blended.

5 In a small skillet, heat the remaining 1 tablespoon of oil over moderate heat for 1 minute. Increase the heat to high and pour the egg mixture into the pan. Swirl pan to distribute the eggs evenly over the surface. Cook, without stirring, for 2 minutes, or until the eggs have set on the bottom. Using a large, metal spatula, turn the egg pancake over and cook for 2 minutes more, or until set. Using the spatula, transfer the egg pancake to a plate and cut it into ¼″ strips.

6 Transfer the fried rice to a serving dish, garnish with egg strips, and serve immediately.

This fried rice dish makes a lovely presentation and it's great tasting, too.

6 SERVINGS
PREP TIME: 30 MINUTES
COOKING TIME: 31 MINUTES

EQUIPMENT LIST

Utility knife
Paring knife
Strainer
Pepper mill
Medium-size saucepan with lid
Wok or large, heavy skillet
Small skillet
Kitchen spoon
Small bowl
Wire whisk
Large, metal spatula
Plate

Vegetable Couscous

Couscous is dried semolina from North Africa. Here it is combined with a variety of vegetables for a tasty, healthful supper dish.

2	tablespoons olive oil
¼	cup chopped yellow onion
2	large cloves garlic, chopped
4	cups chicken stock or canned broth
2	tablespoons tomato paste
1	teaspoon ground cinnamon
½	teaspoon paprika
½	teaspoon ground ginger
2	large carrots, peeled and sliced ¼″ thick (2 cups)
1	large Idaho or other baking potato, peeled and cut in ½″ pieces (1½ cups)
2½	cups sliced green cabbage
1	small zucchini, trimmed and chopped (1 cup)
1	small red bell pepper, cored, seeded, and chopped (½ cup)
1	cup canned chick peas, drained
½	cup dark raisins
1	cup instant couscous

1 In a large saucepan, heat the oil over moderate heat for 1 minute. Add the onion and garlic and sauté for 5 minutes, or until the onion is translucent.

2 Add the stock, tomato paste, cinnamon, paprika, and ginger. Bring the mixture to a boil over high heat. Add the carrots and potato. Reduce the heat to low and cook, uncovered, stirring occasionally, for 10 minutes. Add the cabbage, zucchini, and bell pepper and cook, stirring occasionally, for 10 minutes. Add the chick peas and raisins and cook, stirring occasionally, for 5 minutes more.

3 Transfer 2 cups of the cooking liquid to a medium-size saucepan and bring to a boil over high heat. Add the couscous. Remove the pan from heat and let stand, covered, for 5 minutes, or until couscous is tender and the liquid is absorbed. Fluff the couscous with a fork.

4 Using a large spoon, mound the couscous on a serving platter. Remove the pan from the heat. Ladle some cooking liquid over the couscous. Using a slotted spoon, arrange the vegetables around the couscous and ladle some cooking liquid over them. Serve immediately.

4 SERVINGS
PREP TIME: 35 MINUTES PLUS
5 MINUTES TO STAND
COOKING TIME: 31 MINUTES

EQUIPMENT LIST

Utility knife
Vegetable peeler
Strainer
Large saucepan
Medium-size saucepan with lid
Kitchen spoons
Fork
Ladle
Slotted spoon

Millet Salad Mexicano

Millet, a versatile and easy-to-prepare grain, resembles bright yellow mustard seeds in appearance and size. Toasting millet before it is cooked results in a flavorful grain that retains a slight crunch.

1	cup hulled millet
3	cups boiling water
2	cups frozen corn kernels
6	ripe plum tomatoes, seeded and chopped (2 cups)
1	large ripe avocado

MEXICANO DRESSING (1 CUP)

2	small jalapeño peppers, cored, seeded, and finely chopped (2 tablespoons)
2	shallots, finely chopped (2 tablespoons)
2	tablespoons snipped fresh chives
¼	cup chopped fresh cilantro (coriander leaves)
1	large clove garlic, chopped
¼	cup fresh lemon juice
¼	cup extra virgin olive oil
⅛	teaspoon salt, or to taste

1 In a large, nonstick skillet, toast the millet over moderately high heat, stirring continuously, for 5 minutes, or until fragrant and golden. Stir in the boiling water. Reduce the heat to moderately low and cook, covered, for 20 to 25 minutes, or until the millet is tender and the liquid is absorbed. Remove the skillet from the heat. Fluff the millet with a fork and let cool slightly.

2 Meanwhile, bring a medium-size saucepan of water to a boil over high heat. Add the corn and cook for 2 minutes, or until crisp-tender. Drain well, rinse under cold running water, and drain again.

3 To make the Mexicano Dressing: In a small bowl, combine the jalapeño peppers, shallots, chives, cilantro, garlic, and lemon juice. Slowly add the oil, whisking vigorously until well blended, or place the ingredients in a small jar with a tight-fitting lid and shake to blend. Season to taste with the salt.

4 In a large, shallow serving bowl, combine the millet, corn, and tomatoes. Peel and pit the avocado and cut into ½″ pieces. Add the avocado pieces to the salad. Pour the dressing over the salad, tossing to coat. Serve at room temperature.

4 SERVINGS
PREP TIME: 20 MINUTES
COOKING TIME: 30 MINUTES

EQUIPMENT LIST

Paring knife
Utility knife
Kitchen scissors
Citrus juicer
Large, nonstick skillet with lid
Kitchen spoon
Fork
Medium-size saucepan
Colander
Small bowl
Wire whisk

South-of-the-Border Rice Bake

Serve this brunch dish with freshly squeezed orange juice and fresh fruit.

2 cups water
1 cup long-grain brown rice
5 large eggs plus 1 egg white
⅓ cup lowfat milk
¼ teaspoon salt
Ground white pepper
⅛ teaspoon hot pepper sauce
2 tablespoons unsalted butter
1 large clove garlic, finely chopped
2 medium-size carrots, peeled and shredded (1½ cups)
4 ounces mushrooms, trimmed, cleaned, and sliced (1¼ cups)
1 small yellow onion, chopped (½ cup)
1 small green bell pepper, cored, seeded, and chopped (½ cup)
1 small red bell pepper, cored, seeded, and chopped (½ cup)
2 ounces shredded Cheddar cheese (½ cup)
Apple slices (optional)
Black grapes (optional)
Vine leaves (optional)

1 In a medium-size saucepan, bring the water to a boil over high heat. Stir in the rice. Reduce the heat to low and cook, covered, for 45 to 50 minutes, or until the rice is tender and the liquid is absorbed. Remove the pan from the heat. Fluff the rice with a fork and set aside.

2 In a medium-size bowl, whisk the eggs and egg white with the milk, salt, pepper, and hot pepper sauce until frothy. Set aside.

3 In a large skillet over moderate heat, melt the butter. Add the garlic, carrots, mushrooms, onion, and green and red bell peppers and sauté for 4 minutes, or until the vegetables are softened. Pour the egg mixture over the vegetables, reduce the heat to low, and cook, gently lifting the eggs with a large, metal spatula as they set, for 3 to 4 minutes, or until the mixture is set but still moist.

4 Add the rice and Cheddar cheese to the skillet and cook, stirring continuously, for 1 minute, or until the cheese is melted. Transfer the rice to individual serving plates. Garnish with apple slices, grapes, and vine leaves, if desired. Serve immediately.

6 SERVINGS
PREP TIME: 20 MINUTES
COOKING TIME: 1 HOUR

EQUIPMENT LIST

Small bowl
Utility knife
Vegetable peeler
Grater
Medium-size saucepan with lid
Kitchen spoon
Fork
Medium-size bowl
Wire whisk
Large skillet
Large, metal spatula

Add elegance to a brunch buffet with this Mexican-inspired dish.

Cranberry-Wild Rice Salad

This easy to prepare salad makes a colorful as well as healthful holiday accompaniment to roast pork or poultry, or it can be used as a stuffing for poultry or baked winter squash.

Wild rice has a high moisture level and is best stored in an airtight container in the refrigerator during hot and humid weather. At other times, it should be stored in a cool, dry place.

1   cup wild rice
3   cups water
4   ounces fresh or frozen cranberries, thawed and drained (1 cup)
1   tablespoon granulated sugar
¼   cup cranberry juice
2   green onions (including tops), finely chopped (¼ cup)
1   medium-size carrot, peeled and cut in narrow strips (1 cup)
½   cup dark or golden raisins
1   ounce pecan halves (¼ cup)
2   tablespoons peanut or walnut oil
2   teaspoons cider vinegar
¼   teaspoon salt, or to taste
Freshly ground black pepper

6 SERVINGS
PREP TIME: 5 MINUTES PLUS
30 MINUTES TO CHILL
COOKING TIME: 50 MINUTES

EQUIPMENT LIST

Colander
Utility knife
Vegetable peeler
Pepper mill
Medium-size saucepan with lid
Small saucepan
Kitchen spoons
Large bowl
Small bowl
Wire whisk
Plastic wrap

1 In a medium-size saucepan, combine the wild rice and water. Bring to a boil over high heat. Reduce the heat to moderately low and cook, covered, for 45 minutes, or until the rice is tender and the liquid is absorbed. Drain well and set aside to cool.

2 In a small saucepan, combine the cranberries, sugar, and cranberry juice. Cook, stirring occasionally, over moderate heat for 5 to 6 minutes, or until the cranberries "pop" slightly and give off their juices. Remove the pan from the heat and cool slightly.

3 In a large bowl, combine the wild rice, cranberries, green onions, carrot, raisins, and pecans. In a small bowl, whisk together the peanut oil and cider vinegar. Drizzle the mixture over the salad, tossing to coat. Season to taste with the salt and pepper. Cover the bowl with plastic wrap and chill in the refrigerator for 30 minutes to allow the flavors to blend. Serve chilled or at room temperature.

Cranberries and wild rice—a great combination of flavors and textures.

Risotto with Eggplant Sauce

2⅔ cups chicken stock or canned broth
2 tablespoons olive oil
1 small yellow onion, finely chopped (½ cup)
1 large clove garlic, chopped
1 cup Arborio rice
⅓ cup dry white wine or water
1 tablespoon unsalted butter
1 tablespoon chopped fresh parsley
¼ teaspoon salt, or to taste
2 ounces grated Parmesan cheese (½ cup)

EGGPLANT SAUCE

¼ cup olive oil
1 medium-size eggplant, peeled and chopped (3½ cups)
1 medium-size yellow onion, finely chopped (1 cup)
1 large green or red bell pepper, cored, seeded, and cut in chunks (1 cup)
2 large cloves garlic, chopped
1 16-ounce can whole tomatoes
1 teaspoon dried basil leaves, crumbled
⅛ teaspoon salt, or to taste
Freshly ground black pepper

To achieve risotto's traditional creamy texture, use Arborio rice as it has the ability to absorb more liquid, and therefore flavor, than other kinds of rice. Look for Arborio rice in specialty food stores or Italian markets. Serve this dish on its own or with a meat or poultry entrée.

1 To make the Eggplant Sauce: In a large saucepan, heat the oil over moderate heat for 1 minute. Add the eggplant and sauté for 5 minutes, or until slightly softened. Add the 1 cup of onion, bell pepper, and the 2 cloves of garlic and sauté for 5 minutes, or until the onion is translucent. Add the tomatoes with their juices, gently breaking them with a wooden spoon. Stir in the basil and season to taste with the ⅛ teaspoon of salt and pepper. Reduce the heat to low and simmer, uncovered, for 10 minutes, or until the vegetables are tender. Remove the pan from the heat and set aside.

2 To make the risotto: In a large saucepan, bring the stock to a boil over high heat. Reduce the heat to low and keep the stock simmering. In a medium-size saucepan, heat the oil over moderate heat for 1 minute. Add the ½ cup of onion and the 1 clove of garlic and sauté for 5 minutes, or until the onion is translucent. Add rice and stir to coat with the oil. Stir in the wine and cook, stirring continuously, for 2 minutes, or until the liquid is absorbed.

3 Add ⅓ cup of the hot stock to the rice and cook, stirring continuously, for 5 minutes, or until the stock is absorbed. Continue adding the stock, ⅓ cup at a time, and adding more only when the previous amount is absorbed. The total cooking time is 25 minutes, or until the rice is creamy and just tender. Remove the pan from the heat, cover, and let stand for 2 minutes.

4 Stir the Eggplant Sauce, butter, and parsley into risotto and season to taste with the ¼ teaspoon of salt. Transfer risotto to individual serving dishes and sprinkle with Parmesan cheese. Serve immediately.

4 SERVINGS
PREP TIME: 15 MINUTES
COOKING TIME: 45 MINUTES

EQUIPMENT LIST

Utility knife
Vegetable peeler
Pepper mill
2 large saucepans
Medium-size saucepan with lid
Kitchen spoons
Wooden spoon

Three-Cheese Grits

2½ cups water
½ cup regular grits
2 ounces shredded Cheddar cheese (½ cup)
2 ounces grated Parmesan cheese (½ cup)
2 ounces shredded Swiss cheese (½ cup)
2 tablespoons salted butter or margarine
1 large egg, beaten
1 large clove garlic, finely chopped

Here's a recipe that uses grits as a side dish—not as a breakfast food. Serve it as an accompaniment to roast or grilled pork.

1 Preheat the oven to 350° F. Grease a 1-quart casserole. In a medium-size saucepan, bring the water to a boil over high heat. Slowly stir in the grits and bring the water back to a boil. Reduce the heat to low and simmer, stirring occasionally, for 12 to 14 minutes, or until thickened.

2 Add the Cheddar, Parmesan, and Swiss cheeses and butter and stir until melted. Add the egg and garlic and mix well. Pour the mixture into the casserole and bake for 30 to 35 minutes, or until a knife inserted in the center comes out clean. Remove the casserole from the oven and serve immediately.

4 SERVINGS
PREP TIME: 10 MINUTES
COOKING TIME: 50 MINUTES

EQUIPMENT LIST

Grater
Small bowl
Fork
Utility knife
1-quart casserole
Medium-size saucepan
Kitchen spoon

*N*o family meal is complete without bread, and if freshly baked then all the better. In this chapter bakers are presented with a tempting array of recipes for home baked goods, including spicy applesauce muffins, breakfast loaf, peppery cornbread, dinner rolls, and a fabulous focaccia.

Dinner Roll Assortment.

Dinner Rolls

Buttery dinner rolls are easy to prepare. Below is a basic recipe, together with some exciting variations that everyone will love.

1 In a small saucepan over moderate heat, warm the milk to just below the boiling point. Remove the pan from the heat and cool slightly. In a large bowl, combine the sugar, yeast, and water and let stand for 5 minutes, or until foamy. Stir in the milk, 4 tablespoons of the butter, egg, salt, and 1 cup of the flour until well blended. Add enough of the remaining flour to make a soft but manageable dough.

2 On a lightly floured work surface, knead the dough for 5 minutes, or until smooth and elastic. Place the dough in a large, lightly greased bowl, turning to coat. Cover with plastic wrap and let rise in a warm, draft-free place for 1 hour, or until doubled in volume.

3 Lightly grease 2 baking sheets. Punch down dough and turn out onto a lightly floured work surface. Divide dough into 24 pieces. Shape each piece into a ball. Place on prepared baking sheets, spacing them 2″ apart. Cover loosely with lightly greased plastic wrap and let rise in a warm, draft-free place for 30 minutes, or until doubled in volume.

4 Preheat the oven to 400° F. In a small saucepan over moderate heat, melt the remaining 3 tablespoons of the butter. Brush the rolls with melted butter. Bake for 20 minutes, or until lightly browned. Remove baking sheets from oven. Transfer the rolls to a wire rack and cool slightly. Serve warm.

Ingredients

1 cup milk
⅓ cup granulated sugar
1 package (¼ ounce) active dry yeast
¼ cup warm water (105°-115° F.)
7 tablespoons unsalted butter, softened
1 large egg
1 teaspoon salt
4½ cups all-purpose flour

24 ROLLS
PREP TIME: 30 MINUTES PLUS
1 HOUR 35 MINUTES TO STAND
AND RISE
COOKING TIME: 20 MINUTES

EQUIPMENT LIST
2 small saucepans
2 large bowls
Kitchen spoon
Plastic wrap
2 baking sheets
Pastry brush
Wire rack

Crescents

Prepare the dough as directed up to shaping rolls. Melt 4 tablespoons of unsalted butter. Divide dough in half. Cover one half with a clean kitchen towel. Set aside. Lightly flour a rolling pin. Roll the remaining dough half into a 12″ circle ⅛″ thick. Brush with some of the melted butter. Cut circle into quarters, then cut each quarter into 3 wedges. Starting with the wide end, roll up each wedge tightly. Tuck the point of the wedge underneath the roll and curve the ends towards one another to form a crescent shape. Place the crescents on the prepared baking sheets, spacing them 2″ apart. Repeat as directed with the remaining dough. Proceed as directed from covering with lightly greased plastic wrap and allowing for a second rising.

24 ROLLS
PREP TIME: 35 MINUTES PLUS
1 HOUR 35 MINUTES TO STAND
AND RISE
COOKING TIME: 20 MINUTES

ADDITIONAL EQUIPMENT LIST
Kitchen towel
Rolling pin
Utility knife

Knots

Prepare dough as directed up to shaping rolls. Divide dough in half. Cover one half with a clean kitchen towel. Set aside. Lightly flour a rolling pin. Roll the remaining dough half into a 14″ x 5″ rectangle. Cut the rectangle into fourteen 2″ x 2½″ pieces. Roll each piece into a 10″ long rope. Tie the ropes into loose knots and place on prepared baking sheets, spacing them 2″ apart. Repeat as directed with the remaining dough. Proceed as directed from covering with lightly greased plastic wrap and allowing for a second rising.

28 ROLLS
PREP TIME: 40 MINUTES PLUS
1 HOUR 35 MINUTES TO STAND
AND RISE
COOKING TIME: 20 MINUTES

ADDITIONAL EQUIPMENT LIST
Kitchen towel

Cheese-Filled Focaccia

This focaccia recipe is quick and easy because it calls for frozen bread dough. Best when warm, this Italian bread may be cut into pieces and served with a mixed green salad for lunch.

2	pounds frozen white bread dough, thawed
2	tablespoons olive oil
6	ounces thinly sliced Provolone cheese
6	ounces thinly sliced Jarlsberg cheese
4	teaspoons dried basil leaves, crumbled
1	teaspoon dried rosemary leaves, crumbled
1	teaspoon dried oregano leaves, crumbled
1	teaspoon dried marjoram leaves, crumbled
1	large clove garlic, finely chopped
1	ounce grated Parmesan cheese (¼ cup)

Tomato roses (optional)
Sprigs of fresh rosemary (optional)

1 Lightly grease a 15½" x 10½" jelly roll pan. Divide the bread dough in half. Lightly flour a work surface and a rolling pin. Roll 1 dough half evenly, from the center outward, into a 15" x 10" rectangle. (If the dough shrinks back, let it rest for 10 minutes, then continue rolling it out to the correct size.)

2 Transfer dough to the prepared pan, leaving a ½" border around the edges. Brush the dough with 1 tablespoon of the oil. Arrange the Provolone and Jarlsberg cheese slices over dough. Sprinkle with half of the basil and rosemary and all of the oregano, marjoram, and garlic.

3 On the lightly floured work surface, roll the remaining dough half evenly, from the center outward, into a 15" x 10" rectangle. Place dough on top of the cheese and herbs. Press together the edges of the 2 layers of dough to seal. Brush top with remaining 1 tablespoon of oil. Let rise in a warm, draft-free place for 1 hour, or until puffy.

4 Preheat the oven to 375° F. Just before baking, make several indentations in the dough with your knuckles. Bake for 25 to 30 minutes, or until golden brown and the bread sounds hollow when the bottom is tapped.

5 Remove the pan from the oven and transfer to a wire rack to cool slightly. While still warm, sprinkle with the remaining basil and rosemary and the Parmesan cheese. Cut into rectangles and transfer to individual serving plates. Garnish with the tomato roses and sprigs of fresh rosemary, if desired. Serve warm.

1 LOAF OR 6 PIECES
PREP TIME: 30 MINUTES PLUS
1 HOUR 10 MINUTES TO REST AND RISE
COOKING TIME: 30 MINUTES

EQUIPMENT LIST

Utility knife
15½" x 10½" jelly roll pan
Rolling pin
Pastry brush
Wire rack

Hearty Breakfast Loaf

3½ cups all-purpose flour
1 cup plus 3 tablespoons yellow cornmeal
1 cup whole-wheat flour
1 cup old-fashioned rolled oats
2 packages (¼ ounce each) active dry yeast
1 teaspoon salt
1 tablespoon grated orange rind
5 tablespoons salted butter or margarine, softened
1 cup prune juice or orange juice
1 cup plus 1 tablespoon water
⅓ cup honey
2 large eggs
9 ounces pitted prunes, quartered (1½ cups)
2 ounces sunflower seeds (½ cup)
Unsalted butter (optional)
Marmalade (optional)

This fiber-filled loaf is a great way to begin the day. Healthful and easy to prepare, it contains three different grains, prunes, and sunflower seeds.

1 In a large bowl, mix together 1 cup of the all-purpose flour, 1 cup of the cornmeal, the whole-wheat flour, oats, yeast, salt, orange rind, and butter until well blended.

2 In a small saucepan, heat the prune juice and 1 cup of the water over moderate heat until very warm (120°-130° F.). Slowly pour warm liquid into the flour mixture, stirring until well blended. Add the honey, 1 egg, and enough of the remaining all-purpose flour to make a soft but manageable dough.

3 On a lightly floured work surface, knead the dough for 8 to 10 minutes, or until smooth and elastic. Place dough in a large, lightly greased bowl, turning to coat. Cover loosely with plastic wrap and let rise in a warm, draft-free place for 1 hour, or until doubled in volume.

4 Grease two 9″ x 5″ loaf pans and sprinkle each with 1 tablespoon of the cornmeal. Punch down the dough, turn out onto the lightly floured work surface, and gently knead in the prunes and sunflower seeds. Divide the dough in half, cover with a clean kitchen towel, and let rest for 5 minutes.

5 Shape each dough half into a loaf and place in the prepared loaf pans. Cover loosely with lightly greased plastic wrap and let rise in a warm, draft-free place for 40 to 45 minutes, or until doubled in volume.

6 Preheat the oven to 375° F. In a small bowl, beat the remaining egg with remaining 1 tablespoon of water. Gently brush tops of the loaves with the egg mixture. Sprinkle with remaining 1 tablespoon of cornmeal.

7 Bake for 40 to 45 minutes, or until the tops are brown and the loaves sound hollow when bottoms are tapped. Remove the pans from the oven. Turn the loaves out onto a wire rack and cool for 15 minutes. Serve warm with a little unsalted butter or marmalade, if desired.

2 LOAVES OR 24 SLICES
PREP TIME: 30 MINUTES PLUS
1 HOUR AND 50 MINUTES TO RISE
COOKING TIME: 45 MINUTES

Equipment List

Grater
Paring knife
2 large bowls
Small bowl
Kitchen spoon
Small saucepan
Plastic wrap
2 9″ x 5″ loaf pans
Dish towel
Fork
Pastry brush

Green Onion and Herb Bread

1   package (¼ ounce) active dry yeast
¾   cup warm water (105°-115° F.)
½   cup (1 stick) unsalted butter, softened
2   tablespoons granulated sugar
1   teaspoon salt
3   large eggs plus 1 egg yolk
4   cups all-purpose flour
2   teaspoons milk

GREEN ONION AND HERB FILLING

1   tablespoon unsalted butter
4   green onions (including tops), chopped (½ cup)
1   large egg
4   ounces shredded Swiss cheese (1 cup)
1½   ounces grated Parmesan cheese (⅓ cup)
2   tablespoons chopped fresh tarragon, or 2 teaspoons dried tarragon leaves, crumbled
¼   teaspoon coarsely ground black pepper

1 In a small bowl, combine the yeast and water and let stand for 5 minutes, or until foamy. Meanwhile, in a large bowl, using an electric mixer set on high speed, beat the ½ cup of butter for 1 minute, or until creamy. Reduce mixer speed to medium-low and beat in sugar, salt, 3 eggs, and 1 cup of the flour for 1 minute, or until well combined.

2 Add the yeast mixture to the egg mixture, then add 1 cup of the remaining flour. Beat for 5 minutes, or until well combined. Reduce the mixer speed to low and add enough of the remaining flour to make a soft but manageable dough.

3 On a lightly floured work surface, knead the dough for 5 minutes, or until smooth and elastic, adding additional flour if necessary. Place the dough in a large, lightly greased bowl, turning once to coat. Cover bowl with plastic wrap and let rise in a warm, draft-free place for 1½ hours, or until doubled in volume.

4 Meanwhile, prepare the Green Onion and Herb Filling. In a medium-size skillet over moderate heat, melt the 1 tablespoon of butter. Add the green onions and sauté for 2 minutes, or until softened. Transfer the green onion mixture to a medium-size bowl and stir in the 1 egg, the Swiss and Parmesan cheeses, tarragon, and pepper. Set aside.

5 Grease a 2-quart round baking dish or soufflé dish. Punch down the dough and knead gently for 1 minute. Lightly flour a work surface and a rolling pin. Roll the dough evenly, from the center outward, into a 16″ x 10″ rectangle 1½″ thick. Spread the filling over the dough, leaving a ½″ border around the edge.

6 Starting with a long edge, roll dough, jelly-roll style, into a tight cylinder. With the seam underneath, coil the roll around tightly and tuck end underneath. Place coil, seam-side down, in prepared dish. Cover the dish loosely with plastic wrap, and let rise in a warm, draft-free place for 45 to 60 minutes, or until doubled in volume.

7 Preheat the oven to 350° F. In a small bowl, mix the egg yolk with the milk. Brush top of bread with egg yolk mixture. Bake for 40 to 45 minutes, or until top is golden brown and loaf sounds hollow when bottom is tapped. Remove the dish from the oven and set on a wire rack to cool for 5 minutes. Turn the bread out onto rack and cool completely. Serve sliced.

1 LOAF OR 12 SLICES
PREP TIME: 20 MINUTES PLUS 2 HOURS 30 MINUTES TO RISE
COOKING TIME: 45 MINUTES

EQUIPMENT LIST

2 small bowls
2 large bowls
Medium-size bowl
Utility knife
Grater
Electric mixer
Plastic wrap
Medium-size skillet
Kitchen spoons
2-quart round baking dish
Rolling pin
Fork
Pastry brush
Wire rack

Jalapeño Cornbread

Buttermilk and corn kernels combine to make this cornbread especially moist. Chopped fresh jalapeño peppers add a Southwestern flavor. Serve it with a hearty soup, chili, or baked ham.

½ cup (1 stick) unsalted butter
1 cup yellow cornmeal
1 cup all-purpose flour
2 tablespoons granulated sugar
1 tablespoon baking powder
¼ teaspoon salt
1 cup buttermilk
1 large egg
2 jalapeño peppers, cored, seeded, and finely chopped (2 tablespoons)
1 cup fresh or frozen corn kernels, thawed and drained

1 Preheat the oven to 325° F. Grease a 9″ square pan. In a small saucepan over moderate heat, melt the butter. Remove the pan from the heat and set aside.

2 In a large bowl, combine the cornmeal, flour, sugar, baking powder, and salt.

3 In a small bowl, mix the butter, buttermilk, and egg until well blended. Add to the flour mixture, stirring until the batter is just mixed. Stir in the jalapeño peppers and corn.

4 Spoon the batter into the prepared pan. Bake, uncovered, for 25 to 30 minutes, or until the bread is firm and springy to the touch. Remove pan from the oven and cut the cornbread into approximately 2¼″ squares. Serve warm.

16 SQUARES
PREP TIME: 15 MINUTES
COOKING TIME: 30 MINUTES

EQUIPMENT LIST

Paring knife
Strainer
9″ square pan
Small saucepan
Large bowl
Small bowl
Kitchen spoon
Rubber spatula

Applesauce Muffins

A foolproof muffin recipe is indispensable to every cook, and this one fits the bill. The results are meltingly soft and full of flavor, and the nut topping adds crunch.

½ cup (1 stick) unsalted butter
¾ cup firmly packed light brown sugar
1 large egg
1 cup unsweetened applesauce
1¼ cups all-purpose flour
½ cup wheat bran
1 teaspoon baking powder
½ teaspoon ground cinnamon
1 teaspoon baking soda
¼ teaspoon ground nutmeg
⅛ teaspoon ground cloves

NUT TOPPING

⅓ cup chopped walnuts
3 tablespoons granulated sugar
½ teaspoon ground cinnamon

1 Preheat the oven to 400° F. Grease 12 standard-size muffin pan cups or line them with paper liners.

2 To make the Nut Topping: In a small bowl, combine the walnuts, granulated sugar, and cinnamon and set aside.

3 In a large bowl, using an electric mixer set on medium-high speed, cream butter with the brown sugar until light and fluffy. Beat in the egg and applesauce until well blended.

4 In a medium-size bowl, combine the flour, bran, baking powder, cinnamon, baking soda, nutmeg, and cloves. Add the flour mixture to the applesauce mixture, stirring until batter is just mixed. Spoon the batter into the muffin pan cups, filling them two-thirds full. Sprinkle the topping over the batter.

5 Bake for 15 to 18 minutes, or until the muffins are golden brown and springy to the touch. Remove the muffin pan from the oven and set on a wire rack to cool for 5 minutes. Turn the muffins out onto the rack and cool slightly. Serve warm.

12 STANDARD-SIZE MUFFINS
PREP TIME: 12 MINUTES
COOKING TIME: 18 MINUTES

EQUIPMENT LIST

12-cup muffin pan
Small bowl
Large bowl
Medium-size bowl
Electric mixer
Kitchen spoons
Rubber spatula
Wire rack

DESSERTS

*E*nd midweek meals or family celebrations with a flourish by making one of the desserts featured in this chapter. From strawberry mousse to almond baked apples, banana cream pie to chocolate cake, coffee-walnut pudding to raspberry cookies the selection is truly awesome.

Peach Crisp Desserts.

Peach Crisp Desserts

In this version of a classic dessert, brown rice is combined with juicy peaches and then finished with a crisp topping. Besides its nutritional value, brown rice also adds flavor and texture. Add vanilla ice cream for a great summer dessert.

1   cup water
½   cup long-grain brown rice
3   medium-size ripe peaches, peeled, pitted, and sliced, or 1⅔ cups frozen sliced peaches, thawed and drained
⅔   cup firmly packed light brown sugar
¾   cup whole-wheat or all-purpose flour
½   teaspoon ground cinnamon
¼   teaspoon ground nutmeg
¼   cup (½ stick) unsalted butter, chilled and cut in small pieces
2   ounces chopped walnuts or pecans (½ cup)
1   pint vanilla ice cream or frozen yogurt
1   small ripe peach, quartered (optional)
4   sprigs of fresh mint (optional)

1 In a medium-size saucepan, bring the water to a boil over high heat. Stir in the rice. Reduce the heat to low and cook, covered, for 45 to 50 minutes, or until the rice is tender and the liquid is absorbed. Remove the pan from the heat. Fluff the rice with a fork and cool.

2 Preheat the oven to 350° F. Grease a 9″ square baking pan. In a large bowl, combine the rice, sliced peaches, and ⅓ cup of the sugar. Spread the mixture over the bottom of the pan.

3 In a small bowl, combine the flour, cinnamon, nutmeg, and the remaining ⅓ cup of sugar. Using a pastry blender or 2 knives, cut the butter into the flour mixture until the mixture resembles coarse crumbs. Stir in the walnuts until well combined. Spread the walnut topping evenly over the rice and peach mixture.

4 Bake for 20 to 25 minutes, or until the top is golden and the peaches are tender. Spoon the crisp into individual sherbet glasses. Place a scoop of ice cream on top of the crisp. Garnish each with a peach quarter and a sprig of fresh mint, if desired. Serve warm.

4 SERVINGS
PREP TIME: 20 MINUTES
COOKING TIME: 1 HOUR 15 MINUTES

EQUIPMENT LIST
Vegetable peeler
Utility knife
Medium-size saucepan with lid
Kitchen spoons
Fork
9″ square baking pan
Large bowl
Small bowl
Pastry blender or 2 knives
Ice cream scoop

Marble Cake

1⅓   cups all-purpose flour
⅛   teaspoon salt
2   ounces semisweet chocolate chips (⅓ cup)
½   cup (1 stick) unsalted butter
2   ounces white chocolate chips (⅓ cup)
8   egg whites
¾   cup superfine sugar
1   teaspoon vanilla extract

1 Preheat the oven to 350° F. Grease and flour a 9″ tube pan. Sift together flour and salt onto a sheet of wax paper and set aside.

2 In a double boiler set over simmering (not boiling) water, melt the semisweet chocolate and ¼ cup of the butter, stirring until smooth. Transfer the mixture to a small bowl. In a clean double boiler, repeat as directed with the white chocolate and the remaining ¼ cup of butter and transfer to another small bowl.

3 In a large bowl, using an electric mixer set on high speed, beat egg whites to soft peaks. Slowly add the sugar and beat to stiff peaks. Sift flour mixture over beaten egg whites and, using a rubber spatula, gently fold into the egg whites. Transfer half the batter to a medium-size bowl and fold in the semisweet chocolate mixture. Fold the white chocolate mixture and vanilla into the remaining batter.

4 Place alternating tablespoons of white and dark batters, side by side, in the bottom of the prepared pan. Make a second layer of batter, reversing the pattern of white and dark batters, followed by a third layer, reversing the batters. Swirl batter 4 or 5 times with the point of a knife to blend batters slightly and create a marble pattern.

5 Bake for 50 to 55 minutes, or until a cake tester or toothpick inserted in the center comes out clean. Remove the cake pan from the oven and set on a wire rack to cool for 5 minutes. Turn the cake out onto the wire rack and cool completely.

12 SERVINGS
PREP TIME: 20 MINUTES PLUS
40 MINUTES TO COOL
COOKING TIME: 55 MINUTES

EQUIPMENT LIST
Large bowl
2 small bowls
Medium-size bowl
9″ tube pan
Sifter
Wax paper
Double boiler
Kitchen spoons
2 tablespoons
Electric mixer
2 rubber spatulas
Utility knife
Cake tester or toothpick
Wire rack

Classic Banana Cream Pie

1½ cups all-purpose flour
1 teaspoon granulated sugar
½ teaspoon salt
¼ cup (½ stick) unsalted butter, chilled and cut in pieces
¼ cup cold water
1 egg yolk
1 tablespoon vegetable oil

BANANA CREAM FILLING

2 large eggs
½ cup superfine sugar
¼ cup all-purpose flour
2 cups milk
1 tablespoon vanilla extract
¼ cup (½ stick) unsalted butter, softened
4 medium-size firm, ripe bananas
½ cup heavy cream
Sprigs of fresh mint (optional)
Sliced banana (optional)

Any time of year is the right time to make one of America's favorite pies.

1 To make the pie shell: In a medium-size bowl, mix together the flour, granulated sugar, and salt. Using a pastry blender or 2 knives, cut the ¼ cup of butter into the flour until the mixture resembles coarse crumbs. In a small bowl, combine the water, egg yolk, and oil. Add the egg yolk mixture to the flour mixture, tossing gently with a fork to combine. Gather the pastry into a ball. Flatten it slightly, wrap in wax paper, and chill in the refrigerator for at least 30 minutes.

2 Meanwhile, make the Banana Cream Filling. In a small bowl, beat eggs, superfine sugar, and flour until smooth. In a medium-size saucepan, heat milk over moderate heat to just below the boiling point. Do not boil. Whisk ½ cup of milk into the egg mixture. Pour mixture back into pan and bring to a boil over moderate heat, stirring continuously. Boil for 1 minute. Remove from heat, add vanilla, and stir in the ¼ cup of butter, 1 piece at a time, until melted. Pour the custard into a medium-size bowl. Cover surface with a sheet of wax paper or plastic wrap. Cool to room temperature, then chill in refrigerator for 1 hour.

3 Preheat the oven to 425° F. Lightly flour a work surface and a rolling pin. Roll the dough evenly, from the center outward, and line a 9″ pie pan, fitting it loosely and pressing to fit the side. Trim the edge ¼″ above the rim of the pan, fold this edge under, and press in place with your fingers. Crimp the pastry edge.

4 Prick bottom of pie shell with a fork, line with aluminum foil, and fill with pie weights or dried beans. Bake pie shell for 10 minutes. Remove foil and weights. Bake for 5 minutes more, or until golden. Remove pie shell from the oven and set on a wire rack to cool.

5 In a medium-size bowl, using an electric mixer set on high speed, beat the cream to stiff peaks.

6 Remove the custard from the refrigerator. Slice the bananas thinly and stir into custard. Spoon the mixture into the pie shell and smooth the top. Spoon whipped cream in the center. Garnish with sprigs of fresh mint and banana slices, if desired.

8 SERVINGS
PREP TIME: 40 MINUTES PLUS
1 HOUR 30 MINUTES TO CHILL
COOKING TIME: 30 MINUTES

EQUIPMENT LIST
Utility knife
2 small bowls
3 medium-size bowls
Kitchen spoons
Pastry blender or 2 knives
2 forks
Wax paper
Aluminum foil
Medium-size saucepan
Wire whisk
Rolling pin
9″ pie pan
Pie weights or dried beans
Wire rack
Electric mixer

Lemon Curd Tartlets

5 egg yolks
½ cup granulated sugar
½ cup fresh lemon juice
2 teaspoons grated lemon rind
¼ cup (½ stick) unsalted butter, cut in small pieces
6 3″ prepared tart shells
¼ cup seedless raspberry jam
Fresh raspberries (optional)

Lemon Curd is a favorite British recipe that is used as a spread for toast or muffins, or as a filling for cakes, pastries, and tarts as in the recipe below. It will keep for up to 3 weeks if refrigerated in a jar with a tight-fitting lid. This recipe for the curd makes 1 cup, but it can easily be doubled or tripled. Keep a jar on hand to make a special dessert for unexpected guests.

1 To make the Lemon Curd: In a medium-size, heavy saucepan, mix together the egg yolks, sugar, and lemon juice and rind. Cook over low heat, stirring continuously, for 5 to 8 minutes, or until the mixture thickens.

2 Remove the pan from the heat. Add the butter and stir until melted and well blended. Transfer the Lemon Curd to a medium-size bowl, cover with plastic wrap, and chill for 1 hour.

3 To make Lemon Curd Tartlets: Divide the Lemon Curd among the tart shells. Transfer to a serving plate. Cover with plastic wrap and chill in the refrigerator for 2 hours.

4 In a small saucepan, melt the jam over low heat. Drizzle the jam over the tartlets and garnish with fresh raspberries, if desired. Serve immediately.

6 TARTLETS
PREP TIME: 20 MINUTES PLUS
3 HOURS TO CHILL
COOKING TIME: 8 MINUTES

EQUIPMENT LIST

Small bowl
Citrus juicer
Grater
Utility knife
Medium-size, heavy saucepan
Kitchen spoons
Medium-size bowl
Plastic wrap
Small saucepan

Apricot-Applesauce Cake

1 cup all-purpose flour
1 cup whole-wheat flour
2 teaspoons ground allspice
1 teaspoon baking soda
½ cup granulated sugar
½ cup (1 stick) unsalted butter
1 cup applesauce
2 large eggs
3 ounces dried apricots, chopped (¾ cup)
2 ounces chopped, blanched almonds (½ cup)

This fruit-filled cake can be enjoyed at any time of the year. Try it as a breakfast treat with a little cream cheese, or as a dessert sprinkled with confectioners' sugar or topped with whipped cream. Either way it's delicious and healthful, too.

1 Preheat the oven to 350° F. Grease a 10″ tube or Bundt pan. In a medium-size bowl, combine the all-purpose and whole-wheat flours, allspice, and baking soda.

2 In a large bowl, using an electric mixer set on high speed, cream the butter and sugar. Add the applesauce and eggs and beat until mixture is fluffy. Stir in flour mixture and beat for 2 minutes, scraping down the side of the bowl with a rubber spatula whenever necessary. Stir in apricots and almonds

3 Scrape batter into prepared pan. Bake for 35 to 40 minutes, or until a cake tester inserted in the center comes out clean. Remove pan from the oven and set on a wire rack to cool for 10 minutes. Turn the cake out onto the rack and cool completely.

12 SERVINGS
PREP TIME: 25 MINUTES PLUS
40 MINUTES TO COOL
COOKING TIME: 40 MINUTES

EQUIPMENT LIST

Utility knife
10″ tube pan
Medium-size bowl
Large bowl
Kitchen spoon
Electric mixer
Rubber spatula
Cake tester or toothpick
Wire rack

Lemon and Poppy Seed Bundt Cake

2½ cups all-purpose flour
1 teaspoon baking powder
⅛ teaspoon salt
¾ teaspoon baking soda
2 teaspoons grated lemon rind
1 cup (2 sticks) unsalted butter, softened
1 cup granulated sugar
4 large eggs
1 teaspoon vanilla extract
1 12½-ounce can poppy seed filling
1 cup buttermilk
Sifted confectioners' sugar (optional)

This light and buttery cake, with its lemon accent, has a crunchy texture that is created by the poppy seed filling. Serve this cake with lemon sauce and vanilla ice cream for a special party dessert.

For picnics and lunch boxes, try Poppy Seed Cupcakes: Grease 24 standard-size muffin pan cups or line with paper liners. Spoon the batter into the muffin pan cups, filling them two-thirds full. Bake for 30 minutes, or until a cake tester or toothpick inserted in the center comes out clean. Cool and dust with confectioners' sugar as directed.

1 Preheat the oven to 350° F. Grease and flour a 10″ tube or Bundt pan. In a medium-size bowl, combine the flour, baking powder, salt, baking soda, and lemon rind.

2 In a large bowl, using an electric mixer set on medium speed, cream the butter with the granulated sugar until light and fluffy. Add the eggs, 1 at a time, beating well after each addition. Add the vanilla and the poppy seed filling and mix well.

3 Reduce the mixer speed to low and alternately beat in the flour mixture and the buttermilk until well blended. Scrape the batter into the prepared pan. Tap the pan firmly on a flat surface 2 or 3 times to remove any air pockets.

4 Bake for 45 to 50 minutes, or until the cake is golden and well risen and a cake tester or toothpick inserted in the center comes out clean. Remove the cake from the oven and set on a wire rack to cool for 10 minutes. Turn the cake out onto the rack and cool for 20 minutes.

5 Dust the cake with the confectioners' sugar, if desired, and serve sliced.

Delicious and portable, this lemon cake is always a welcome treat.

12 SERVINGS
PREP TIME: 25 MINUTES PLUS
30 MINUTES TO COOL
COOKING TIME: 50 MINUTES

Equipment List
Grater
10″ tube or Bundt pan
Medium-size bowl
Large bowl
Kitchen spoon
Electric mixer
Rubber spatula
Cake tester or toothpick
Wire rack

Almond-Filled Baked Apples

These baked apples are a beloved comfort food. Easy to prepare, they are wonderful served warm with heavy cream poured over them.

4   medium-size McIntosh or other red-skinned apples (2 pounds)
¾   cup water
Heavy cream (optional)

ALMOND FILLING

1   ounce sliced almonds (¼ cup)
1   tablespoon unsalted butter
½   cup firmly packed light brown sugar
¼   cup dark or golden raisins
¼   cup chopped candied cherries
¼   teaspoon ground cinnamon

1   Preheat the oven to 350° F. To make the Almond Filling: Spread the almonds in a thin layer on a baking sheet. Toast in the oven for 7 to 10 minutes, or until golden brown. Stir the almonds occasionally while toasting to prevent them from burning. Remove baking sheet from the oven, transfer almonds to a small bowl, and cool slightly.

2   Increase the oven temperature to 375° F. In a medium-size bowl, using a pastry blender or 2 knives, cut the butter into the sugar until the mixture resembles coarse crumbs. Stir in the almonds, raisins, cherries, and cinnamon until well blended.

3   Rinse the apples under cold running water and pat dry with paper towels. Using a paring knife, remove the core from each apple, leaving about ½" on the bottom.

4   Make a horizontal cut in the skin around the middle of each apple. Place the apples in a shallow 8" square baking dish. Spoon the filling into the apples. Pour water into bottom of the dish. Cover with aluminum foil and bake for 45 to 50 minutes, or until apples are tender.

5   Remove baking dish from the oven and let stand for 10 minutes. Using a large, metal spatula, transfer the baked apples to individual serving plates. Top the baked apples with heavy cream, if desired, and serve warm.

4 SERVINGS
PREP TIME: 20 MINUTES PLUS
10 MINUTES TO STAND
COOKING TIME: 50 MINUTES

EQUIPMENT LIST
Baking sheet
Kitchen spoons
Small bowl
Medium-size bowl
Pastry blender or 2 knives
Paper towels
Aluminum foil
Paring knife
Shallow 8" square baking dish

Chilled Strawberry Mousse

This mousse is the perfect choice when the occasion calls for a simple, light, and refreshing dessert.

1½   cups fresh strawberries or frozen strawberries without syrup, thawed
1   envelope (¼ ounce) unflavored gelatin
¼   cup water or sweet vermouth
6   tablespoons granulated sugar
2   cups heavy cream
Fresh strawberries (optional)

1   Place the 1½ cups of strawberries in a blender or food processor fitted with the metal blade. Blend or process for 1 to 2 minutes, or until the strawberries are puréed. Strain the strawberry purée through a fine sieve into a small bowl and discard the solids.

2   In a small saucepan, sprinkle the gelatin over the water and cook over low heat, stirring continuously, for 15 seconds, or until the gelatin is dissolved. Stir in the strawberry purée and 4 tablespoons of the sugar. Cook over moderately low heat, stirring frequently, for 5 minutes, or until the sugar has dissolved. Remove the pan from the heat. Transfer strawberry mixture to a small bowl and cool completely.

3   In a medium-size bowl, using an electric mixer set on high speed, beat cream and the remaining 2 tablespoons of sugar to stiff peaks.

4   Using a rubber spatula, gently and thoroughly fold the cooled strawberry mixture into the whipped cream. Spoon the mousse into individual serving glasses or bowls. Chill in the refrigerator for 30 minutes, or until the mousse is set. Garnish with fresh strawberries, if desired, and serve chilled.

8 SERVINGS
PREP TIME: 15 MINUTES PLUS
45 MINUTES TO COOL AND CHILL
COOKING TIME: 5 MINUTES

EQUIPMENT LIST
Blender or food processor with metal blade
Fine sieve
2 small bowls
Medium-size bowl
Small saucepan
Kitchen spoons
Electric mixer
Rubber spatula

Pineapple Meringue Cake

1 cup sifted cake flour
2 teaspoons baking powder
⅛ teaspoon salt
½ cup (1 stick) unsalted butter
1½ cups granulated sugar
4 large eggs, separated
5 tablespoons milk
2 teaspoons vanilla extract
3 ounces finely chopped pecans (¾ cup)

PINEAPPLE CREAM FILLING

1 cup heavy cream
1½ teaspoons confectioners' sugar (optional)
¼ teaspoon vanilla extract
2 8-ounce cans crushed pineapple, well drained (1 cup)

1 Preheat the oven to 350° F. Grease two 9″ layer cake pans and line the bottoms with wax paper.

2 To make the cake: In a small bowl, resift cake flour with baking powder and salt and set aside. In a medium-size bowl, using an electric mixer set on medium speed, cream butter with ½ cup of the granulated sugar until fluffy. Add egg yolks, 1 at a time, beating well after each addition. Stir in milk and 1 teaspoon of the vanilla. Slowly beat in flour mixture. Spoon batter into prepared cake pans; set aside.

3 In a medium-size, clean bowl, using an electric mixer set on high speed, beat egg whites to soft peaks. Slowly add remaining 1 cup of granulated sugar, and continue beating the meringue to stiff peaks. Fold in the remaining 1 teaspoon of vanilla. Spoon the meringue on top of the cake mixture in the pans without flattening it too much. Sprinkle the pecans over both layers.

4 Bake the layers for 35 to 45 minutes, or until the meringue is golden and a cake tester or toothpick inserted in the centers of the cake layers comes out clean. Remove the cake pans from the oven and set on wire racks to cool completely.

5 Meanwhile, make the Pineapple Cream Filling. In a medium-size bowl, using an electric mixer set on high speed, beat the cream to soft peaks. Add the confectioners' sugar, if desired, and stir in the ¼ teaspoon of vanilla and pineapple.

6 To assemble: Using a thin, metal spatula, loosen the edges of the cake layers. Turn out 1 layer onto a large plate and peel off the wax paper.

7 Place a serving platter on top of the sponge base and quickly invert the cake so that the meringue is on the top. Spoon the filling on top of the meringue. Turn out the second layer and place on top with the meringue layer facing up. Serve immediately or cover lightly with plastic wrap and refrigerate for up to 6 hours.

This meringue cake with its alternating texture layers will get taste buds tingling.

12 SERVINGS
PREP TIME: 35 MINUTES PLUS
30 MINUTES TO COOL
COOKING TIME: 45 MINUTES

EQUIPMENT LIST

Sifter
2 small bowls
3 medium-size bowls
Strainer
2 9″ layer cake pans
Wax paper
Plastic wrap
Electric mixer
Kitchen spoons
Rubber spatula
Thin, metal spatula
Cake tester or toothpick
Wire racks
Large plate

Chocolate-Walnut Cake
with Chocolate Frosting

½ cup boiling water
½ cup unsweetened cocoa
   powder
2¼ cups cake flour
2 ounces finely ground walnuts
   (½ cup)
1 teaspoon baking soda
½ teaspoon salt
⅔ cup unsalted butter, softened
1¾ cups granulated sugar
1 teaspoon vanilla extract
2 large eggs, lightly beaten
1⅓ cups milk
8 ounces chopped walnuts
   (2 cups) (optional)
8 walnut halves (optional)

CHOCOLATE FROSTING

1 cup heavy cream
1 cup confectioners' sugar
6 ounces semisweet chocolate,
   chopped (1 cup)
½ cup (1 stick) unsalted butter
1 teaspoon vanilla extract

1 To make Chocolate Frosting: In a medium-size saucepan, heat the cream and confectioners' sugar over moderate heat, stirring frequently, for 5 minutes, or until sugar is dissolved. Bring to a boil. Reduce heat to low and cook, stirring continuously, for 5 minutes. Remove pan from the heat. Add chocolate all at once, stirring until chocolate is melted and mixture is smooth. Stir in the ½ cup of butter and the 1 teaspoon of vanilla. Transfer to a medium-size bowl, cover with plastic wrap, and chill in the refrigerator for 2 hours, or until thickened.

2 Preheat the oven to 350° F. Grease and flour two 9″ round layer cake pans. In a small bowl, combine the water and cocoa until well blended. In another small bowl, combine the flour, ½ cup of walnuts, baking soda, and salt.

3 In a large bowl, using an electric mixer set on medium speed, cream the ⅔ cup of butter and granulated sugar until light and fluffy. Beat in the 1 teaspoon of vanilla and the eggs. Alternately beat in flour mixture and milk. Stir in the cocoa mixture until well blended.

4 Pour batter into prepared cake pans. Bake for 40 minutes, or until a cake tester or toothpick inserted in the center comes out clean. Remove from the oven and set on wire racks to cool for 10 minutes. Turn the cakes out onto the racks and cool completely.

5 Remove frosting from the refrigerator. Using clean beaters, beat on high speed until light and fluffy. Reserve 1 cup of frosting.

6 To assemble: Place 1 cake layer on a serving platter and spread with ⅓ cup of the frosting. Top with second cake layer. Frost top and side of the cake with the remaining frosting. Press the chopped walnuts into the side of the cake, if desired.

7 Spoon the reserved frosting into a pastry bag fitted with a star tip. Pipe the frosting around top edge. Decorate piping with walnut halves, if desired.

Chocolate lovers won't be able to resist this fabulous cake.

12 SERVINGS
PREP TIME: 45 MINUTES PLUS
2 HOURS TO CHILL
COOKING TIME: 50 MINUTES

EQUIPMENT LIST

3 small bowls
Medium-size bowl
Large bowl
Wire whisk
Utility knife
Medium-size saucepan
Kitchen spoons
Plastic wrap
2 9″ layer cake pans
Electric mixer
Cake tester or toothpick
2 wire racks
Thin, metal spatula
Pastry bag with star tip

Raspberry Linzer Cookies

These cookies are perfect for holiday gift-giving. They can be prepared up to 2 weeks ahead and stored in an airtight container.

2⅓ cups all-purpose flour
1 teaspoon baking powder
½ teaspoon salt
½ teaspoon ground cinnamon
¾ cup (1½ sticks) unsalted butter, softened
1 cup granulated sugar
½ teaspoon almond extract
2 large eggs
¾ cup seedless raspberry jam
½ cup confectioners' sugar

1 In a medium-size bowl, combine the flour, baking powder, salt, and cinnamon. In a large bowl, using an electric mixer set on medium speed, cream the butter with the sugar until light and fluffy. Beat in the almond extract and the eggs, 1 at a time, beating well after each addition. Reduce the mixer speed to low and beat in the flour mixture until well blended.

2 Divide the dough in half and wrap each half in plastic wrap. Chill the dough in the refrigerator for 1 hour, or until firm.

3 Preheat the oven to 350° F. Lightly flour a work surface and a rolling pin. Remove 1 dough half from refrigerator and unwrap. Roll the dough evenly, from the center outward, to ⅛" thick. Using a 2½" fluted round, star, or heart-shaped cookie cutter, cut out 36 cookies from the dough. Place cookies on ungreased baking sheets, spacing them 1" apart. Bake for 8 to 10 minutes, or until edges are just golden. Remove baking sheets from the oven, set on wire racks, and cool for 2 minutes. Using a thin, metal spatula, transfer cookies to racks to cool for 15 minutes.

4 Roll out the remaining dough half and the trimmings and cut out 36 more cookies as directed. Using a 1" fluted round, star, or heart-shaped cookie cutter, cut out the centers of the unbaked cookies. Place cookies on ungreased baking sheets and bake and cool as directed.

5 To assemble: Using a thin, metal spatula, spread 1 teaspoon of the jam on the flat side of each whole cookie. Sprinkle confectioners' sugar over the cookies with the centers cut out and place, sugar side up, on top of jam-topped cookies to form sandwiches.

Present friends with a box of these superb cookies—they will be well appreciated.

3 DOZEN COOKIES
PREP TIME: 30 MINUTES PLUS
1 HOUR 15 MINUTES
TO CHILL AND COOL
COOKING TIME: 20 MINUTES

EQUIPMENT LIST
Medium-size bowl
Large bowl
Kitchen spoon
Electric mixer
Plastic wrap
Rolling pin
2½" fluted, round, star, or heart-shaped cookie cutter
1" fluted, round, star, or heart-shaped cookie cutter
2 baking sheets
2 wire racks
2 thin, metal spatulas

Coffee-Walnut Pudding
with Butterscotch Sauce

1   cup (2 sticks) unsalted butter, softened
1   cup firmly packed dark brown sugar
2   large eggs
2   cups all-purpose flour
2   teaspoons baking powder
¼   cup instant coffee powder
¼   cup hot water
⅓   cup milk
⅓   cup vegetable oil
4   ounces chopped walnuts (1 cup)
½   cup dark raisins
Whipped cream (optional)

BUTTERSCOTCH SAUCE (1½ CUPS)

6   tablespoons unsalted butter
½   cup firmly packed brown sugar
1   tablespoon water
2   teaspoons vanilla extract
1   tablespoon hazelnut liqueur (optional)
2   ounces chopped walnuts (½ cup)
½   cup heavy cream

1 Preheat the oven to 325° F. Grease and flour a 2-quart casserole or baking dish.

2 To make the pudding: In a large bowl, using an electric mixer set on medium speed, cream the 1 cup of butter with the 1 cup of sugar until light and fluffy. Add the eggs, 1 at a time, beating well after each addition.

3 Sift the flour and the baking powder onto a sheet of wax paper. In a small bowl, dissolve the coffee powder in the ¼ cup of hot water. Add the flour to the butter mixture, alternately with the coffee, mixing until well blended. Gradually add the milk and oil and mix well. Stir in the 4 ounces of walnuts and the raisins.

4 Spoon pudding into the prepared dish. Bake for 40 to 45 minutes, or until firm and a toothpick inserted in the center comes out clean.

5 Meanwhile, make the Butterscotch Sauce. In a medium-size saucepan, heat the 6 tablespoons of butter, ½ cup of sugar, and the 1 tablespoon of water over moderate heat for 5 minutes, or until butter is melted. Increase the heat to moderately high and bring the mixture to a boil, stirring continuously. Boil for 5 minutes, without stirring.

6 Remove pan from the heat and stir in the vanilla and liqueur, if desired. Let cool for 5 minutes, stirring occasionally. Add the 2 ounces of walnuts and heavy cream to the sauce and stir well. Keep warm. Remove the casserole from the oven and set on a wire rack to cool for 5 minutes.

7 Spoon the pudding into individual serving dishes. Pour some of the sauce over the pudding, garnish with whipped cream, if desired, and serve immediately.

12 SERVINGS
PREP TIME: 30 MINUTES
COOKING TIME: 45 MINUTES

EQUIPMENT LIST

2-quart casserole
Large bowl
Small bowl
Electric mixer
Sifter
Wax paper
Kitchen spoons
Toothpick
Medium-size saucepan
Wire rack

Citrus Pudding

1   tablespoon unsalted butter, softened
¾   cup granulated sugar
2   large eggs, separated
2   tablespoons fresh lemon juice
2   tablespoons orange juice
2   tablespoons sifted all-purpose flour
1   cup milk
1   teaspoon grated orange rind
½   cup pomegranate seeds (optional)

1 Preheat the oven to 350° F. Grease four 1½-cup ramekins. In a medium-size bowl, using an electric mixer set on medium speed, cream the butter with ½ cup of the sugar until fluffy. Beat in the egg yolks, lemon and orange juices, and flour. Reduce the mixer speed to low and slowly beat in the milk. Stir in the orange rind.

2 In a small bowl, using clean beaters, beat the egg whites on medium-high speed until foamy. Slowly add the remaining ¼ cup of sugar and beat to stiff peaks.

3 Gently and thoroughly fold egg whites into egg yolk mixture. Spoon mixture into ramekins and place in a baking pan. Carefully pour enough water into bottom of baking pan to come 1″ up the sides of ramekins. Bake for 35 minutes, or until tops are puffed and golden. Remove ramekins from water. Let cool slightly. Chill in refrigerator for 3 hours. Garnish with pomegranate seeds, if desired, and serve chilled.

4 SERVINGS
PREP TIME: 20 MINUTES PLUS
3 HOURS TO CHILL
COOKING TIME: 35 MINUTES

EQUIPMENT LIST

3 small bowls
Medium-size bowl
Citrus juicer
Sifter
Grater
4 1½-cup ramekins
Electric mixer
Kitchen spoon
Rubber spatula

UTUMN CELEBRATION DINNER

Autumn is traditionally the time of festivals, and what better way to celebrate the change of seasons than with a dinner party. This menu features roast chicken with a superb Dried Fruit Stuffing— everyone will ask for the recipe—and Marinated Garden Vegetables, which uses the last of the summer produce in a wonderful way. Finish off with an autumnal squash soufflé.

Chicken with Dried Fruit Stuffing

Marinated Garden Vegetables
(page 91)

Spiced Squash Soufflé

PREPARATION TIME-SAVERS

• *The night before*, prepare the Dried Fruit Stuffing for the chicken—be sure to use day-old bread cubes. Cover with plastic wrap and refrigerate until ready to use.

• Prepare the vegetables for the Marinated Garden Vegetables and proceed up until draining. Transfer the drained vegetables to a plastic or glass dish, cover with plastic wrap, and refrigerate until needed.

• Prepare the acorn squash, wrap in plastic wrap, and refrigerate until ready to use.

Chicken with Dried Fruit Stuffing

1   5-pound roasting chicken
Fresh sage leaves (optional)
Cherry tomatoes (optional)

DRIED FRUIT STUFFING (6 CUPS)

½   cup dark raisins
1   cup boiling water
¼   cup (½ stick) unsalted butter
1   medium-size yellow onion,
      finely chopped (1 cup)
6   ounces whole dried apricots
      (1½ cups)
2   ounces coarsely chopped
      walnuts (½ cup)
½   teaspoon dried sage leaves,
      crumbled
½   teaspoon dried thyme leaves,
      crumbled
⅛   teaspoon ground allspice
¼   teaspoon coarsely ground
      black pepper
5   cups 1″ day-old bread cubes
¾   cup chicken stock or canned
      broth

1 Preheat the oven to 350° F. Rinse the chicken, inside and out, under cold running water and pat dry with paper towels.

2 To make Dried Fruit Stuffing: In a small bowl, soak raisins in the boiling water for 15 minutes. Drain well and discard liquid. In a large skillet over moderate heat, melt the butter. Add onion and sauté for 5 minutes, or until translucent. Add the raisins, apricots, walnuts, sage, thyme, allspice, and pepper. Add bread cubes, tossing to combine. Stir in stock. Remove skillet from the heat and let cool slightly.

3 Spoon stuffing into main cavity of chicken. Tie drumsticks together with kitchen twine or secure with a metal skewer. Place any remaining stuffing in a small baking dish. Cover with aluminum foil.

4 Place chicken on a rack in a roasting pan and roast, uncovered, basting frequently with pan juices, for 2 hours, or until a meat thermometer inserted into thigh registers 175° F. and juices run clear when the thigh is pierced with a knife. Thirty minutes before the end of cooking, place the covered baking dish of stuffing in the oven.

5 Remove the pan and baking dish from oven. Cover the chicken with foil and let stand for 15 minutes. Line a serving platter with the sage leaves, if desired. Transfer chicken to the serving platter and remove the kitchen twine or metal skewer. Garnish with the cherry tomatoes, if desired. Carve and serve immediately with the stuffing.

6 SERVINGS
PREP TIME: 20 MINUTES PLUS
30 MINUTES TO SOAK AND STAND
COOKING TIME: 2 HOURS

EQUIPMENT LIST

Utility knife
Carving knife
Paper towels
Aluminum foil
Small bowl
Strainer
Large skillet
Kitchen spoon
Kitchen twine or metal skewer
Small baking dish
Roasting pan with rack
Meat thermometer

Spiced Squash Soufflé

1   large acorn squash, peeled,
      seeded, and cut in 1″ pieces
      (2 cups)
3   tablespoons unsalted butter
3   tablespoons all-purpose flour
¾   cup milk
2   tablespoons granulated sugar
5   large eggs, separated
1   small Granny Smith or other
      tart apple, peeled, cored, and
      grated (½ cup)
½   teaspoon ground cinnamon
½   teaspoon ground ginger
¼   teaspoon cream of tartar
Confectioners' sugar (optional)

1 Preheat the oven to 375° F. In a medium-size saucepan, combine squash with enough cold water to cover. Bring to a boil over high heat. Reduce the heat to low and cook, covered, for 10 minutes, or until the squash is tender. Drain well and cool slightly. Transfer squash to a blender or food processor fitted with the metal blade. Blend or process for 1 minute, or until smooth. Set aside.

2 In a large saucepan over moderate heat, melt butter. Stir in flour until well blended. Cook, stirring continuously, for 1 to 2 minutes, or until it becomes a pale straw color. Slowly add milk and granulated sugar and cook, stirring continuously, for 1 minute, or until sugar dissolves and mixture thickens slightly. Remove pan from heat.

3 In a small bowl, whisk a little milk mixture into egg yolks, then add yolks to the pan. Cook, stirring continuously, for 2 minutes. Stir in squash purée, apple, cinnamon, and ginger until well blended.

4 In a large bowl, using an electric mixer set on medium-high speed, beat egg whites until foamy. Add cream of tartar and beat to stiff peaks. Spoon mixture into a 1½-quart soufflé dish. Mix some stiffly beaten egg whites into the soufflé base to lighten it, then fold in the remaining egg whites. Bake soufflé for 30 minutes, or until puffed and golden. Remove from the oven, sprinkle with the confectioners' sugar, if desired, and serve immediately.

6 SERVINGS
PREP TIME: 20 MINUTES
COOKING TIME: 46 MINUTES

EQUIPMENT LIST

Vegetable peeler
Utility knife
3 small bowls
Large bowl
Medium-size saucepan with lid
Large saucepan
Colander
Blender or food processor with
      metal blade
Electric mixer
Kitchen spoon
Wire whisk
Rubber spatula
1½-quart soufflé dish

Evening à la Bretagne

Brittany, in northwest France, is an area renowned for its fish, and this menu capitalizes on it in the main course casserole which contains shrimp and monkfish in a vegetable mixture and a topping of crunchy garlic croutons. A very French salad of pears and goat cheese precedes it, and the meal concludes with a warming pudding. Bon appétit!

Pear and Goat Cheese Salad

Fish Breton with Garlic Croutons

Coffee-Walnut Pudding with Butterscotch Sauce
(page 129)

PREPARATION TIME-SAVERS

• *The night before,* prepare the onion for the Pear and Goat Cheese Salad, wrap in plastic wrap, and refrigerate until ready to use. Do not slice the pears as they will turn brown. Prepare the Dill Dressing, cover with plastic wrap, and refrigerate until ready to use.

• Prepare the shrimp, monkfish, snow peas, and carrots for the Fish Breton and wrap in plastic wrap. Rinse and slice the leeks and wrap in paper towels. Refrigerate until ready to use.

• Prepare the Butterscotch Sauce for the Coffee-Walnut Pudding, cover with plastic wrap, and refrigerate until ready to use.

Pear and Goat Cheese Salad

This salad makes a perfect starter for a substantial entrée such as a fish, chicken, or beef casserole. Anjou or Red Bartlett pears are best to use. Serve it with crackers or crusty French bread.

3	medium-size pears, cored and thickly sliced (2¼ cups)
2	tablespoons fresh lemon juice
1	small red onion, chopped (1 cup)
3	stalks celery, sliced (1½ cups)
2	ounces pecans (½ cup)
8	ounces mild goat cheese, sliced ½" thick
	Sprigs for fresh dill (optional)

DILL DRESSING (⅓ CUP)

2	tablespoons fresh lemon juice
½	teaspoon dried dill weed, crumbled
¼	cup olive oil
⅛	teaspoon salt, or to taste

4 SERVINGS
PREP TIME: 15 MINUTES

EQUIPMENT LIST

Utility knife
Citrus juicer
Medium-size bowl
Small bowl
Wire whisk
Kitchen spoon
Salad servers

1 Place the pear slices in a medium-size bowl with the 2 tablespoons of lemon juice. Toss gently to coat the pears. Add the red onion, celery, and pecans, stirring to combine. It is important that the pears not be prepared too long before they are combined with the other ingredients as they will turn brown.

2 To make the Dill Dressing: In a small bowl, whisk together the 2 tablespoons of lemon juice and dried dill. Slowly add the oil, whisking vigorously until well blended, or place the ingredients in a small jar with a tight-fitting lid and shake to blend. Season to taste with the salt. Pour the dressing over the pear mixture, tossing gently to coat.

3 Spoon the salad onto individual serving plates and place the slices of goat cheese on top. Garnish with sprigs of fresh dill, if desired, and serve immediately.

Fish Breton with Garlic Croutons

For lovers of French cooking, here's a fish casserole that is truly magnifique and surprisingly easy to prepare.

2	tablespoons unsalted butter, softened
3	tablespoons all-purpose flour
1	large leek (white part only), trimmed, rinsed, and thinly sliced (½ cup)
3	cups fish stock or bottled clam juice
1	cup dry white wine or water
2	tablespoons chopped fresh parsley
1	teaspoon dried tarragon leaves, crumbled
12	ounces medium-size uncooked shrimp, peeled and deveined (16-20 shrimp)
1	pound monkfish fillet, cut in 1" pieces
5	ounces snow peas, trimmed and strings removed (2½ cups)
2	medium-size carrots, peeled and thinly sliced (1½ cups)
⅛	teaspoon salt, or to taste

GARLIC CROUTONS

2	tablespoons olive oil
1	large clove garlic, chopped
2½	cups 1" French bread cubes

4 SERVINGS
PREP TIME: 45 MINUTES
COOKING TIME: 30 MINUTES

EQUIPMENT LIST

Utility knife
Paring knife
Vegetable peeler
Small bowl
Kitchen spoons
Large saucepan
Wire whisk
3-quart casserole
Medium-size skillet

1 Preheat the oven to 375° F. In a small bowl, mix 1 tablespoon of the butter with the flour to form a smooth paste.

2 In a large saucepan over moderate heat, melt the remaining 1 tablespoon of butter. Add the leek and sauté for 3 minutes, or until softened. Add stock and wine and bring the mixture to a simmer.

3 Whisk in the flour paste until well blended. Increase the heat to moderately high and bring the mixture to a boil, stirring continuously. Reduce the heat to moderately low and cook, stirring frequently, for 15 minutes, or until the mixture has thickened slightly.

4 Add the parsley and tarragon to the mixture. Stir in the shrimp, monkfish, snow peas, and carrots. Season to taste.

5 Spoon the fish and vegetable mixture into a 3-quart casserole. Bake the fish casserole for 30 minutes, or until the sauce is bubbly and the carrots are tender.

6 Meanwhile, make the Garlic Croutons. In a medium-size skillet, heat the oil over moderate heat for 1 minute. Add the garlic and sauté for 30 seconds, or until fragrant. Add the bread cubes, tossing to coat. Cook, stirring frequently, for 10 minutes, or until the croutons are lightly golden brown. Remove the skillet from the heat.

7 Remove the casserole from the oven. Sprinkle the croutons around the edge of the fish casserole. Serve immediately.

ℱIRESIDE SUPPER

A supper around the fireside is perfect to ward off the chilly winds of winter. The Root Vegetable Stew featured in this menu is simplicity itself, in addition to being flavorful and warming, and the Green Onion and Herb Bread will fill the house with a delicious aroma as it bakes. As an added treat, there's spicy English Gingerbread—seconds will be hard to refuse.

Root Vegetable Stew

Green Onion and Herb Bread
(page 118)

English Gingerbread

PREPARATION TIME-SAVERS

• *The night before,* prepare and cook the Root Vegetable Stew. Transfer the stew to a large bowl, cover with plastic wrap, and cool. Refrigerate until needed.

• Prepare and bake the English Gingerbread, turn out on a wire rack, and cool. Wrap in plastic wrap and keep at room temperature.

• Prepare and bake the Green Onion and Herb Bread.

Root Vegetable Stew

2 tablespoons olive oil
2 medium-size yellow onions, chopped (2 cups)
2 large cloves garlic, chopped
1 teaspoon dried oregano leaves, crumbled
2⅓ cups water
3 cups chicken stock or canned broth
1 16-ounce can plum tomatoes
½ cup chopped fresh parsley
4 small California white or other boiling potatoes, peeled and cut in ½″ pieces (2 cups)
3 small parsnips, peeled and cut in ½″ pieces (1½ cups)
3 small carrots, peeled and cut in ½″ pieces (1½ cups)
2 stalks celery, chopped (1 cup)
1 small yellow turnip, peeled and cut in ½″ pieces (¾ cup)
4 teaspoons cornstarch
1 16-ounce can chick peas, drained and rinsed
Sprigs of flat-leaf parsley (optional)

This fragrant stew with its mixture of root vegetables and chick peas is especially appealing during the winter months.

1 In a 5-quart Dutch oven, heat the oil over moderate heat for 1 minute. Add the onions and garlic and sauté for 5 minutes, or until the onions are translucent.

2 Stir in the oregano and sauté for 1 minute more. Add 2 cups of the water, the stock, tomatoes with their juice, ¼ cup of the parsley, the potatoes, parsnips, carrots, celery, and turnip. Bring the mixture to a boil over moderately high heat, stirring frequently. Reduce the heat to low and cook, covered, stirring occasionally, for 30 minutes, or until the vegetables are tender.

3 In a small bowl, mix the cornstarch with the remaining ⅓ cup of water. Stir the cornstarch mixture into the stew until well blended. Add the chick peas and the remaining ¼ cup of parsley. Cook, uncovered, stirring occasionally, for 15 minutes, or until thickened slightly and heated through.

4 Ladle the stew onto individual serving plates. Garnish with the sprigs of flat-leaf parsley, if desired, and serve immediately.

6 SERVINGS
PREP TIME: 30 MINUTES
COOKING TIME: 55 MINUTES

EQUIPMENT LIST

Utility knife
Vegetable peeler
Colander
5-quart Dutch oven
Kitchen spoons
Small bowl

English Gingerbread

2½ cups all-purpose flour
2 teaspoons baking soda
1½ teaspoons ground ginger
1 teaspoon ground cinnamon
½ teaspoon ground cloves
¼ teaspoon salt
½ cup (1 stick) unsalted butter, softened
½ cup firmly packed dark brown sugar
½ cup dark molasses
½ cup dark corn syrup
1 tablespoon peeled, grated fresh ginger
1 teaspoon grated lemon rind
2 large eggs
1 cup water
Crystallized orange rind (optional)
Sliced strawberries (optional)
Whipped cream (optional)

This dark, moist gingerbread is perfectly accented by a variety of garnishes. Fresh seasonal fruit and whipped cream fit the bill if time is short, but a lemon icing drizzled over the top is well worth the effort when there is a little extra time available.

1 Preheat the oven to 350° F. Grease and flour an 8″ square baking pan. In a large bowl, sift together the flour, baking soda, ground ginger, cinnamon, cloves, and salt.

2 In a medium-size saucepan, combine butter, sugar, molasses, and corn syrup. Cook, stirring continuously, over moderately low heat for 2 minutes, or until butter is melted and sugar is dissolved. Remove pan from heat. Cool slightly. Stir in grated ginger and lemon rind. Slowly stir molasses mixture into dry ingredients. Add eggs, 1 at a time, beating well after each addition. Stir in water until well blended.

3 Scrape batter into prepared pan. Bake for 35 to 40 minutes, or until a cake tester or toothpick inserted in the center comes out clean. Remove from the oven and set on a wire rack to cool for 20 minutes.

4 Turn the gingerbread out onto a wire rack. Garnish with the crystallized orange rind, sliced strawberries, and whipped cream, if desired. Cut into 2″ squares and serve warm or at room temperature.

16 SQUARES
PREP TIME: 15 MINUTES PLUS
20 MINUTES TO COOL
COOKING TIME: 40 MINUTES

EQUIPMENT LIST

Vegetable peeler
Grater
8″ square baking pan
Large bowl
Sifter
Medium-size saucepan
Kitchen spoon
Rubber spatula
Cake tester or toothpick
Wire rack

Nutritional Information

Unless otherwise noted, the analyses are based on a single serving.

Bruschetta *Calories 364; Cholesterol 0 mg; Sodium 183 mg; Protein 4 g; Total Fat 29 g; Saturated Fat 4 g* — page 13

Index

Photo Credits

Grateful acknowledgment is made to the following sources for use of their photographs. All photographs not otherwise credited were taken by Gus Francisco and Allan Baillie. **Aaron Rezny, Inc.:** Pasta Nostra Italiano, p. 102. **American Lamb Council:** Grilled Lamb Steaks with Barbecue Sauce, p. 51; Shoulder Lamb Chops with Triple Apricot Sauce, p. 52. **Bertolli Olive Oil:** Tri-Colored Pasta Salad with Mustard-Garlic Dressing, p. 97. **Bridgford Foods Corporation:** Cheese-Filled Focaccia, p. 116. **The Catfish Institute:** Mixed Fish Paella, p. 64. **California Prune Board:** Hearty Breakfast Loaf, p. 117. **California Tree Fruit Agreement:** Haddock Fillets with Pears Jardinière, p. 62. **Clear Springs Trout Company:** Rainbow Trout with Vegetable Salsa, p. 61. **Thom DeSanto:** Scandinavian Picnic Loaf, p. 39. **Dole® Food Company:** Classic Banana Cream Pie, p. 122. **Hazelnut Marketing Board:** Chinese Chicken Wings with 5-Spice Mayonnaise, p. 16. **Martin Jacobs:** Summer Pea Combo, p. 80. **Kraft Creative Kitchens:** Double Rice and Bell Pepper Salad, p. 98. **Vincent Lee:** Chilled Peach and Pistachio Dessert Soup, p. 27; Roast Turkey with Chorizo Stuffing, p. 77. **National Broiler Council:** Hearty Broiled Chicken and Potatoes, p. 66. **National Pork Producer's Council:** Pork and Mixed Vegetable Stir-Fry, p. 46; Choucroute Garni, p. 47. **National Turkey Federation:** Turkey Swirls, p. 74. Norwegian Jarlsberg Cheese: Pasta-Stuffed Peppers, p. 103. **Ocean Spray Cranberries, Inc.:** Cranberry-Wild Rice Salad, p. 112. **Sokol and Company:** Lemon and Poppy Seed Bundt Cake, p. 124. **USA Rice Council:** Hearty Chicken and Rice Soup, p. 25; Vegetable and Rice Casserole, p. 106; South-of-the-Border Rice Bake, p. 110; Peach Crisp Desserts, p. 120. **Wisconsin Milk Marketing Board:** Cheese and Onion Pie, p. 35.